Brad Waggoner is one of the leading evangelicals in the field and ministry of discipleship. He has a passion to see people become followers of Christ and to see those followers grow up in their walk with Christ. Dr. Waggoner takes that passion and combines it with one of the most comprehensive research projects on discipleship ever undertaken. This book truly gives us insight into the shape of faith to come among Christians in America. This work is both descriptive and prescriptive and will be seen as one of the best books ever written on what is really taking place in the discipleship process of Christians.

—Thom S. Rainer
President and CEO
LifeWay Christian Resources

The elephant in the room of evangelicalism is the surprising lack of discipled believers in all different kinds of churches. We have produced a cafeteria Christianity rather than a robust orthodoxy and Jesus-shaped spirituality. In this challenging and disturbing book, Brad Waggoner draws on twenty years of research in discipleship and spiritual formation not to show us just who we are, but to point us to what we must do. *The Shape of Faith to Come* will become a milestone as evangelicals begin to take discipleship seriously once again.

—Ed Stetzer
Director of LifeWay Research and coauthor of *Lost and Found: The Younger Unchurched and Churches that Reach Them*

Brad Waggoner, backed up by extensive research, has taken a hard look at contemporary American church life. What he sees raises alarm. Yet, realistically facing the evidence of mediocrity in average Christian experience, he charts a course of action for the future. It is a serious call to biblical discipleship, a lifestyle of faith that overflows in obedient witness and service to a lost world. Sobering reading, to be sure, but taken to heart, the message of this book points the way to real revival.

—Robert E. Coleman

Distinguished Professor of Evangelism and Discipleship

Gordon-Conwell Theological Seminary

Brad Waggoner has set out on a bold and daring undertaking in *The Shape of Faith to Come*. Every spiritual leader who takes the mission of making disciples seriously should read this book. While others have examined the attitudes of those outside of faith, Brad has charted a new course in research by examining the spiritual formation of those who are followers of Jesus Christ. In many ways this book is our long overdue report card.

—David Putman

Author of *Breaking the Discipleship Code*

Brad Waggoner's roots run deep in discipleship back to his relationship with the Navigators. His keen insights and observations regarding discipleship in the church are on the mark! As a fellow publisher committed to the recovery of biblical discipleship in the church, I highly recommend this book!

—Michael D. Miller

President and Executive Publisher

NavPress

THE SHAPE OF FAITH TO COME

THE SHAPE OF FAITH TO COME

SPIRITUAL FORMATION AND THE FUTURE OF DISCIPLESHIP

BRAD J. WAGGONER

Nashville, Tennessee

Printed in the United States of America

978-0-8054-4824-5

Published by B&H Publishing Group
Nashville, Tennessee

Dewey Decimal Classification: 261
Subject Heading: SPIRITUAL FORMATION \ CHRISTIANITY—UNITED STATES \ DISCIPLESHIP

1 2 3 4 5 6 7 8 9 10 • 12 11 10 09 08

To my wife Patti for her consistent love and support.

To my sons, Brandt and Blake, who seek after God and desire to be used by Him.

"I am sure of this, that He who started
a good work in you will carry it on to
completion until the day of Christ Jesus."
—Philippians 1:6

Acknowledgments

Many people have invested in my life. I am grateful for my parents, who insisted that I attend church. It was never an option. Because of this I was exposed to the gospel and by the grace of God was "adopted through Jesus Christ for Himself" (Eph. 1:5). I am indebted to the ministry of Pastor West, who faithfully preached God's Word during my childhood and teen years.

I am grateful to those who have discipled and mentored me: Dave Edwards, Bob Anderson, Billie Hanks Jr., Dr. Warren Benson, and Dr. Robert Coleman.

I am honored to have served alongside three pastors: Dr. T. C. Melton, Dr. Kenny Mahanes, and Dr. Tim Beougher.

I am deeply appreciative of the three churches I have served over the years and for all of the wonderful people I grew to love within these local communities of faith: Elmcrest Baptist Church in Abilene, Texas; Far Hills Baptist Church in Dayton, Ohio; and Cedar Creek Baptist Church in Louisville, Kentucky. These churches have contributed much to my love for the local church and my desire to help pastors, staff, and other spiritual leaders to be fruitful in their service.

I am grateful for the opportunity to colabor with Dr. Thom Rainer for nearly a decade in various ministry settings. His love for Christ, concern for the lost, and love for the local church has inspired and motivated me to give my best for the cause of Christ.

A special word of thanks goes to the LifeWay Research team for their invaluable help related to the research for this book: Ed Stetzer, Scott McConnell, Sandra Wilson, and Lizette Beard. I am also very grateful for the B&H team who helped bring this writing project to fruition: Tom Walters, Sue Farmer, Kim Stanford, David Chandler, and others.

Last but not least, I am honored to have the support of my wife Patti and my sons, Brandt and Blake, and daughter-in-law Jill. They all love God, and as a team we are seeking to serve and honor Him. What more could a husband and father ask for?

Contents

Introduction

Imagine

Imagine a church filled with believers who are spiritually alive, hungry for God, filled with wisdom, and living lives of impeccable character. Imagine a local community seasoned with Christians like this who truly desire to live as salt and light in the midst of their neighbors, coworkers, and friends. Wouldn't it be encouraging to know that the watching world would see a collective witness that reflected the truths of the gospel? Consider what it would be like if the majority of Christians shared the good news of Jesus regularly with those in their sphere of influence.

What if your walk with God was consistently characterized by love, obedience, loyalty, praise, purpose, prayer, service, and passion? Visualize the experience of feasting upon God's Word and having it captivate your thoughts, feelings, and perspectives. Contemplate the joy of knowing your life is bringing glory and pleasure to our eternal God.

Consider living in a community of faith, the body of Christ, where fellow believers actually love, honor, respect, and care for one another. Think about what it would be like to be encouraged, admonished, supported, and challenged by other followers of Christ. Wouldn't it be great to hang out in an environment with little selfishness or harmful comments? Imagine standing shoulder to shoulder with people of like mind and faith praising God and serving Him and others.

Imagine the kind of faith that grows, stretches, and matures over time. I have seen some parents who use wall space or a hallway to display pictures of their children one year at a time, reflecting observable maturation. What if we could view our spiritual formation in this way? Would most years show noticeable development?

Some people may say, "Yes, I can imagine this kind of existence. I often live in this spiritual dynamic." Others may say, "No way! I know nothing about this kind of Christianity." I wonder how many Christians concur with the former.

I often contemplate the condition of "American Christianity." I wonder what God thinks about our individual and collective faith. Are we healthy? How much of a gap exists between God's standards for our lives and how we actually live? We know there is a gap, but how much of one?

This book provides a "gap analysis" of twenty-five hundred Protestant churchgoers. The findings of our research paint a graphic picture of the health of Protestant Christianity. Few studies of this kind have been attempted. We have sought to measure the spiritual formation of these regular churchgoers over the course of one year.

We endeavored to determine how spiritually mature they are and how much growth they demonstrated over time. I think the results are fascinating. Let's see what you think.

Editors will tell any author he or she needs to define the audience for which their book is written. I felt torn when encouraged to define my audience. On one hand, I can see any believer benefiting from this book. Yet, much of the content is aimed at what I will broadly call "spiritual leaders." As an individual Christian you can gain much from reading this book as you evaluate the quality of your own spiritual formation. As a spiritual leader, whether you are a pastor, staff member, or layperson interested and involved in the spiritual development of others, you will be challenged to reject the mediocrity of the present and seek more diligently the spiritual transformation of others.

Many leaders measure the "success" of churches by common metrics such as the number of people who attend worship on a weekly basis, or the size of the budget, or the quality of the buildings, or the number of programs. While these metrics are not unimportant, they fall short of the most crucial issue: spiritual transformation.

It is my prayer that this book will ignite your passion for spiritual growth and will deepen your commitment to the spiritual development of others. Much is at stake. I am convinced that things must change. At present I believe that too many of us are settling for easy goals. It is one thing to grow a church numerically. It is quite another to seek the transformation of heart, mind, and character.

Before going further you can make the reading of this book much more personal and life changing by completing the Spiritual Formation Inventory (SFI). The SFI was the survey we used in gathering the data for this book.

By completing this survey online, you can evaluate your own spiritual development and reflect upon your own life as you interact with the analysis contained in the following chapters. After completing the survey, you will be provided with a detailed assessment of your own spiritual development and a set of suggestions and guidelines pertaining to your ongoing growth.

For the first edition of this book, access to the SFI is provided free of charge. All you need is an access code. You can find the access code on the inside of the book jacket (sometimes called the dust-cover). Take the jacket off and look on the inside. Once you locate the code, go to www.lifeway.com/sfi and follow the instructions.

Let the journey begin. The first chapter will explain the nature and scope of our study and will define current reality. I encourage you to pray that God will give you insight and a deep desire to redefine the reality of your own spiritual life. I also challenge you to seek to enhance the spiritual vitality of your local church, first by the influence of your own walk with God and then by your service within your community of faith.

Chapter One

Defining Reality

I am sure of this, that He who started a good work in you will carry it on to completion until the day of Christ Jesus.

—Philippians 1:6

Biblical Truth: God is at work in our churches and among our members, and He will carry on until His work is complete.

Defining Reality: We are confident that God is at work in His church, but at the same time we must be realistic about what we're doing well and what needs improvement.

Although I like all sports, the one I am most passionate about is college football. At the risk of losing some readers right from the kickoff, I must say I am a big Nebraska Cornhuskers fan. Nebraska fans were spoiled for more than four decades.

But the 2007 season is one we Huskers want to forget.

Historically, Nebraska football was known for its defense. The "Black Shirts," as we called them, put fear into the eyes of many opponents.

Not in 2007: we gave up more yards and touchdowns than McDonald's sold McNuggets, and so Nebraska fans started referring to our defense as the "Pink Shirts." For one game, my son Blake and I traveled to Lincoln for the Nebraska–Oklahoma State game. OSU seemed to score every time they touched the football, and by halftime the score was 38–0. (The zero being Nebraska!) The game ended 45–14.

I still break into a sweat thinking about that game. However, like most fans, I will forget about last year and anticipate the coming season with joy, buying all the college football magazines I can get my hands on in order to read about next year. I will pretend last year did not happen and will optimistically buy into all of the hype about this coming season.

During the preseason it is easy to think your team is better than it really is. You listen to the players and coaches talk about how well the players are doing in the weight room and how they are performing in practice. But then September rolls around, and after the usual game against a nonconference sacrificial goat, you watch your team perform against a real opponent.

By the end of September, coaches and fans learn what kind of football teams they really have. And if they are serious about winning, they begin to make adjustments, recognizing the current reality and creating a new one. If the coaching staff is smart, they will find the balance of building on the positives while changing the negatives.

Building on the positives and changing the negatives is what our research in general, and this book specifically, is all about. We will look at the challenges but also celebrate some good news. I will seek to avoid two extremes: the Chicken Little Syndrome and the Pollyanna Bubble.

Avoiding the Chicken Little Syndrome and the Pollyanna Bubble

When Dr. Thom Rainer and I began to lay the groundwork for LifeWay Research, I told myself that I did not want to become "Chicken Little" to the church crying, "The sky is falling!" Even though our research reveals reasons for concern, my underlying theology allows me to maintain confidence. I believe God is on His throne without any threat to His sovereign rule. The church, the body and bride of Christ, will be triumphant. The Great Commission is firmly underway and is proceeding according to God's plan. One day Christ will return and reveal His preeminence. Finally, all true believers will enjoy our "heavenly rest" and will eternally worship and serve our Lord and Savior. There is much cause for optimism and rejoicing.

A *Pollyanna* is an excessively or blindly optimistic person. It is a challenge when conducting research to keep a balance of biblically grounded optimism while facing the hard facts of reality. The apostle Paul is a great example. He did not dodge, ignore, or sugarcoat problems within the early church. In fact, he confronted problems head-on without losing his ultimate confidence in the church. One of my favorite examples of this biblically based optimism is found in Paul's letter to the Philippians.

> I am sure of this, that He who started a good work in you will carry it on to completion until the day of Christ Jesus. (Phil. 1:6)

Paul knew not all of the people in the church in Philippi were where they needed to be spiritually. He knew they would face strong opposition from Satan and his forces. He also knew some likely would walk away from God. Yet he remained confident enough to state his ultimate assurance in their spiritual formation. His great confidence in their being made into complete disciples was placed in the source of their transformation and discipleship—God.

We can likewise remain confident in God's work in the church today. All true believers, or disciples, can find hope and encouragement in God's promise to complete His transforming work in us and in His church.

Much of what we have today in the Bible came out of the context of biblical authors confronting problems in the church. God always brings good out of bad situations. We do not always see or understand what He is doing, but we can trust Him. An example of how we are to view God this way comes from Solomon's message to Israel.

> [Solomon] stood and blessed the whole congregation of Israel with a loud voice: "May the LORD be praised! He has given rest to His people Israel according to all He has said. Not one of all the good promises He made through His servant Moses has failed. May the LORD our God be with us as He was with our ancestors. May He not abandon us or leave us. May He incline our hearts toward Him to walk in all His ways and to keep His commands, ordinances, and judgments, which He commanded our ancestors. May my words I have made my petition with before the LORD be near the LORD our God day and night, so that He may uphold His servant's cause and the cause of His people Israel, as each day requires, and so that all the peoples of the earth may know that the LORD is God. There is no other! Let your heart be completely devoted to the LORD our God to walk in His ordinances and to keep His commands, as it is today." (1 Kings 8:55–61)

Praise God! Not one of the good promises of God failed. There is no other! This is the kind of biblical optimism we can embrace as we evaluate brutal facts. Let's not stick our heads in the sand. Let's not make things look worse or better than they are. We must embrace the truth. We must set aside whatever self-centered or self-serving, biased filter we look through. No one is helped by our dodging or spinning the truth. Let's own up to the facts and work on the solutions.

The Shape of Faith in the Past, Today, and Tomorrow

This book could be titled *The Shape of Faith in the Past, Today, and Tomorrow* because it describes what I hope to accomplish in the rest of this book.

The Shape of Faith in the Past

Let's start with the end in mind. As leaders, in order for us to lead our people to be the disciples they should be, we need first to look to the past, to the Bible. What should mature, obedient, loving followers of Christ look like? The Bible describes what our church members should look like, and in this chapter I provide a summary of how the Bible defines and describes a disciple of Jesus Christ. If we do not have a clear understanding of what a disciple looks like, then how can we produce what God expects?

When someone asked a well-known sculptor how he carved such beautiful sculptures, he stated, "I remove anything that does not look like what I am sculpting." All painters and sculptors begin with the end in mind. They have some idea of what their result should look like before they start. Every block of stone has a statue inside it and it is the task of the sculptor to discover it.

Defining Reality: The Shape of Faith Today

Many of us rely on anecdotal evidence when it comes to forming our concepts of reality. It reminds me of the story of the three blind men trying to describe an elephant. One man, feeling the ear, described the elephant as big and floppy like a fan. The next man, touching the elephant's side, described the animal as high and wide like a wall. The third man grabbed the tail and said the elephant was small and round like a rope.

In the same way, most people describe the condition of the church based on their most recent church experience. Some think the church in America is healthier than it really is; others think the church is nearly extinct.

The research that led to this book is substantial. First, it is substantial in its scope. We surveyed twenty-five hundred Protestants who attend church on a regular basis. It is also substantial in that it is a longitudinal study: repeated observations of the same items over a period of time.

We surveyed our sample in May 2007 and then again in May 2008. Few studies of this sort are longitudinal due to the cost and difficulty. But this provides us with a unique perspective, especially when dealing with a topic like spiritual formation. We were able to see what, if any, spiritual progress participants made over the course of one year.

With a study of this magnitude, we can define current reality, at least as it relates to Protestant Christianity. Depending on your theological and denominational view, much of what you will see will be troubling. But, just as when you go for your annual physical, you should want to know the truth. There is no spin in this study. You will see the exact questions we asked and the exact responses.

In one of my favorite leadership books, *Good to Great,* author Jim Collins explains what he calls the Stockdale Paradox. This refers to Vice Admiral James Stockdale, who, as a commander, was the highest-ranking United States naval officer held as a prisoner of war during the Vietnam War. He was tortured more than twenty times during his eight-year imprisonment and lived out the war without prisoner's rights and no set release date. When asked why he thought he survived, he stated, "I never lost faith in the end of the story." He never doubted that he would prevail and get out.

When asked who did not survive, he commented, "Oh that is easy. The optimists. They were the ones who said, 'We are going to be out by Christmas,' and Christmas would come, and then Christmas would go." He indicated that this process of optimism followed by disappointment continued to the point that they died of a broken heart. He indicated that he was hopeful but realistic.[1]

I hope we can find this balance of defining reality without losing hope for the future. I think this perspective is biblical. Paul exemplifies the attitude of dealing with the brutal facts without any wavering regarding the sovereignty of God or the ultimate destination of the church. He often described evil, sin, and heresy, both in and outside of the church; yet he continued to refer to the local church as the bride of Christ and knew it would prevail.

The Shape of Faith Tomorrow

This book is not an attempt to predict the next fad in spiritual formation or cutting-edge methodology of discipleship. It is an attempt based on clear biblical admonitions, combined with an analysis of the current state of affairs, to indicate the direction I believe we need to go.

The prescriptions are scattered throughout the book, and you will find a summary of guidance in the final chapter. The prescriptions and applications are based on my understanding of the expectations of Scripture, my own nearly thirty years of church experience, several years of church consultation, the input of other leaders, and, finally, the statistically significant correlations in this study between spiritual maturity and certain beliefs and practices.

Can Spiritual Formation Be Observed and Measured?

The first step is to provide a biblical foundation for what it means to be a disciple. This involves both an analysis of relevant texts and a comprehensive review of literature related to what it means to be and live as a disciple.

I have studied the Gospels and reviewed scholarly documents related to Scripture. The Gospels, most notably in the teachings and ministry of Christ, represent a significant amount of what we know of God's expectation for living as disciples. Following is a brief summary of what the Bible, my mentors, and important books have taught me regarding growing spiritually and living as a disciple of Jesus Christ.

Two historic Christians provide particular insight into the ministry and teachings of Christ on this subject. A. B. Bruce wrote the classic book, *The Training of the Twelve,* which has helped many understand what it means to be a disciple of Christ.

Later, Robert Coleman helped us with his phenomenal work, *The Master Plan of Evangelism*.

In addition to these important influences on my understanding of the Gospels, the rest of God's revealed Word added further insight into what it means to be and live as a disciple. An analysis of the book of Acts, the Pauline epistles, and the remainder of the Bible helped provide a comprehensive understanding of what it means to be a disciple.

In the greatest sermon ever delivered, the Sermon on the Mount, Jesus set forth several observable characteristics of faith. Jesus was establishing the ideal of what a follower of His should and will look like. He uses descriptions: gentle, merciful, pure in heart, peacemaker, salt of the earth, and light of the world. He goes on to condemn attitudes and behaviors that run counter to faith, such as: murder, adultery, divorce, practicing righteousness before men, materialistic pursuits, and judging others. Both the positive traits, referred to as Beatitudes, and the contrary sinful practices can be observed and examined.

In the Gospel of John, chapter 15, we find the exhortation of Christ on abiding in the vine, bearing fruit, and keeping His commandments. Several aspects of this are deeply internal, fully within the recesses of the mind and heart, yet believers in Christ will display evidence of their relationship with God.

In Paul's letter to the church at Colossae, we find themes similar to those expressed by the Gospel writers. In chapter 3, verses 12–14, we find the admonition for believers to "put on" specific attitudes and behaviors: compassion, kindness, humility, gentleness, patience, bearing with one another, forgiving one another, love, and unity.

In Galatians 5:16–26 Paul describes two contrasting and contradictory lifestyles. One is evidenced by living out the gospel through the power of the Holy Spirit, resulting in observable attitudes and behaviors such as love, joy, peace, patience, kindness, goodness, faithfulness, gentleness, and self-control. Paul contrasts this with an ugly, deceitful, disdainful lifestyle depicted by immorality, impurity, sensuality, idolatry, sorcery, enmities, strife, jealousy, outbursts of anger, disputes, dissensions, factions, envying, drunkenness, carousing, and the like.

God intends a radically different lifestyle for His followers, and this regenerate lifestyle is inherently observable. Since spiritual maturity can be seen, it can also be measured.

The Church Is Commanded to Produce Something

The Great Commission is the prime directive of the church. I have many good friends who teach theology, and they remind all of us that the most significant prime directive is to bring glory to God (see 1 Cor. 10:31). Part of bringing glory to God is obeying His commands. When it comes to the mission of the church, a succinct command is found in the Gospel of Matthew.

> Then Jesus came near and said to them, "All authority has been given to Me in heaven and on earth. Go therefore, and make disciples of all nations, baptizing them in the name of the Father and of the Son and of the Holy Spirit, teaching

them to observe everything that I have commanded you.
And remember, I am with you always, to the end of the age."
(Matt. 28:18–20).

The church is called, directed, gifted, and empowered to make disciples. Having a proper understanding of the meaning of *disciple* is essential. Dr. Scot McKnight, professor of New Testament theology, says, "If one understands discipleship as 'daily routine,' then one will produce those who have daily routines. If one understands discipleship as 'evangelistic ministry,' then one will produce evangelists. If one understands discipleship as 'Bible study,' then one will produce biblical scholars. If one understands discipleship as 'effective operations,' then one will produce administrative geniuses."[2]

What does the Bible mean when it uses the term *disciple*? The Latin term *discipulus,* derived from its verb form *discere,* means "to learn." Some related words are *pupil*, *scholar*, *apprentice*, and *adherent*.[3]

The most common term used in the New Testament is *mathetes*. In early classical times it was generally used to refer to a learner. Sometimes it meant "adherent." Other New Testament words related to *disciple* are *mathano* (to learn), *katamanthano* (to examine, to consider), *symmathetes* (fellow disciple), *mathetria* (woman disciple), and *matheteuo* (to become a pupil or to make disciples).

The verb *mathano* occurs 25 times in the New Testament and generally means "to learn something new." The term *mathetes* occurs 259 times. Most are references to the disciples of Jesus, John the

Baptist, and the Pharisees. Therefore, this term is generally understood to refer to the adherents of a leader.

Bill Hull is a pastor who has written extensively on discipleship. He makes the following observation:

> Therefore, a clear identification of a disciple is imperative. Understanding what a disciple is and what a disciple does are top priority for the church. The irony of the church is that we throw the word disciple around freely, but too often with no definition. . . . The definition has proven elusive. Is a disciple a convert, one who has simply trusted in Christ alone for his salvation? Is it more, a fruit-bearing, reproducing believer described by Jesus in other passages?[4]

What about the word *discipleship*? Technically there is no biblical word for discipleship. What follows are various quotes from biblical scholars regarding the meaning of discipleship.

> As an abstract term, "discipleship" does not appear in the New Testament. Rather, it is derived from the account of the relationship between Jesus and his followers as recorded in the gospels. It is characterized by two terms found frequently in the gospel material: Mathetes (disciple) and Akolothein (to follow).[5]

> [Discipleship consists of] the teachings of Jesus which pertain to being His follower. I do not use the term for the process of developing new believers into mature believers. I am using it abstractly for the teaching of Jesus regarding following Him.[6]

> Discipleship in the New Testament is the big overarching concept which includes becoming a disciple, living as a disciple and growing as a disciple.[7]

For this study, *disciple* means "to be a learner and a follower of Jesus Christ." It implies obedience. It implies a lifestyle that demonstrates spiritual formation in terms of character and service. It means "to be like Christ." The word *discipleship* refers to a deliberate process of moving Christians forward spiritually. Paul summarizes this process in his letter to the Colossian church.

> We proclaim Him, warning and teaching everyone with all wisdom, so that we may present everyone mature in Christ. I labor for this, striving with His strength that works powerfully in me. (Col. 1:28–29)

This passage and many others show that discipleship begins with proclamation. This proclamation includes preaching the gospel to the lost. Then, for those who repent and believe, we teach them God's wisdom, God's Word. And we do so with the goal of Christlike maturity.

We are not satisfied with people just sitting in a pew. We aim for far more than attendance. We seek life transformation. We also see from this passage that spiritual formation is hard work. Paul said that he labored at this task. Finally, we must recognize that real transformation, real discipleship, is possible only through the power of the Holy Spirit. We work hard to disciple others, but only God can transform them.

Characteristics and Domains

We are familiar with the term *IQ*, short for "intelligence quotient." IQ scores are used in many ways, including as predictors of educational achievement and job performance. Working off of the idea of IQ, I have sought to develop an instrument that can quantify, measure, and benchmark the degree to which self-professed Christians think and act in accordance with biblical characteristics of a disciple of Jesus Christ.

The Spiritual Formation Inventory, the survey instrument used in this study, was developed from extensive research. The foundational element of the survey design was a thorough analysis of Scripture and various articles, books, and commentaries written by many respected theologians and scholars relating to the nature of a New Testament disciple. With validation by a panel of experts, I identified twenty-one functional characteristics of a disciple. These are clear biblical expectations of any follower of Christ that can be observed and, thus to some degree, measured. Eventually, these characteristics are categorized by some common affinity into seven domains of spiritual formation.

The Learning Quotient
Domain One: Learning Truth

The Obedience Quotient
Domain Two: Obeying God and Denying Self

The Service Quotient
Domain Three: Serving God and Others

The Evangelism Quotient
Domain Four: Sharing Christ

The Faith Quotient
Domain Five: Exercising Faith

The Worship Quotient
Domain Six: Seeking God

The Relational Quotient
Domain Seven: Building Relationships

In the following chapters we will examine the biblical basis for each domain (referred to as the biblical ideal), and then we will look at what I call "current reality" by analyzing the results of our study.

A Sample of Twenty-five Hundred Protestants

The sample is composed of twenty-five hundred Protestant regular church attendees. Attendance was determined as attending at least one worship service a month. This sample is representative of America in terms of geography, gender, and age.

The respondents, or participants, can be identified by denominational preference and belief systems, such as evangelical, born-again Christian, and nonevangelical. Born-again Christians are those who have made a personal commitment to Jesus Christ and believe they will go to heaven because they have confessed their sins and accepted Christ as their Savior. Based on some of the research of George Barna, evangelicals are born-again Christians who also hold the following beliefs or doctrines:

- God-inspired accuracy of the Bible
- Reality of Satan
- Personal responsibility to share Christ with others
- Importance of Christianity in their daily lives
- View of Jesus as sinless on earth
- View of God as all-knowing, all-powerful deity
- View of salvation by grace alone[8]

Keep in mind there are various belief systems in all the denominational categories. For example, there are evangelicals (according to belief system) in both mainline and evangelical churches. Not everyone who affiliates with an evangelical church affirms all of the above doctrinal convictions; therefore, they are categorized as "nonevangelical" regardless of the church they attend.

Types of Questions

Most of the questions used for this study are called Likert-type. This means that there is a range of possible answers along a continuum of "strongly agree" to "strongly disagree." This is a common approach when seeking to determine attitudes, perceptions, opinions, and behaviors.

There are three ways to measure overall performance within each domain:

1. The proportion who gave the "ideal" response on *every one* of the elements of the domain
2. The *average* proportion who gave the "ideal" response for the elements within the domain
3. The overall score for each domain on a 0 to 100 scale (with 0 being the least ideal score and 100 being the most ideal score), based on the averages of questions with normalized scales.

For the first two types of measurement, there are two levels:

1. Top (including only the top expected levels of response, the closest to the ideal)
2. Positive (also including levels of response that are positive but not at the top). For example, "agree strongly" that "I believe everything I have belongs to God" would be a top response, while a positive response would be either "agree strongly" or "agree somewhat" with that statement.

In most cases a positive or top-two response is "agree strongly" and "agree somewhat." Occasionally a question is asked from the negative perspective, and in such cases a positive response is "disagree somewhat" or "disagree strongly."

Overall Spiritual Formation Scores

I will provide detailed analysis of the spiritual formation study in the following chapters as we look at the results through the lens of the seven domains. At this point I want to provide an overall big picture of the findings. Here is a table showing the percentage of our sample of churchgoers who provided either a top response (usually "strongly agree") to the questions in the survey and those who provided a positive or top-two response. Further, the table compares scores by various categories such as the size of the church, the frequency of attendance, and the belief systems.

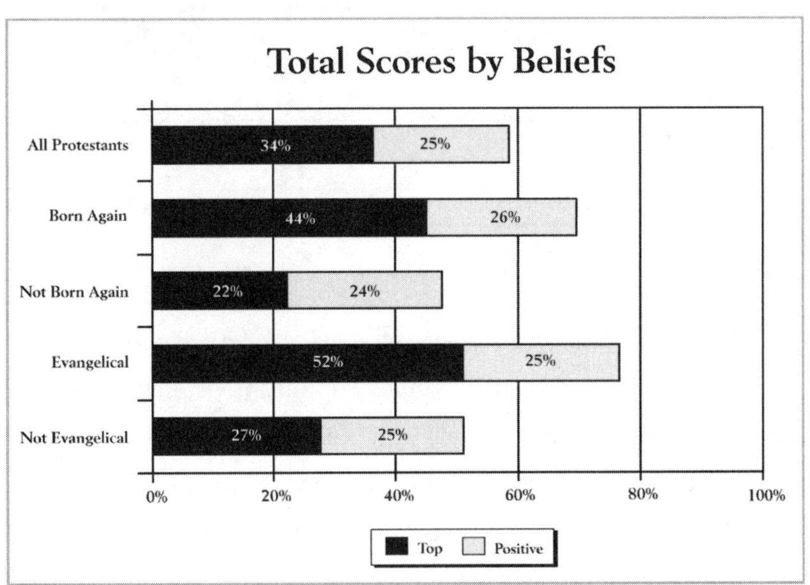

A more helpful table (below) shows the percentage of our sample scoring the equivalent of an 80 or higher. We can usually relate to this type of scoring system as it is the same as the system we grew up with at school. Assuming you agree that a score of 80 is somewhat respectable but not spectacular, we can say that 17 percent of our twenty-five-hundred churchgoers received a decent discipleship or spiritual formation score.

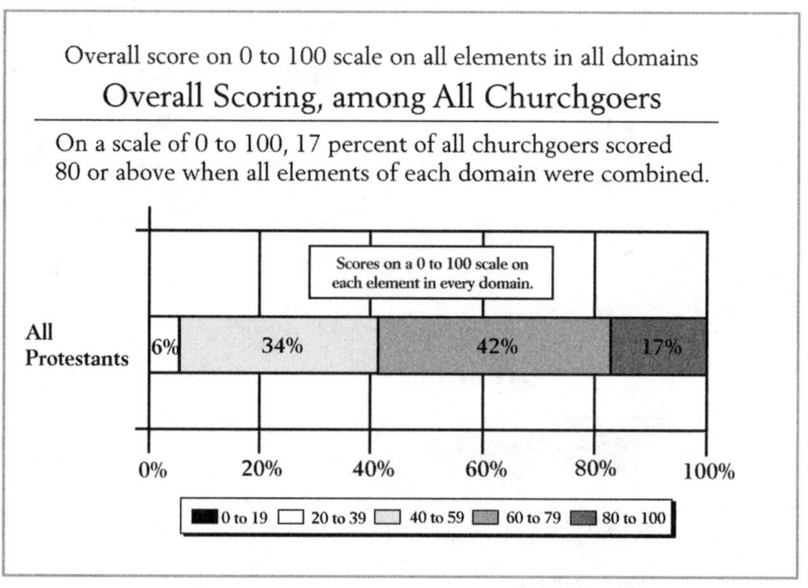

I don't think many leaders will get excited over this score. Surely, by God's grace and through His means of maturation, we can do better. In the chapters that follow, we break this study into several parts for more detailed analysis. Chapter 2 provides a summary of the basic beliefs of our churchgoers. Some would call this a picture of the "worldview of Protestantism." In the next several chapters we look at seven specific aspects of spiritual formation and biblical discipleship.

Take an Honest, Unflinching Look

Many of the results are disturbing, but this is not the time to stick our heads in the sand. When you consider the cultural context in which we reside, this is not the time for weak or average Christians or the time for weak or average churches.

If you are an individual believer active in your church, do not make the mistake of comparing yourself to those in this study. A natural human tendency is to play the comparison game without integrity. By that I mean that we tend to compare our strengths to other people's weaknesses. We need to compare ourselves by the standards set forth in the Bible.

If you are a leader in the church—pastor, staff member, or lay leader—I encourage you to be honest in assessing your leadership and the true condition of your church. I caution you about assuming the findings of this study do not apply to your setting. My guess is that your church is not far from the mean scores in this study.

This is a time for courage. The stakes are high. We need to evaluate our churches by far more than the typical quantitative metrics. This study is about qualitative perspectives related to spiritual formation. We need to be satisfied with nothing less than true biblical transformation.

Let's raise the bar of expectation for ourselves and our fellow believers. I fear mediocrity. Someday all of us will stand before God with reference to the stewardship of our own faith and ministry to others. My hope is this book will be a stimulus for many who, like me, want to move from mediocrity to excellence.

---

1. Jim Collins, *Good to Great* (New York, NY: HarperCollins, 2001), 85.

2. Scot McKnight, "Jesus and Discipleship," Lecture Notes, Trinity Evangelical Divinity School, Deerfield, IL, 1.

3. See http://humanum.arts.cuhk.edu.hk/Lexis/Latin.

4. Bill Hull, *The Disciple Making Pastor* (Old Tappan, NJ: Fleming H. Revell, 1988), 54.

5. Patricia A. Schoelles, "Discipleship and Social Ethics: A Study in the Light of the Works of Dietrich Bonhoeffer and Johann B. Metz" (Ph.D. diss., Notre Dame University, 1984), 29.

6. McKnight, "Jesus and Discipleship," 1.

7. Rwin J. Kolb, "Teaching Discipleship," *Discipling: American Festival of Evangelism* 3 (1982), 2.

8. See www.barna.org, Evangelical Christians, 2007.

Chapter Two

Surprised by What They Believe

> **Biblical Truth:** Our worldview should emerge from biblical truth.
>
> **Biblical Worldview:** Our beliefs should align with the truths taught in the Bible, and our behavior should match our beliefs.

Several years ago I was serving at a church encountering growth problems: we were growing faster than we could keep up with space. To provide some relief for the crowded conditions during our 9:30 a.m. worship service and Bible study, we started offering Sunday school classes at 8:00 a.m. I volunteered to teach one of those early classes. One of our key single male leaders and a good friend of his became faithful members of the class. They seemed committed to the beliefs and teachings of the church. Over time, however, I began to suspect that their friendship was more than the kind men typically have.

One week they mentioned that they would miss a Sunday or two because they were going to Hawaii for a few days. When they came back, I noticed both were wearing wedding rings. I knew neither of them had been dating any girls, so I asked if I could meet with them and they agreed. In the process of the meeting, they told me they were gay and had committed themselves to each other in marriage.

Now this may not be all that uncommon in many churches today, but this was a conservative church that taught a biblical perspective on marriage, one that did not include homosexuality.

The point of this story is not to engage in a lengthy apologetic for heterosexual marriage, but rather to illustrate that most pastors would be surprised to discover what some of their members believe and practice. Things are not always as they appear.

Worldviews in Conflict

We cannot separate spiritual formation, or spirituality, from matters of worldview and beliefs. Much of the Bible is dedicated to teaching doctrine and confronting falsehoods.

Large sections of Paul's letter to the Romans, for example, aim at correcting false beliefs related to Judaism and other perversions of the gospel, sin, and Christian liberty, just to name a few. When addressing the many problems in the Corinthian church, Paul confronted false ideas about the resurrection of Christ. Some people were teaching that Jesus did not actually rise from the dead.

In response Paul declared:

> Now if Christ is preached as raised from the dead, how can some of you say, "There is no resurrection of the dead"? But if there is no resurrection of the dead, then Christ has not been raised; and if Christ has not been raised, then our preaching is without foundation, and so is your faith. In addition, we are found to be false witnesses about God, because we have testified about God that He raised up Christ—whom He did not raise up if in fact the dead are not raised. For if the dead are not raised, Christ has not been raised. And if Christ has not been raised, your faith is worthless; you are still in your sins. (1 Cor. 15:12–17)

> There are some who are troubling you and want to change the gospel of Christ. But even if we or an angel from heaven should preach to you a gospel other than what we have preached to you, a curse be on him! As we have said before, I now say again: if anyone preaches to you a gospel contrary to what you received, a curse be on him! (Gal. 1:7–9)

> You foolish Galatians! Who has hypnotized you, before whose eyes Jesus Christ was vividly portrayed as crucified? I only want to learn this from you: Did you receive the Spirit by the works of the law or by hearing with faith? Are you so foolish? After beginning with the Spirit, are you now going to be made complete by the flesh? (Gal. 3:1–3)

In Colossians, Paul warns: "Be careful that no one takes you captive through philosophy and empty deceit based on human tradition, based on the elemental forces of the world, and not based on Christ" (Col. 2:8). We also see the importance of teaching doctrine and confronting falsehoods when we look at Paul's admonitions to the young pastor Timothy:

> Teach and encourage these things. If anyone teaches other doctrine and does not agree with the sound teaching of our Lord Jesus Christ and with the teaching that promotes godliness, he is conceited, understanding nothing. (1 Tim. 6:2–4)

> Evil people and imposters will become worse, deceiving and being deceived. But as for you, continue in what you have learned and firmly believed, knowing those from whom you learned, and that from childhood you have known the sacred Scriptures, which are able to instruct you for salvation through faith in Christ Jesus. (2 Tim. 3:13–16)

The Boat Is Leaking

The apostle Paul spent much time and energy teaching doctrine and refuting false theological concepts. In our day we have downplayed the role of doctrine at times, perhaps because we have been influenced by our relativistic culture, which insists that one person's truth is as good as another's. Yet we diminish our emphasis on doctrinal truth to our own harm. We are like the captain who is unconcerned about the leak in his ship. While it may not seem like a big deal at the time, eventually it will sink the ship.

Throughout this book I refer to "cultural seepage," the incipient invasion of ideas, perspectives, and beliefs that are contrary to a biblical worldview. Cultural seepage often occurs so gradually that we do not notice the deadly consequences until it is too late, like the tragedy of the premature death of professional golfer Payne Stewart on October 25, 1999. Stewart set out in a private jet, flying from Florida to Texas. Everything seemed normal during the routine flight. He, and those flying with him, had no idea they were gradually losing oxygen out of a small leak in the cabin of the aircraft. Eventually, however, the passengers and crew lost consciousness. The plane crashed in the open plains of South Dakota. No one survived.

There is abundant evidence of a leaking boat and cultural seepage in the church. I recently read two news stories highlighting the erosion of a biblical worldview. I was reading the ***USA Today*** online and saw the heading, "Survey: More have dropped dogma for spirituality in U.S." The article summarized some of the findings of a research project from the Pew Forum designed to measure the religious views of thirty-five thousand Americans. Here are a couple of disturbing findings:

- 70 percent, including a majority of all major Christian and non-Christian groups except Mormons, say "many religions can lead to eternal life."

- 51 percent have a certain belief in a personal God, but 27 percent say they are less certain of this, 14 percent call God "an impersonal force," and 5 percent reject any kind of God.[1]

It gets worse. The Cooperative Baptist Fellowship invited John Killinger to teach a workshop at their June 2008 General Assembly in Memphis, Tennessee. Here are some disturbing remarks he made at this event and from his book, *The Changing Shape of Our Salvation*.

- "Now we are reevaluating and we're approaching everything with a humbler perspective and seeing God's hand in working in Christ, but not necessarily as the incarnate God in our midst."[2]
- In the computer age, Killinger argues, religion moved from a belief in doctrines to a quest for self-fulfillment drawing on useful tidbits from an eclectic variety of faith traditions. "Doctrine isn't the driving force to many people today" except "to the fundamentalists who insist on it," Killinger said. "But doctrine is a thing of the past now religiously."[3]
- "But my notion of salvation has been considerably transformed from the simple one I was given as a young Christian. Now, I am quite certain that it is more like what the ministers talked about when they spoke of 'self-realization' and 'self-fulfilment.' It has to do with being so well integrated as a self, so comfortable with the presence of God and the world around me, that I am already in a kind of heaven, even in this highly imperfect world."[4]

Connecting the Dots

Many other examples of doctrinal erosion and biblical compromise could be cited. As a part of our study, we wanted to determine the degree to which cultural seepage had impacted our sample. We also were curious to see the possible correlation between the sample's denominational affiliation, belief system, and overall spiritual maturity scores.

We decided to use three broad distinctions found in George Barna's basic categories of belief systems:

- "Born-again Christians" are those who have made a personal commitment to Jesus Christ and believe they will go to heaven because they have confessed their sins and accepted Christ as their Savior.
- "Evangelicals" are defined according to theology. There is also a second concept of "evangelical church" versus "mainline church," which is defined by the denomination of church they attend. Evangelicals are not defined by denomination; they can be found in both mainline and evangelical churches (and not everyone in an evangelical church has evangelical beliefs). As explained in chapter 1, Barna defines an evangelical as someone who believes in the:
    - God-inspired accuracy of the Bible
    - Reality of Satan
    - Personal responsibility to share Christ with others
    - Importance of Christianity in their daily lives
    - View of Jesus as sinless on earth

- ✦ View of God as all-knowing, all-powerful deity
- ✦ View of salvation as by grace alone

- "Nonevangelicals" are those who are unable to affirm all seven of the doctrines listed above.[5]

The following table illustrates the substantial differences between evangelicals and nonevangelicals identified in our study. For example, 77 percent of evangelicals gave at least a positive response to the questions in the survey versus 52 percent of nonevangelicals. The major difference can be seen when looking at the top or ideal responses: 52 percent of evangelicals provided a top response compared to only 27 percent of nonevangelicals. This is a significant difference.

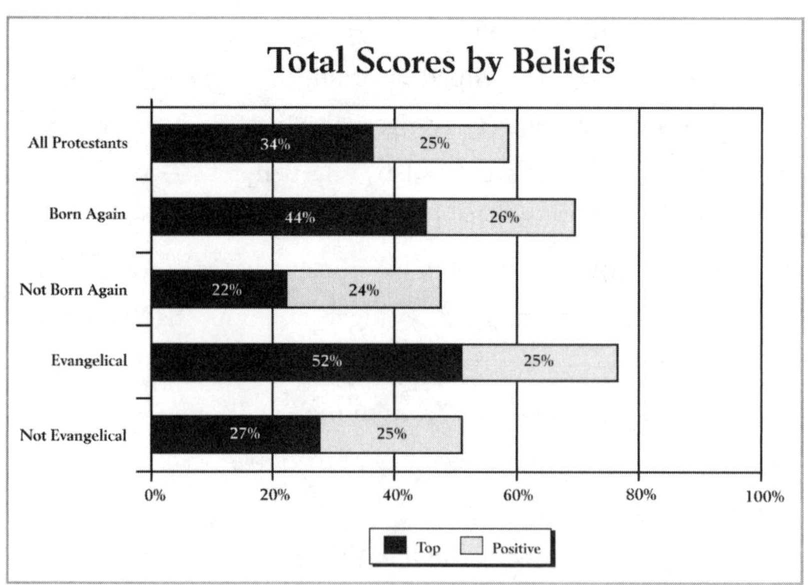

We found also a strong correlation between spiritual formation scores and the belief systems of the respondents. A person's view of basic doctrine—how he views God, the Scripture, the church, etc.—will clearly affect how that person lives out the Christian faith.

A Dozen Doctrines

The Christian faith has many important doctrinal components. Claiming to be a follower of Jesus Christ implies that a person embraces a Christian worldview. Over time, a strong correlation must exist between a person's claim to believe in Jesus and his or her understanding and belief in what the Bible teaches.

No one expects a new convert to understand fully all the Bible's essential teachings. However, we can legitimately expect that, within a reasonable period of time, a Christian will learn and embrace the foundational doctrines of the Christian faith. Far too many churchgoers hang around the Christian faith for long periods of time without making appropriate advances in their knowledge of God's Word.

The author of Hebrews rebuked Christians for that very thing:

> We have a great deal to say about this, and it's difficult to explain, since you have become slow to understand. For though by this time you ought to be teachers, you need someone to teach you again the basic principles of God's revelation. You need milk, not solid food. Now everyone who lives on milk is inexperienced with the message about

> righteousness, because he is an infant. But solid food is for the mature—for those whose senses have been trained to distinguish between good and evil. (Heb. 5:11–14)

For this study we decided to measure twelve basic Christian beliefs. We kept the questions simple and straightforward. What follows is a brief explanation of these twelve beliefs, why they are important, and how our sample of churchgoers responded.

Is the Bible Accurate?

A person's view of the Bible pretty much determines the rest of his or her faith. Faith is based on a person's worldview, which itself is grounded in an understanding of what truth is and where it comes from.

Several years ago I was on a flight from Richmond, Virginia, to Dayton, Ohio. I initiated a conversation with the young man sitting next to me, hoping to be able to share the gospel with him. As I brought spiritual subjects into the conversation, he began to share his ideas about spirituality and life after death. Essentially he believed that everyone would end up in heaven.

He said he believed that right before death everyone experiences a light, a full revelation of truth about God, and that the resulting understanding leads to true faith and entrance into a heavenly existence. "That is an intriguing view," I said. "What do you base that belief on?"

The young man stared at me for a moment as if no one had ever asked him to provide some authoritative source for his ideas. Then he said, "Well, that is just what I believe."

I replied that I would never want to trust my own creativity or intellect to come up with an accurate understanding of such significant issues as faith and life after death. This led us into a discussion about the concept of revelation and God's provision of His truth through the Bible.

Regardless of the issue, the Bible must be the starting point. If a person does not regard the Bible as given by God and fully trustworthy, faith and spiritual formation have no solid basis. An abundance of historical evidence demonstrates that once a person, church, or denomination begins to depart from strong conviction about the trustworthiness of the Bible, it is merely a matter of time before any sense of godliness evaporates.

With this in mind, we asked our sample of churchgoers a basic question about the Bible:

How much do you agree/disagree:
The Bible is the written Word of God and is totally accurate in all that it teaches?

Only 54 percent of those we surveyed "agreed strongly" with this question. Another 18 percent said they "agreed somewhat."

Earlier in this book, I mentioned that I consider "agree somewhat" a positive response for many of the questions. When it comes to the doctrinal questions, however, I believe the only solid answer is "agree strongly." Doctrinal questions are so basic and essential to the Christian faith that anything less than "agree strongly" ought to be viewed with great caution.

We can confidently say that six out of ten churchgoers surveyed appear to have a high view of the Bible. This percentage will prove to be telling as we look at the other doctrinal issues.

Salvation: What Is It? How Do I Obtain It?

The waters have often been muddied, even among evangelicals, about the basis of our faith. Years ago, as I was learning how to share my faith, I found that questions like, "Are you a Christian?" or "Do you believe in Jesus?" were not helpful in determining a person's spiritual status. Perhaps you have heard the statement, "Same words, different dictionary." When it comes to talking about the basis of someone's faith, many questions are not helpful because the same word can mean different things to different people.

For example, someone may confidently tell you he or she believes in Jesus but mean nothing more than intellectual agreement that Jesus was a real person, much as someone might acknowledge the historical reality of George Washington. For some people the word *believe* does not include the biblical notion of faith.

LifeWay Research regularly polls American teenagers for insight into their beliefs and practices. Our last study found that 69 percent of teenagers strongly or somewhat agree that they will go to heaven because Jesus Christ died for their sins. However, out of this 69 percent, 60 percent *also* stated that they believe they will go to heaven because they are religious, and 60 percent *also* agree that they will go to heaven because they are kind to others. Clearly this group of teenagers does not understand the concept of salvation through faith alone in Christ alone.

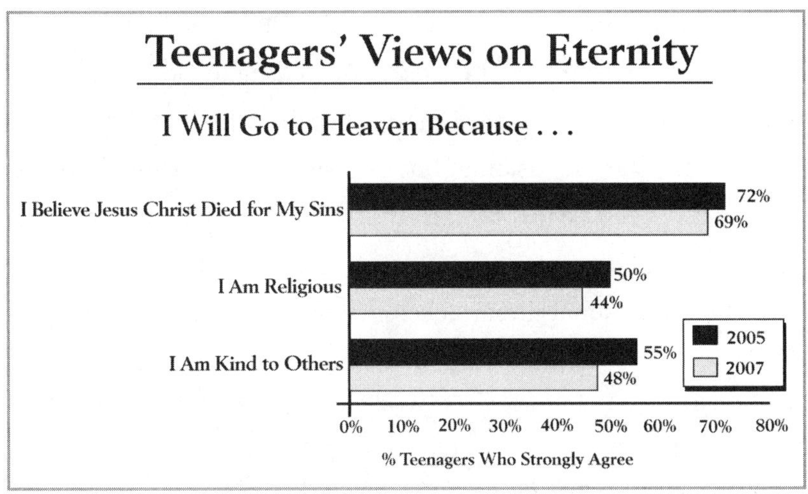

Understanding the nature of the gospel and the basis for salvation is essential. Many of the problems we see in churches today can be traced to an inadequate view of the gospel. Several prominent evangelical leaders today are expressing concern that many church members are simply unregenerate.

It should go without saying that spiritual formation cannot happen in the life of someone who has not experienced regeneration. Salvation is based solely on the substitutionary death of Jesus Christ on the cross. Human effort, as pertaining to salvation, is useless. Confusion and uncertainty as to what constitutes salvation raise serious questions about a person's salvation and his or her resulting spiritual formation. If a person thinks his salvation is dependent, even in part, on his ability to earn or sustain it, then all his attempts at spiritual growth will be unsuccessful because they are based on the wrong foundation.

In his letter to the Corinthian church, Paul explained that there can be only one source of salvation: "According to God's grace that was given to me, as a skilled master builder I have laid a foundation, and another builds on it. But each one must be careful how he builds on it, because no one can lay any other foundation than what has been laid—that is, Jesus Christ" (1 Cor. 3:10–11).

The foundational importance of conversion to all other aspects of the Christian faith led us to ask our sample of churchgoers two related questions:

How much do you agree/disagree:
Christians must continually work toward their salvation or risk losing it?

Only 23 percent of the sample "disagreed strongly" with this statement and another 10 percent "disagreed somewhat." These are deeply discouraging numbers. Just in case you are tempted to blame these low numbers on the fact the sample is broadly Protestant, I should point out that within the portion of the sample that was Southern Baptist—a denomination historically teaching that salvation is based solely on the redemptive work of Christ—only 50 percent "strongly disagreed" with the statement.

The second question was:

How much do you agree/disagree:
Eternal salvation is possible through God's grace alone; nothing we do can earn salvation?

Of our sample, 58 percent "agreed strongly" with this question while another 14 percent said they "agreed somewhat." Among Southern Baptists 75 percent "agreed strongly" that salvation is by grace alone.

These responses should be a major wake-up call for leaders and churches that care about the gospel and biblical fidelity. The fact that so few regular churchgoers have an accurate biblical understanding and conviction about salvation says we are a long way from where we need to be.

Is Jesus the Only Way?

Just as salvation cannot be earned by human merit, neither can it be obtained from any source other than the atoning work of Jesus Christ. This has been taught by the true church from its earliest days. When Peter was arrested and brought before the Jewish religious leaders, he made this great proclamation:

> There is salvation in no one else, for there is no other name under heaven given to people by which we must be saved. (Acts 4:12)

As with other doctrines discussed earlier, the exclusivity of the gospel of Jesus Christ is foundational not only for faith, but also for growing as a Christian. To think that salvation can be obtained through some other faith is to deny the essence of Christianity.

How much do you agree/disagree: If a person is sincerely seeking God, he/she can obtain eternal life through religions other than Christianity?

Only 32 percent of our sample "disagreed strongly" with this question; another 8 percent "disagreed somewhat." Only 46 percent of the Southern Baptist sample "disagreed strongly," meaning that fewer than half of the Southern Baptists surveyed firmly believe in the exclusivity of the gospel, that Jesus is the only way to salvation.

These are disturbing findings! Talk about cultural seepage! Our pluralistic society has encroached on Christianity, which, combined with inadequate teaching and discipling, has left us with results such as these. This raises serious questions about the future of many Protestant churches. If substantial numbers of churchgoers believe Christ's death on the cross is not the only means of salvation, then

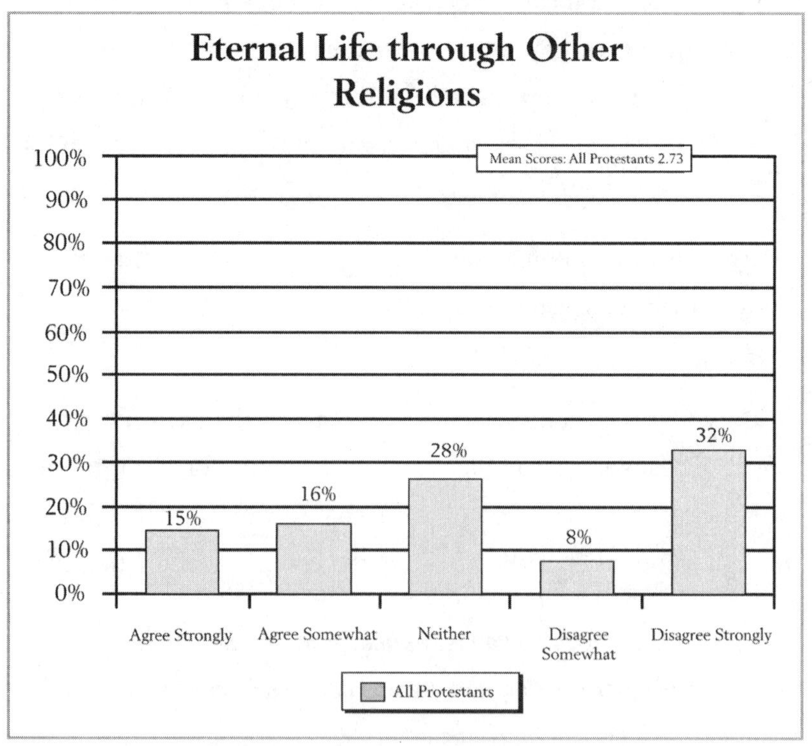

we have serious problems now and for the future. The shape of faith to come will continue to weaken unless leaders take corrective action.

Was I Born a Sinner?

Another foundational teaching of Christianity is the doctrine of original sin. Since the fall of Adam and Eve, all humans have inherited a sinful nature. Theologians use the term *imputed* to refer to the idea that Adam's sin nature has been transferred to the entire human race. They use the same term to assert that the righteousness of Christ is transferred to those who, by faith, have been regenerated. Understanding this doctrine is essential to having a proper grasp of the gospel. Paul explained it this way: "Therefore, just as sin entered the world through one man, and death through sin, in this way death spread to all men, because all sinned" (Rom. 5:12).

With this in mind, we asked our sample of churchgoers:

How much do you agree/disagree:
Every person is born a sinner due to the sin of Adam
being passed on to all persons?

Of our sample, 56 percent said they "agreed strongly" with this statement, and another 15 percent "agreed somewhat."

At the risk of sounding repetitive, these responses show serious erosion of doctrinal integrity in our churches. Apparently, either significant principles of Scripture are not taught adequately in many churches, or individuals have chosen to construct their faith in their own terms.

Did Jesus Literally Rise from the Dead?

Paul said this about those who denied the resurrection:

> Now if Christ is preached, that He has been raised from the dead, how do some among you say that there is no resurrection of the dead? But if there is no resurrection of the dead, not even Christ has been raised; and if Christ has not been raised, then our preaching is vain, your faith also is vain. Moreover we are even found *to be* false witnesses of God, because we testified against God that He raised Christ, whom He did not raise, if in fact the dead are not raised. For if the dead are not raised, not even Christ has been raised; and if Christ has not been raised, your faith is worthless; you are still in your sins. Then those also who have fallen asleep in Christ have perished. If we have hoped in Christ in this life only, we are of all men most to be pitied. (1 Cor. 15:12–19 NASB, emphasis added)

Without the literal resurrection of Christ from a literal death, Paul says, we Christians are to be pitied more than anyone. Without Christ's victory over sin, proven by His resurrection, our faith is in vain. Paul's words are unequivocal. We would expect something stated so clearly in the Bible to find unanimous support among regular churchgoers.

To discover whether this was the case, we asked our sample:

How much do you agree/disagree: Jesus died on the cross and was physically resurrected from the dead?

Of our sample, 72 percent "agreed strongly," while another 12 percent "agreed somewhat." More churchgoers affirmed the resurrection of Christ than the doctrine of inerrancy. It would be interesting to ask churchgoers what belief in the resurrection of Christ can be based on other than the Word of God.

If leaders are biblically to shape the faith to come, they will work hard to equip church members and fellow believers with solid doctrinal beliefs and convictions. They will be taught why they can confidently believe key truths like the resurrection of Christ. They need to understand how the doctrine of inerrancy is foundational to all other doctrines. If you cannot trust God's Word completely, how can you know which of its teachings to believe?

The Trinity

Another foundational teaching of Christianity is the Trinity, the idea that there is one God in three persons—Father, Son, and Holy Spirit. This doctrine is so essential that it is used to distinguish between genuine Christian followers and false believers. In fact, the majority of scholars say that not affirming the Trinity is so far out of line with historical Christianity that it is cultic. The Church of Jesus Christ of Latter-day Saints (Mormon), Jehovah's Witness, and Unitarians, for example, do not believe in the Trinity, and most scholars consequently view them as outside of the Christian faith.

Due to the essential nature of this doctrine, we asked our sample of churchgoers:

How much do you agree/disagree: There is one true God who reveals Himself to humanity as God the Father, God the Son, and God the Holy Spirit (commonly referred to as the Trinity)?

Of those we surveyed, 70 percent said they "agreed strongly" with the doctrine of the Trinity; another 13 percent "agreed somewhat."

The fact that nearly a third of our sample could not clearly affirm the historical, orthodox understanding of the Trinity should greatly concern spiritual leaders. Pastors and church leaders need to be aggressive in providing foundational teaching on the nature of God. There must be no confusion about this essential biblical belief.

Jesus: Was He Sinless?

In recent years many progressive secularists and liberal "Christians" have tried to recast the person and work of Jesus Christ. The Jesus Seminar, *The Da Vinci Code*, and other heretical efforts have tried to undermine the biblical view of Jesus Christ. Apparently these efforts, compounded by a lack of solid biblical preaching and teaching, have resulted in significant aberration from the essential doctrine of the sinlessness of Christ.

The question we asked related to the sinless nature of Christ was:

How much do you agree/disagree: Jesus may have committed sins while in human form on earth?

This question was asked in the negative so we were hoping for a large number of "disagree strongly" responses. What we discovered was that only 54 percent of our sample said they "strongly disagreed," and another 6 percent "disagreed somewhat." Among Southern Baptists 76 percent said they "disagreed strongly."

I have to admit the responses to all these doctrinal questions deeply bother me, but this one really stings! How any Protestant can fail to affirm strongly the sinless nature of Christ is beyond me. Why follow a mere sinful human? Thinking that Jesus may have sinned goes well beyond the typical liberal or pluralistic view that Jesus was a prophet or a great moral teacher but not God.

Is God in Full Control?

Throughout history skeptics and cynics have questioned the nature of God. The orthodox view of God has been that He is all-present, all-knowing, and all-powerful. Scholars use the words *omniscient*, *omnipresent*, and *omnipotent* to describe these divine characteristics. These perceptions of God's nature are as basic to the church as the notions of freedom and liberty are to America. Just as it would be considered un-American to question liberty and freedom, it is likewise un-Christian to doubt the all-knowing, all-present, and all-powerful attributes of God.

In recent years an old heresy dressed up in new clothing, "open theism," has come onto the scene. *Open theism* is defined this way:

> Practically, open theism makes the case for a personal God who is able to be influenced through prayer, decisions, and actions of people. Although unknowing of the future, God has predictive (anticipatory) foreknowledge of the future through His intimate knowledge of each individual.[6]

With all the onslaughts from secular progressives and liberals, every evangelical leader must be concerned about corrupt concepts taking hold in our churches. With this in mind, we asked our sample of churchgoers:

How much do you agree/disagree: God is the all-knowing, all-powerful, perfect Deity who created the universe and still rules it today?

Of our sample, 74 percent said they "agreed strongly" with the view that God is all-knowing and all-powerful; another 12 percent "agreed somewhat."

Clearly, some theological erosion is going on within Protestantism. More than a quarter of our sample was unable to affirm confidently the classical understanding of the nature of God. While determining the influences that led to this slippage was outside the scope of this research project, open theism has likely made some inroads. Evangelical leaders must vigilantly bolster the theological depth and convictions of our churches. A great deal is at stake. Once you begin to limit your view of the nature of God, it is only a matter of time before the entire foundation of Christianity will wash away.

Will Jesus Christ Return as He Left?

From the first days of Christianity, believers have been eagerly awaiting the return of Jesus Christ. Here are a few glimpses from the Bible about the proper disposition of believers regarding the Second Coming:

> You also be ready, because the Son of Man is coming at an hour that you do not expect. (Luke 12:40)

> They are focused on earthly things, but our citizenship is in heaven, from which we also eagerly wait for a Savior, the Lord Jesus Christ. (Phil. 3:19–20)

> So also the Messiah, having been offered once to bear the sins of many, will appear a second time, not to bear sin, but to bring salvation to those who are waiting for Him. (Heb. 9:28)

While eschatology, the study of end times, is often debated and Christians lack solid consensus about many of the details, the belief that Jesus Christ will physically return is widely held. This expectation is so widely recognized in our culture that when Michael Jordan came out of retirement to play professional basketball again, many of the nation's secular newspapers referred to it as the "Second Coming." Even people outside the church are familiar with the terminology of the Second Coming.

Since this is the case, one would expect near total consensus in Protestantism regarding the Second Coming. We asked our sample of churchgoers:

How much do you agree/disagree: Christ will return a second time to gather believers to Himself?

Of our sample, 67 percent said they "agreed strongly," while another 13 percent "agreed somewhat."

Is Satan Real?

Our culture is familiar with the notion of demons. Hollywood has produced many movies involving Satan or demons. Comedian Flip Wilson popularized the phrase, "The devil made me do it."

The person of Satan enters the biblical record early, and he holds a prominent position throughout biblical revelation. In the third chapter of Genesis, we see Satan in the form of a serpent tempting Eve to disobey God. The Gospels record this diabolical figure tempting Jesus to disobey the Father.

Jesus understood that Satan is behind all efforts to discourage or deceive the church. On one occasion, He confronted the scribes and Pharisees with:

> Why don't you understand what I say? Because you cannot listen to My word. You are of your father the Devil, and you want to carry out your father's desires. He was a murderer from the beginning and has not stood in the truth, because there is no truth in him. When he tells a lie, he speaks from his own nature, because he is a liar and the father of liars. (John 8:43–44)

Paul explains the nature of the enemy this way: "And no wonder! For Satan himself is disguised as an angel of light" (2 Cor. 11:14).

Later, in his letter to Timothy, Paul said: "For some have already turned away to follow Satan" (1 Tim. 5:15).

Without any doubt there has been clear belief in the person and evil actions of Satan throughout Judeo-Christian history. Within the current Christian context, two extreme views on Satan and his demonic forces emerge. On one hand, phony preachers on "Christian" television programs act as if there is a demon behind every bush, a perversion of the Bible that has tainted many people's view of Christianity. At the other extreme, some people never even think about or discuss the reality of Satan and the demonic. I would guess many of the churches represented by our sample rarely, if ever, discuss Satan and his evil domain.

In order to determine where our sample stood on this issue, we asked this question:

How much do you agree/disagree:
Satan is a real being,
not just a symbol of evil?

Only 58 percent "agreed strongly" with the belief in a literal being called Satan; another 14 percent "agreed somewhat."

What about Hell?

Similar to the issue of Satan, the concept of hell is widely understood not only within Christianity but in American culture as well. Many, however, have difficulty holding the idea that hell is a literal place where those who reject the gospel spend eternity. Many liberal theologians have dismissed the notion of hell altogether by spinning it as merely metaphorical. Others have tried to lessen the severity of the concept by teaching annihilation, the idea that nonbelievers merely cease to exist when they die.

In 2000, *U.S. News & World Report* conducted a survey of Americans' view of hell. Here is a quote from *Religion Today* regarding this study:

> Hell has lost its fire and brimstone in the minds of most Americans. A *U.S. News & World Report* poll shows that more people believe in hell today than they did in the 1950s, but think of hell as a state of existence where a person suffers deprivation from God rather than as a physical place. While 64 percent of respondents said there was a hell, 53 percent agreed it is "more of an anguished state of existence eternally separated from God" than an actual place. Thirty-four percent said hell is an actual place where people suffer eternal fiery torments.[7]

Historically, those who have a high view of the Bible support the clear teaching that a literal place called hell exists and that those who deny Christ will spend eternity there. This is based in part on the fact that Jesus viewed hell as a literal place: "Don't fear those who kill the body but are not able to kill the soul; rather, fear Him who is able to destroy both soul and body in hell" (Matt. 10:28).

How much do you agree/disagree: There is a literal place called hell?

Of our sample, 54 percent "agreed strongly" with the existence of hell, and another 16 percent "agreed somewhat."

The Shape of Faith to Come

An average of 58.5 percent of our sample provided a top or ideal response to the twelve doctrinal questions.

These numbers are unacceptable. I urge all church leaders who desire to see the body of Christ built up and mobilized for eternal purposes to reinforce our efforts to preach and teach the full counsel of God's Word. This task starts in the pulpit. We need men of God to step into the pulpits of our churches to edify and build up believers. We need sermons that are well prepared, biblically substantive, and delivered by sincere, humble preachers who model what they teach.

We have too many leaders who appear to be more concerned about attracting a crowd than fostering genuine spiritual transformation among believers. When they step into the pulpit, spiritual leaders need to ask themselves who their audience is. While we need to be warm and welcoming to visitors and nonbelievers in our midst, we must keep the community of faith clearly in view. Otherwise, our churches will continue to be a mile wide and an inch deep, as our study shows.

Training believers in the Word of God must not, however, be limited to the Sunday morning pulpit. Churches that are serious about producing disciples seek to provide a wide variety of opportunities for Bible study, discipleship, and life transformation in the microcosm of a biblical community. Small groups, Sunday school, discipleship classes, men's and women's ministry events, and the like are all useful strategies for teaching God's Word. Churches need to equip parents to foster spiritual depth in the home. Children and youth ministries must move beyond fun and games and seek life transformation.

I have a friend who pastors a church in Alabama who is seeking to teach God's Word in a substantive manner. He has taken some exciting steps to mature his flock. He began leading a few of his key leaders in a study of a substantive book about Christian doctrine. His leaders responded enthusiastically. They loved learning and being challenged beyond their previous knowledge of God's Word. Once they completed the book, each leader then led a small group of other church members through the same study. This process of taking small groups through a substantive study of Christian theology has continued to the point where hundreds of members have been challenged and stretched to new levels of biblical knowledge.

This is just one example of a pastor's raising the bar of expectation for his church. Christians need to be challenged to grow and learn. Most Christians will respond when challenged. If we lead them, they will follow.

---

1. Cathy Lynn Grossman, "Survey: More have dropped dogma for spirituality in U.S., *USA Today*, www.usatoday.com, June 23, 2008.

2. David Roach, "CBF presenter questions Christ's deity," *Baptist Press*, www.baptistpress.com, June 19, 2008.

3. Ibid.

4. John Killinger, *The Changing Shape of Our Salvation* (New York, NY: Crossroad Publishing Company, 2007), 103.

5. See www.barna.org, Evangelical Christian, 2007.

6. See www.wikipedia.com.

7. *Religion Today*, January 27, 2000.

Chapter Three

Domain One

Learning Truth: The Learning Quotient

When the Spirit of truth comes, He will guide you into all the truth. For He will not speak on His own, but He will speak whatever He hears. He will also declare to you what is to come.

—John 16:13

Biblical Truth: Seeking God and His truth is the essence of being a Christian.

The Learning Quotient: The Christian life is a journey of learning and applying biblical truth.

Paul Kwak is an amazing guy. I met Paul in Dayton, Ohio, in 1991 when he was an elementary student. I was in a worship service one Sunday, and this little kid walked up to the platform and sat at the piano. My first thought was this kid had escaped his parents' grasp and was about to interrupt the worship service. To my amazement he began to play a baby grand piano with ability I had never heard before. After the service I asked who this young kid was. I found he was no ordinary elementary-school kid. He not only was winning national awards as a piano player, but he was an even better violinist!

Over the next few years, I watched this young man grow up. His private school evaluated his intellectual capacity and advanced him one entire grade on the spot. He spoke French so fluently that French people would swear he grew up in France.

After graduating with honors from high school, he went on to receive an undergraduate degree from Harvard, a master's degree from Oxford, a master's degree from Juilliard, and is working on a medical degree from Case Western Reserve University.

Clearly Paul Kwak is not an ordinary young man. He is very gifted. But his vast knowledge and skill came from hard work. From the time he was young, he worked hard to learn and grow his varied talents. He has a tremendous thirst for learning, and he is highly motivated to learn and grow.

Most of us know someone who is passionate to learn. While they may not have the raw talent of a Paul Kwak, they are hungry to grow in knowledge and wisdom. We can't help but notice this attitude and spirit. Teachers remember students who showed thirst for knowledge and insight. They are a delight to teach, and we wish we knew more people who love to learn.

Following Christ is a lifelong journey of adventure and learning, and there is a connection between learning, spiritual formation, and living as a disciple of Jesus Christ.

Biblical Truth

The essence of being a Christian is being a learner, learning the truth of God, but we have a major barrier to learning. In studying the doctrine of man, we accept that all people are born sinners and affected by the fall of man, a reference to original sin and rebellion of the first man, Adam. Paul expressed in his letter to the church at Rome that:

> Therefore, just as sin entered the world through one man, and death through sin, in this way death spread to all men, because all sinned. (Rom. 5:12)

We know that original sin is not only legal in nature—we stand condemned before a holy God—but there are also other widespread effects. Scholars and theologians discuss total depravity, meaning that original sin affects every aspect of a person, including his or her knowledge and the capacity to understand spiritual truth. Paul expressed it this way:

> But the natural man does not welcome what comes from God's Spirit, because it is foolishness to him; he is not able to know it since it is evaluated spiritually. (1 Cor. 2:14)

In Scripture, however, we find a different description of those who are regenerate or saved and, thus, adopted into God's family.

A regenerate person is not only spared the legal condemnation of sin, but can now understand spiritual truth. Paul puts it this way:

> Now we have not received the spirit of the world, but the Spirit who is from God, in order to know what has been freely given to us by God. We also speak these things, not in words taught by human wisdom, but in those taught by the Spirit, explaining spiritual things to spiritual people. (1 Cor. 2:12–13)

One of the joys of knowing Christ and being adopted into His family, the community of faith, is to learn and value truth. We are no longer in bondage to our former state of deception and blindness. We see ourselves and others through a new lens.

The disciple John noted an important proclamation by Jesus: "If you continue in My word, you really are My disciples. You will know the truth, and the truth will set you free" (John 8:31–32). This is the nature of truth, disclosing deception, and pointing to a better way. That is the nature of God, His will and ways. It doesn't lead to perfection, but to a journey of gaining and applying biblical truth leading to Christlikeness.

Becoming a Christian does not automatically lead to an abundance of knowledge and wisdom. Rather, it leads to the ability to comprehend and apply biblical truth. At the point of regeneration, the Holy Spirit takes up residence within us and we start a wonderful journey of learning and growing. Jesus referenced the role of the Holy Spirit in making truth known to believers:

"When the Spirit of truth comes, He will guide you into all the truth" (John 16:13).

Donald Whitney reminds us that spiritual transformation cannot happen without learning. "Growth in godliness involves a mental renewal that cannot happen without learning. And the alternative to transformation via learning is conformity to the world."[1]

As believers we must apply diligence to learn. We have the capacity to learn—we have the indwelling Spirit—but we must apply the *will* to learn. While believers are free from enslavement to sin, we can still experience ignorance and deception.

Learning truth is an active process, requiring desire, will, energy, discipline, and determination. It demands that we invest time in exposing ourselves to biblical truth, and it requires a sense of humility. It also demands constant remorse in that we must often confess our willful rebellion against the truth and seek a new disposition and behavior.

The Bible contains many references to teaching and learning. Jesus was called Rabbi or Teacher. The Bible has many references to Jesus teaching those who gathered to hear Him and accounts of His withdrawing from the crowds to teach the twelve disciples. Luke reported that even after the resurrection and before the ascension of Christ, "He told them [his disciples], 'These are My words that I spoke to you while I was still with you—that everything written about Me in the Law of Moses, the Prophets, and the Psalms must be fulfilled.' Then He opened their minds to understand the Scriptures" (Luke 24:44–45).

After Christ's ascension and Pentecost (fulfilling God's promise to send the Holy Spirit recorded in Acts 2:1–4), the early church was characterized by teaching and learning.

> So those who accepted His message were baptized, and that day about 3,000 people were added to them. And they devoted themselves to the apostles' teaching, to fellowship, to the breaking of bread, and to prayers. (Acts 2:41–42)

Teaching and learning biblical truth has continued throughout church history. Teaching God's Word is one of the primary works of the church. Worship services for more than two thousand years have centered on song, praise, prayer, fellowship, and the study of God's Word. Scripture makes clear that one of the qualifying characteristics for church leadership is the ability to teach (see 1 Tim. 3:2; Titus 1:9).

Learning biblical truth is the core of transformation. Paul, in his letters to the churches, provided many urgings about learning and renewing the mind.

> Do not be conformed to this age, but be transformed by the renewing of your mind, so that you may discern what is the good, pleasing, and perfect will of God. (Rom. 12:2)

> Do what you have learned and received and heard and seen in me, and the God of peace will be with you. (Phil. 4:9)

> We proclaim Him, warning and teaching everyone with all wisdom, so that we may present everyone mature in Christ. (Col. 1:28)

> Let the message about the Messiah dwell richly among you, teaching and admonishing one another in all wisdom, and singing psalms, hymns, and spiritual songs, with gratitude in your hearts to God. (Col. 3:16)

> All Scripture is inspired by God and is profitable for teaching, for rebuking, for correcting, for training in righteousness, so that the man of God may be complete, equipped for every good work. (2 Tim. 3:16–17)

A major part of the spiritual formation process is to be a diligent student of the Word of God and to have a hungry, teachable spirit. To be a disciple means being a learner. Being a learner involves both attitude and behavior. Therefore, the Spiritual Formation Inventory contains questions allowing the respondent to describe perspectives and practices that will help provide a basis for evaluation. Here are the questions:

- How much do you agree/disagree: I desire to please and honor Jesus in all that I do?
- How much do you agree/disagree: I have made a serious attempt to discover God's will for my life?
- How much do you agree/disagree: I tend to accept the constructive criticism and correction of other Christians?
- How much do you agree/disagree: I am open to those who teach the Bible?
- How often do you read the Bible?
- How often do you study the Bible (more in-depth than just reading it)?

- Have you ever gone through a class for new Christians?
- Have you ever been discipled or mentored one-on-one by a more spiritually mature Christian who spent time with you on a regular basis (at least once a month) for the purpose of helping in your spiritual development?
- How much do you agree/disagree: A Christian should consider himself/herself accountable to other Christians?

These questions are designed to measure both attitudes toward learning and behaviors that would lead to learning. Motivation is a central issue related to spiritual formation. It is easy to lean toward measuring performance. Yet we must be reminded that Jesus rebuked individuals who appeared religious and spiritual on the outside without a corresponding heart for God and love for others.

> Woe to you, scribes and Pharisees, hypocrites! You are like whitewashed tombs, which appear beautiful on the outside, but inside are full of dead men's bones and every impurity. In the same way, on the outside you seem righteous to people, but inside you are full of hypocrisy and lawlessness. (Matt. 23:27–28)

We can fall for the same self-deception. During my years of local church ministry, some of the most difficult people I dealt with were those who possessed an outward appearance of godliness. But inside they had hearts of self-righteousness and the absence of the fruit of the Holy Spirit.

The Truth Quotient: Real Numbers

Now that we have a biblical standard, let's examine how our sample of twenty-five hundred churchgoers measured up to the biblical standards related to being a learner.

Only 3 percent of the respondents provided a top or ideal response on every question; 16 percent had a positive response. On a scale of 0–100, the average for all respondents was 64.9 out of 100. Only 23 percent scored above 80 out of 100. Most church leaders expect more than 3 percent of their people to give the top response or more than 23 percent to score above 80.

Truth Emerges from the Inside Out

Jesus said we honor Him from the inside out. Truth emerges from inside. The truth transforms our lives, not merely facts or knowledge. Otherwise, we are like the scribes and Pharisees, who "clean the outside of the cup and dish, but inside they are full of greed and self-indulgence! . . . First clean the inside of the cup, so the outside of it may also become clean" (Matt. 23:25–26).

This "inside out" teaching suggests that if we answer the "why" question we'll receive insight into what is working its way out of a believer, truth or mere facts. We attempt to measure motivations by asking this question:

How much do you agree/disagree: I desire to please and honor Jesus in all that I do?

This first question in Domain One is an attempt to get at the true heart or motive of learning. An essential manifestation of true regeneration and genuine spirituality is the desire to honor and please God. This is modeled in the heart of Jesus the Son toward God the Father: "My food is to do the will of Him who sent me" (John 4:34).

We see admonitions throughout the Bible for all believers to seek to please, glorify, and honor God: "Do everything for God's glory" (1 Cor. 10:31); "Discerning what is pleasing to the Lord" (Eph. 5:10). As we attempt to measure behavior that typifies a learner, we want to inquire about intrinsic motivation, the heart of the learner.

We found that only 54 percent of our sample responded with "agree strongly" to this question. Another 29 percent chose "agree somewhat." Notice the question includes "I desire." It is one thing if many Christians believe they fall short of pleasing and honoring God through their conduct. But this question aimed at the degree to which they *wanted* to "please and honor Jesus." This is alarming! You would think that when it comes to desire, rather than actual practice, the response would be close to 100 percent.

Comparing Belief Systems

As mentioned earlier, this study allows us to compare our sample in various ways, including the general belief categories of "evangelical" versus "nonevangelical" and "born again" versus "not born again." From time to time, I will show differences in some of these categories.

In our first question in Domain One only 44 percent of those identified as "nonevangelical" agreed strongly that they desire to "please and honor Jesus in all that they do" compared with 86 percent of those identified as "evangelical." This represents a sizable difference between these two groups of churchgoers. Nearly twice as many evangelicals express the internal motivation, or desire, to please and honor Christ. As you can see, doctrinal perspective matters significantly in terms of spiritual formation.

Seeking God's Will

Think about it. There is an all-powerful, ever-present, all-knowing, eternal, perfect Creator, the God of the universe. This reality is mind-boggling! Then, to make it even more phenomenal, He actually loves us and desires to direct and guide us in and along His perfect path of wisdom. Why wouldn't any true believer and follower be eager to discover the will and ways of this perfect, divine Being?

To determine the degree to which our sample of churchgoers are learners, we asked them this question:

How much do you agree/disagree: I have made a serious attempt to discover God's will for my life?

This is different from the one related to desiring to honor and please Jesus. This question is related more to practical application than to intrinsic motivation or attitude. We would expect higher numbers related to questions about desire than questions related to practice. And yet, this time only 37 percent said they strongly agree they have made a serious attempt to discover God's will. Another 36 percent said they "agreed somewhat."

Attempting to discover God's will is essential for anyone claiming to be a learner or a disciple of Jesus Christ. This should be as natural for a believer as breathing. For only 37 percent of our sample to affirm strongly the pursuit of God's will should be a cause for concern to any church leader. This reality raises serious questions about our churchgoers' understanding of the nature of salvation.

Is My Life Your Business?

In the New Testament one of the greatest examples of openness to correction is when the apostle Paul stood before the Sanhedrin. When one of the group ordered Paul be slapped hard across the mouth, Paul rebuked the man who gave the command: "God is going to strike you, you whitewashed wall! You are sitting there judging me according to the law, and in violation of the law are you ordering me to be struck?" (Acts 23:3).

The men standing next to Paul asked, "Do you dare revile God's high priest?" (v. 4). Despite a bloody lip, Paul immediately took the correction, responding to the truth, saying he did not realize Ananias was the high priest. Paul knew that the Scriptures taught: "You must not speak evil of a ruler of your people" (v. 5).

We have a teachable spirit when we can quickly respond to the truth. Leaders will biblically shape the faith to come by demonstrating and teaching that spirituality is no longer, nor was it ever, a private matter. The truth is, we are connected to a community of faith that not only brings encouragement and support but also requires transparency and accountability.

In order to measure openness to corrective truth, we asked the following question:

How much do you agree/disagree: I tend to accept the constructive criticism and correction of other Christians?

Only 17 percent of our sample "agreed strongly" with this statement, while another 41 percent "agreed somewhat." Among evangelicals 28 percent "agreed strongly" and 49 percent "agreed somewhat," compared to mainline scores of 11 percent and 40 percent.

Clearly the majority of our churchgoers do not readily embrace the idea of correction. Yet accepting correction is an essential part of being a learner. Jesus trained His twelve disciples through intensive exposure of their lives to one another. Their daily interaction resulted in an intense community of faith. But one can fake the Christian life in our "go to church once a week" culture where you can reflect the appearance of godliness without any true scrutiny.

I do not suggest communal living, nor do I support zealous intrusion into one another's lives. I merely suggest that to live as a biblical disciple, one must have exposure, access, openness, and accountability translating into constructive input and correction. When was the last time anyone knew enough about your life, and loved you enough, to offer constructive criticism, or had permission to correct or guide you?

Do Disciples Listen? Are They Open?

If you have ever taught or preached, you can recall how encouraging it is when you see a few attentive faces and expressions of interest or agreement on the part of some in the audience. I have often wondered after a sermon how many people really tuned in and thought about what I said. There is no question that one of the issues is the quality of the presentation, but the attitude of those listening is more important. Are they hungry? Are they open? Are they eager to learn?

The New Testament believers in the city of Beroea are an example of attentive, teachable Christians. "As soon as it was night, the brothers sent Paul and Silas off to Beroea. On arrival, they went into the synagogue of the Jews. The people here were more open-minded than those in Thessalonica, since they welcomed the message with eagerness and examined the Scriptures daily to see if these things were so" (Acts 17:10–12).

One of the characteristics of a learner is intentional exposure and openness to those called by God to preach and teach His Word. With this in mind, we asked this question:

How much do you agree/disagree:
I am open and responsive to those in my church
who teach the Bible?

Of our sample 36 percent indicated they "agreed strongly" with the question, and another 38 percent said they "agreed somewhat";

63 percent of evangelicals responded "agree strongly" compared to only 27 percent of nonevangelicals.

The scores related to Domain One were higher than some of those in the other domains. Historically, denominations and churches have anchored their worship services on teaching and preaching. A characteristic of Christianity is that the Bible is to be prominent in worship. While there are differences in both the quality and quantity of time given to teaching and preaching, most churches put a high value on preaching.

Several Bible passages refer to the importance of teaching and preaching. Paul reminded Timothy that "all Scripture is inspired by God and profitable for teaching, for reproof, for correction, for training in righteousness; so that the man of God may be complete, equipped for every good work" (2 Tim. 3:16–17 NASB). A couple of verses later Paul urged Timothy to "preach the word; be ready in season and out of season; reprove, rebuke, exhort, with great patience and instruction" (2 Tim. 4:2 NASB).

Another example of a teachable person is in Jesus' parable of the soils. Jesus describes the good soil: "But the one sown on the good ground—this is one who hears and understands the word, who does bear fruit and yields: some 100, some 60, some 30 times" (Matt. 13:23). A hungry, teachable attitude is essential to fruitfulness in the Christian life.

The good news is that most evangelicals display openness and receptivity to those who preach and teach God's Word. We celebrate and take hope in this finding. All leaders, especially preachers, should be encouraged about the high level of openness of the laity to the teaching and preaching ministry of the church.

The Bible Factor

Our study of churchgoers included the measurement of more than sixty factors characteristic of biblical spiritual development. After the first round of surveys in May 2007, we hired a professional statistician to help determine which of the factors included in our survey were most strongly correlated to spiritual maturity. Keep in mind that research cannot prove cause and effect. That is limited to scientific experiment, like putting chemicals into a test tube and measuring empirically verifiable phenomenon. But in a study like this, we can measure statistically significant correlations.

Our statistician applied sophisticated procedures to our data to produce a rank-ordered list of correlations. The number one factor, or characteristic, most correlated to the highest maturity scores is the practice of "reading the Bible." I almost had to laugh when I saw this. Sometimes we complicate things. The simple discipline of reading the Bible has a major impact on Christians.

Spiritual leaders need to take note of this. We put a lot of time and energy into preparing sermons, as we should. But we make a huge mistake if we think our sermons, regardless of their quality, are enough to create sustained life transformation or sanctification in the lives of our fellow believers. Our people need daily exposure to the life-transforming power of God through His revealed Word.

With this in mind, we asked these questions pertaining to Bible reading and Bible study:

How often do you do each of the following:
Read the Bible?

Study the Bible (more in-depth than just reading it)?

Among those surveyed, 16 percent said they read their Bible every day. Another 20 percent read it "a few times a week," and 12 percent read it "weekly." On one hand, we find it encouraging that 48 percent of churchgoers read the Bible at least once a week. We can take heart that nearly half of our members are looking to the Word at least weekly, but it should be much better.

Seven percent said they study the Bible every day, and 14 percent said they study the Bible "a few times each week." Another 14 percent do so weekly, meaning 35 percent of active churchgoers study the Bible at least once a week. That's more encouraging than I expected. More than a third of the average congregation goes beyond just reading the Bible and seeks to analyze it in study.

But what is the standard? What does God expect of us? Is this a satisfactory performance for a church to be spiritually healthy and effective? Can any believer grow in Christ without a steady diet of Bible study, reflection, and meditation? These questions are almost rhetorical. Clearly we need to set the bar of expectation high and then enjoy watching our people reach for new heights. One of the most rewarding experiences in my ministry over the years has been watching God's Word take on rich, new meaning in the lives of those who begin to drink deeply from it.

To biblically shape the faith to come, spiritual leaders will first establish credibility with reference to drinking deeply from God's Word. We will lead by example. Let's be honest. You know when you are around a leader who spends time meditating and reflecting on God's Word. During the times in my life when I am consistently in God's Word, it comes out my pores. You cannot keep it contained. It bleeds out into your thinking and into your conversations.

> May the words of my mouth and the meditation of my heart
> be acceptable to You, LORD, my rock and my Redeemer.
> (Ps. 19:14)

There is a clear connection between the meditations of our hearts and the words of our mouths.

> Let no unwholesome word proceed from your mouth, but only such a word as is good for edification according to the need of the moment, so that it will give grace to those who hear. (Eph. 4:29 NASB)

Furthermore, to biblically shape the faith to come, spiritual leaders will do whatever it takes to equip believers in the disciplines of reading, studying, memorizing, and meditating upon God's Word. It is not that complicated. Our discipleship strategies should include a consistent emphasis on getting our people into God's Word and God's Word into them.

There is no lack of resources for this task. But more important than resources is intent. What we value will become part of the culture of our churches. It starts with the heart and then moves to strategy.

As an example, after my wife, Patti, and I moved to the Nashville area, we began looking for a church home. While we were visiting one church, we were encouraged that the middle schoolers were memorizing the entire book of Philippians. One Sunday several of these young people stood before the congregation and quoted this book from memory. Wow! Thank God for a church that loves God's Word and works to get it into the hearts of our young people!

Training in the Truth

The book *Band of Brothers* by Stephen Ambrose follows a United States Army Airborne Unit during World War II as E Company goes from basic training through battles in Normandy and Bastogne, all the way to the end of the war. In describing the training of E Company, Ambrose mentions that they were pushed beyond normal endurance in their training to the point that they were more physically fit than any professional athlete. This physical fitness not only helped the company respond quickly under battle conditions, it also gave each man an edge on survival.[2]

As members of the Truth Company, our training for the Christian walk and for the battles ahead should be equally important. Our pursuit of biblical training will not only enable us to respond quickly in any situation, it will also support our growth toward Christlikeness.

I have noted that believers who are teachable will seek and take advantage of training. They know they need to learn and grow. They expect their church to provide this training.

My mother called me recently to mention that Bonnie, one of our lifelong family friends, who is at an age where it would be easy to coast spiritually, was taking an online theology class. I was not surprised. As long as I have known Bonnie, she has been studying the Bible, reading books, and getting all the training she can. Furthermore, she uses her knowledge to help many women whom she teaches and trains.

Knowing that the pursuit of training is evidence of a learner, we asked our sample of churchgoers these questions:

Have you ever gone through a class or training group for new believers or new Christians?

Have you ever been discipled or mentored one-on-one by a more spiritually mature Christian who spent time with you on a regular basis (at least once a month) for the purpose of helping in your spiritual development?

Fifty-two percent of our sample said they had participated in a class for new believers; 46 percent said they had been mentored or discipled.

The response to the first question was not entirely surprising although it was higher than I expected. Such training has become prevalent in most denominations. We were unable to determine the nature or quality of the training, but it is encouraging to note that more than half of churchgoers have demonstrated some interest in learning about the Christian faith.

I was more surprised that nearly half our sample has been mentored or discipled. From personal experience with local churches, I can't recall seeing that much participation. Based on many of the other scores in this study, you have to wonder what is being taught in these classes and in the discipling process. But it is encouraging that so many have demonstrated an interest in learning by participating in such activities.

True biblical disciples, those who have experienced genuine regeneration, will clearly demonstrate that they want to learn and grow. Most will seek help in understanding the Bible and their newfound faith. Peter reminds us of this hunger in 1 Peter 2:1–3: "So rid yourselves of all wickedness, all deceit, hypocrisy, envy, and all slander. Like newborn infants, desire the unadulterated spiritual milk, so that you may grow by it in your salvation, since you have tasted that the Lord is good."

Individually, it should be natural for believers to learn and grow. They will sincerely look to the Word of God for insight and wisdom and will seek out assistance in their growth.

In Colossians, Paul passionately spoke about presenting every man complete in Christ (see Col. 1:28). He added, "For this purpose also I labor" (Col. 1:29 NIV). For churches to "present every man complete" (Col. 1:28 NASB) it requires focus, energy, and hard work. This is not an easy task. In the shape of faith to come, spiritual leaders will give high priority to recruiting and training believers.

Churches will become equipping centers. The preaching ministry of the church will be an essential part of the training strategy, but not the only part. A variety of classes will be aimed at equipping people to serve and guiding them into involvement. It is not enough to preach *at* people, seeking to make them feel guilty for being mere pew sitters. We need to raise the bar of expectation, provide opportunities for our members to discover how God has wired them, and then move them to some appropriate form of involvement.

Truth Leads to Honest Worship

As expected, we found a strong correlation between worship attendance and overall spiritual maturity and being a learner. We found that those who attend church weekly received a score of 69.1 on a 100-point scale compared to 55.4 for those who attend less than weekly.

With reference just to *Domain One: Learning Truth,* we found that those who attend weekly received an overall maturity score of 70.3 compared to 55.9 for those who attend less than weekly. Clearly attendance in worship matters. We were told this nearly two thousand years ago.

> And let us be concerned about one another in order to promote love and good works, not staying away from our meetings, as some habitually do, but encouraging each other, and all the more as you see the day drawing near. (Heb. 10:24–25)

This underscores once more the importance of fighting cultural seepage. Our culture promotes an unbiblical individualism. People are comfortable with a privatized spirituality. Can you really worship God on the golf course? Biblical spirituality is not consistent with a Lone Ranger attitude. We need one another for support and encouragement. We need to bring ourselves before those gifted in the areas of preaching and teaching.

Truth Partners with Accountability

We believe a lie when we believe that the rugged individualism of our culture is based on biblical truth. In reality the Bible teaches that we are all interconnected. The English poet and preacher John Donne wrote a meditation to explain that we are designed to live in Christian community and be accountable to one another:

> No man is an island, entire of itself; every man is a piece of the continent, a part of the main. If a clod be washed away by the sea, Europe is the less . . . any man's death diminishes me, because I am involved in mankind, and therefore never send to know for whom the bell tolls; it tolls for thee.[3]

A good measurement of being a learner must include openness to accountability. So we asked this question:

How much do you agree/disagree:
A Christian should consider himself/herself
accountable to other Christians?

Of those surveyed 62 percent expressed belief in accountability (30 percent "agreed strongly" and 32 percent "agreed somewhat"). Only 15 percent expressed disagreement with the importance of accountability while 23 percent held a neutral view. On one hand, I am encouraged that most churchgoers agree to accountability. I would like, however, to see more than 30 percent of churchgoers "strongly" support this idea. But we find some encouragement in the fact that the majority of believers agree a Christian life is not lived in isolation.

The Truth Quotient—Conclusions

To be a disciple is the same as being a learner. The foundation of spiritual formation is exposure to God's revealed truth, and this truth, when clarified by the Holy Spirit and received by faith, results in transformation. Genuine spiritual formation cannot and will not take place without significant and consistent participation in God's Word. This is why Paul challenged the church at Colossae to:

> Let the word of Christ richly dwell within you, with all wisdom teaching and admonishing one another with psalms and hymns and spiritual songs, singing with thankfulness in your hearts to God. (Col. 3:16 NASB)

Several years ago I attended a weekend retreat where the speaker provided some insight on how spiritual transformation takes place. He explained that as truth is embraced, it transforms perspective, renewing mind-set, and, when grounded in one's heart and soul, defines one's character. To know the quality of your character, reverse the process. The foundation for godly character is the existence of a biblical worldview, but deception and ignorance lie at the root of ungodly behavior.

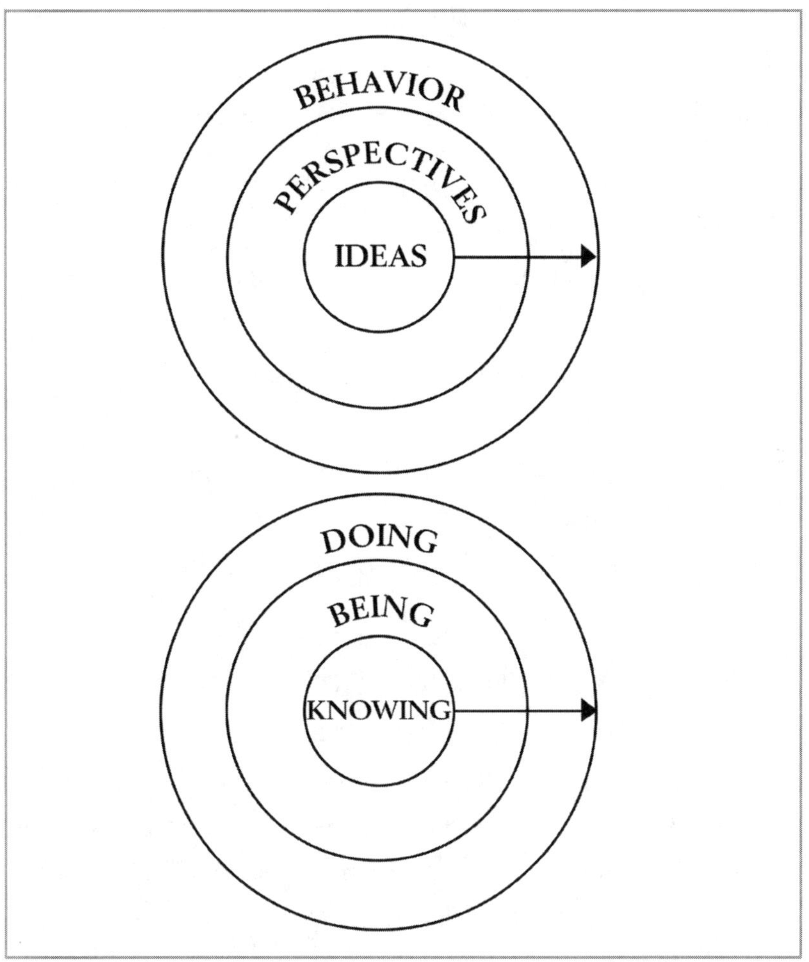

Christians often look in the wrong place to grow spiritually. They focus on changing behavior, but the real battle is in perspective or patterns of thinking. This is why Paul said:

> Do not be conformed to this age, but be transformed by the renewing of your mind, so that you may discern what is the good, pleasing, and perfect will of God. (Rom. 12:2)

Transformation begins with the mind. It starts with your daily thought patterns. It's not, "You are what you eat" but "You are what you think." An unknown writer sums it up this way:

> There is an orderly sequence of events in the shaping of our lives.
> As I think, I make choices. As I make choices, I form habits.
> As I form habits, I fix the direction of my life.
> So, if I am to live differently, I must form new habits.
> If I am to form new habits, I must make new choices.
> If I am to make new choices, I must do new thinking.

There are no shortcuts to biblical spiritual formation. We can tweak our behavior, but this will not last. We must do the difficult work of cultivating the mind-set of Christ.

So if we want to grow and if we want our people to grow, we must increase our exposure to truth. We must read, study, memorize, and reflect on biblical truth. We must increase and take advantage of educational opportunities. We must all listen to sound biblical preaching, read substantive books, and surround ourselves with people who challenge the way we think and act. We must all become open, vulnerable, and transparent within the community of faith. Spiritual formation is not private or individualized. We learn through relationships. Let's push ourselves to become dedicated learners.

---

1. Donald Whitney, *Spiritual Disciplines for the Christian Life* (Colorado Springs, CO: NavPress, 1991), 227.

2. Stephen E. Ambrose, *Band of Brothers* (New York, NY: Simon & Schuster, 2001), 17.

3. John Donne, "Meditation XVII," *Devotions Upon Emergent Occasions*, 1623.

Chapter Four

Domain Two

Obeying God and Denying Self: The Obedience Quotient

"If you love Me, you will keep My commandments."

—John 14:15

"If anyone wants to come with Me, he must deny himself, take up his cross and follow Me."

—Matthew 16:24

Biblical Truth: God commands us to be obedient to Him in all things and to deny self.

The Obedience Quotient: Jesus said that by following His commands we show our love for Him. Our love for God and our obedience to Him are inseparable.

Biblical Obedience

Our faith becomes genuine, according to the apostle John, through our obedience to God: "This is how we are sure that we have come to know Him: by keeping His commands" (1 John 2:3).

Our faith shows in our service to others, according to James, who argues that our works, our obedience, verify our faith: "In the same way faith, if it doesn't have works, is dead by itself. But someone will say, 'You have faith, and I have works.' Show me your faith without works, and I will show you faith from my works. You believe that God is one; you do well. The demons also believe—and they shudder. Foolish man! Are you willing to learn that faith without works is useless?" (James 2:17–20).

When a rich young ruler claimed he followed all the commandments, he was stunned when Jesus said he still needed to deny himself by selling everything he had and giving it to the poor before he could follow Him (see Mark 10:17–22).

"Obeying God" and "denying self" are the two discipleship characteristics we seek to measure in Domain Two.

Jesus said that to be His disciples we must deny self in service to Him, loving Him by being obedient: "If anyone wants to come with Me, he must deny himself, take up his cross, and follow Me" (Matt. 16:24). As gravity is indistinguishable from the law of gravity, our call to be obedient and to deny self is meant to be indistinguishable from our faith.

In order to assess the levels of obedience and self-denial among our sample of churchgoers, we asked the following questions:

- How much do you agree/disagree: A Christian must learn to deny himself/herself in order to serve Christ?
- How much do you agree/disagree: I try to avoid situations in which I might be tempted to think or do immoral things?
- How much do you agree/disagree: When convinced of sin in my life, I readily confess it to God as sin?
- How much do you agree/disagree: When I come to realize that some aspect of my life is not right in God's eyes, I make the necessary changes?
- How much do you agree/disagree: I feel sorrow and regret when I realize I have sinned?
- How much do you agree/disagree: Reading and studying the Bible has not made significant changes in the way I live my life?
- How much do you agree/disagree: I am generally a different person in public than I am in private?
- How much do you agree/disagree: When I realize that I have a choice between "my way" and "God's way," I usually choose my way?
- How often do you confess sins and wrongdoings to God and ask for forgiveness?
- Have you been baptized?

The Obedience Quotient: Real Numbers

We could ask hundreds of questions about obedience and self-denial. But these ten questions provide us with a good picture of the degree to which our churchgoers' lives reflect biblical standards.

Only 2 percent of the respondents, about 50 of the 2,500, gave an *ideal response* to all ten questions. When you include *positive responses* to the questions, the percentage increases to 14 percent, nearly 350 of the 2,500.

Considering how basic the questions are, it is surprising that so few Protestant believers strongly affirm the attitudes and practices measured in Domain Two. Yielding control of our lives to God is fundamental to our Christian faith. Our obedience requires self-denial, struggling with the tension between our fallen nature and the will and ways of God.

Obedience through Self-Denial

As we emerge from the womb, we are already seeking our own self-interests. You don't have to teach selfishness to a two-year-old. My wife taught two-year-olds in Sunday school for fifteen years, and I would occasionally join her. Much of the time we had a blast working with these cute children. Yet these adorable, self-focused kids had to be constantly taught to think of others.

Part of becoming an adult is learning to put others first. We saw a great example of this recently when Sara Tucholsky, a softball player for Western Oregon University, was playing against rival Central Washington University. Sara hit the first home run of her life. Excited, she began to run around the bases. When she missed first base, she turned back awkwardly, injuring her knee and dropping to the ground in pain. She crawled back to first base but could go no farther.

Her first base coach correctly shouted that Sara would be called out if helped by a teammate. A pinch runner could take her place, but the home run would count only as a single as Sara had made it only to first base. Coaches and umpires gathered to discuss the options. Then Mallory Holtman, the first baseman for the opposing team, asked them, "What if we helped her around the bases?" The umpire noted there was no rule against that. So Mallory and teammate Liz Wallace picked up Sara and carried her around the bases, carefully allowing her to touch each base with her good leg. Sara's first-ever home run counted, and her team won the game by that one run.

As a result of their sacrificial kindness, Mallory and Liz's team lost the game and the opportunity to advance in their divisional playoffs. It was an act of self-denial on the part of these young ladies, so rarely seen in sports, and it was celebrated across the nation in the media.

I would love to know more about Mallory Holtman and what motivated her willingness to deny self for the good of someone else. I don't know if there was any faith-based motivation for what she did, but such behavior must be learned; it does not come naturally.

Such an attitude and behavior are not natural for most Christians either, at least for some I know. Through God's Word, the transforming work of the Holy Spirit and encouragement from the community of faith, we learn to think of others. Note the statement in the following verse: "Make your own attitude that of Christ Jesus." Effort and thought are needed to deny self and think about others.

> Do nothing out of rivalry or conceit, but in humility consider others as more important than yourselves. Everyone should look out not only for his own interests, but also for the interests of others. Make your own attitude that of Christ Jesus. (Phil. 2:3–5)

Since the Bible clearly expects all Christians to deny self, we asked our sample of churchgoers this question:

How much do you agree/disagree: A Christian must learn to deny himself/herself in order to serve Christ?

We found that 28 percent "agreed strongly" with this question, and another 28 percent said they "agreed somewhat." So we have a way to go in learning to deny self.

Gary Nikal is a friend from my hometown in Wyoming. During a trip home for Christmas, Gary took my boys and me duck hunting. Gary, a retired coach, showed up wearing a T-shirt that read, "I will do today what you won't, so I can do tomorrow what you can't." Matters of great importance always require self-denying sacrifice.

Of course, following Christ—including the realities of sacrifice and self-denial—must be viewed from an eternal perspective to be understood properly. Any sacrifice we make today pales in significance compared to bringing glory to God and experiencing the rewards of obedience.

The famed missionary martyr Jim Elliot is known for saying, "He is no fool who gives what he cannot keep to gain what he cannot lose."[1]

He properly understood the teachings of Christ on this matter:

> Then Jesus said to His disciples, "If anyone wants to come with Me, he must deny himself, take up his cross, and follow Me. For whoever wants to save his life will lose it, but whoever loses his life because of Me will find it. What will it benefit a man if he gains the whole world yet loses his life? Or what will a man give in exchange for his life?" (Matt. 16:24–26)

In the end self-denial is never a loss. To the contrary, when we abandon all for Christ, we gain precious benefits that He richly pours upon us. The Bible says we'll experience many of these blessings in the age to come.[2] In the Sermon on the Mount, Jesus spoke about the reward that awaits God's people: "Rejoice in that day and leap for joy! Take note—your reward is great in heaven" (Luke 6:23).

My favorite book on leadership is the classic *Spiritual Leadership* by J. Oswald Sanders. He writes:

> Self-sacrifice is part of the price that must be paid daily. A cross stands in the way of spiritual leadership, a cross upon which the leader must consent to be impaled. Heaven's demands are absolute. "He laid down his life for us; and we ought to lay down our lives for the brethren" (1 John 3:16). The degree to which we allow the cross of Christ to work in us will be the measure in which the resurrection life of Christ can be manifested through us. "Death worketh in me, but life in you." To evade the cross is to forfeit leadership.[3]

Sanders is speaking mainly to pastors, but the same truth applies to any believer. Denying self, sacrifice, obedience—whatever term you want to use—applies to everyone who seeks to walk in God's ways.

An Obedient Response to Sin

A key evidence of obedience is how a professing follower of Christ responds to sin. The Bible never portrays the Christian life as perfect obedience. Many spiritual journeys look more like a rough wagon ride over rugged terrain than a smooth automobile ride on the interstate. Most of the great leaders whose lives are chronicled in Scripture had moments of sin and rebellion against God.

Nonetheless, the Bible requires obedience. Jesus told the woman at the well, "Go and sin no more" (John 8:11). That's a high standard. The Christian life is "walking the talk."

As long as we live with the effects of humanity's fall into sin, we are faced with a difficult journey. Every believer I know confesses to instances of sin and rebellion. The Christian life, however, should never be characterized by a pattern of disobedience. You can tell a lot about the spirituality of other believers by watching how they react after realizing they have sinned.

Because there is a clear connection between obeying God and confessing sin, we asked our sample this question:

How much do you agree/disagree: When convinced of sin in my life, I readily confess it to God as sin?

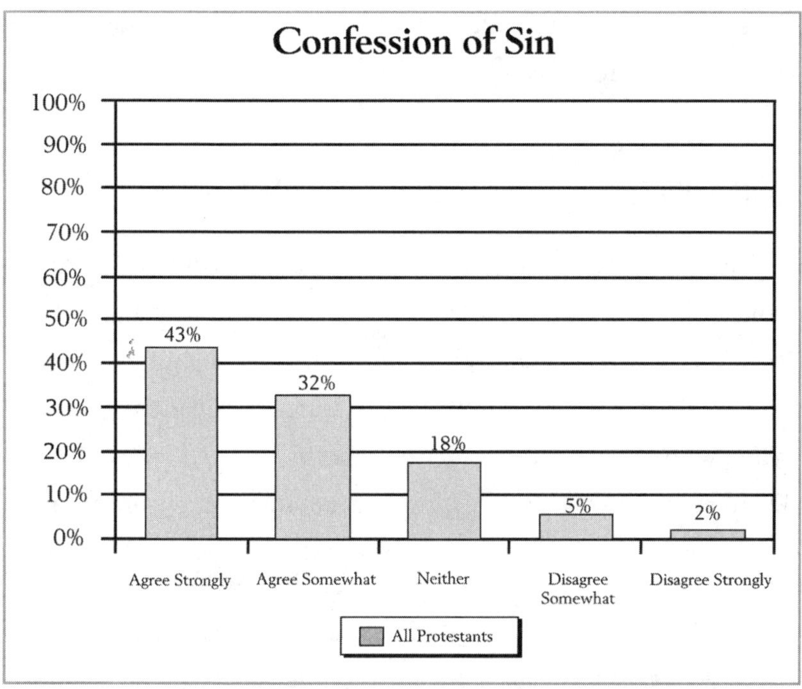

You can see that 43 percent could confidently say they are committed to readily confessing sin to God. The results speak for themselves.

To gain additional insight, we asked another question about the frequency of confession:

How often do you do each of the following: Confess my sins and wrongdoings to God and ask for forgiveness?

Interestingly we found this to be one of the ten strongest statistical correlations to overall spiritual maturity: 35 percent of our sample said they confessed sin daily; 23 percent said "a few times a week"; 10 percent chose "weekly."

Obedience Quotient: Repentance Equals Change

Biblical confession includes repentance. In other words, biblical confession calls for turning from wrong and seeking to follow God. There is, however, widespread misunderstanding of confession. Individuals in the church often see confession as merely admitting wrong without any commitment to change.

To make sure we were getting an accurate read on our sample of churchgoers, we asked these questions related to repentance:

How much do you agree/disagree: When I come to realize that some aspect of my life is not right in God's eyes, I make the necessary changes?

Only 23 percent "agreed strongly" with this question. That's not very encouraging as an indication of obedience among Protestant churchgoers. Notice the specific wording of the question. Even after realizing some aspect of their life is not right, the majority remain unchanged.

Biblical discipleship and spiritual formation involve making changes. Walking with God necessitates constant change in our attitudes: how we think, how we treat others, how we handle our money, how we respond to our desires, how we use our time, and how we speak to others. Faith is change; repentance is change;

obedience is change. If you cannot easily recall a time when you stopped doing something your way and chose to do it God's way, then you need to seriously evaluate your faith.

In his classic work *Celebration of Discipline*, Richard J. Foster makes an important connection between worship and change:

> If worship does not change us, it has not been worship. To stand before the Holy One of eternity is to change. . . . In worship, an increased power steals its way into the heart sanctuary; an increased compassion grows in the soul. To worship is to change. If worship does not propel us into greater obedience, it has not been worship. Just as worship begins in holy expectancy, it ends in holy obedience. Holy obedience saves worship from becoming an opiate, an escape from the pressing needs of modern life. Worship enables us to hear the call to service clearly so that we respond, "Here I am! Send me!" (Isa. 6:8)[4]

One reason we see a lack of repentance among many Christians is cultural seepage. Our culture is permeated with rugged individualism and the exaltation of self. It tells us to do what we want as long as we do not violate the law or get caught.

Our culture also espouses relativism. It tells us that what's wrong for someone else may be all right for you. Many people believe they can do what they want as long as they do not hurt others.

Dr. Ed Stetzer, one of my colleagues at LifeWay, observes that "Americans prefer religion when it says yes. They do not like religion when it says no."

People who are not a regular part of a faith community still want to be "spiritual" people but without a clear faith. Many people create a "tame" God for themselves, a generic god for a generic spirituality, not a God who actually intervened in the world through the death of Christ and calls us to live differently. Many people want all the benefits of spirituality without the challenging truth claims of a vigorous faith.

Many communities of faith espouse a gospel-lite, discipleship-lite ethos. The gospel often is presented as a how-to guide for improving one's life, and the costs and demands of Christian faith are seldom explained.

Recall Jesus' encounter with the rich young ruler:

> A ruler asked Him, "Good Teacher, what must I do to inherit eternal life?" "Why do you call Me good?" Jesus asked him. "No one is good but One—God. You know the commandments: Do not commit adultery; do not murder; do not steal; do not bear false witness; honor your father and mother."
>
> "I have kept all these from my youth," he said.
>
> When Jesus heard this, He told him, "You still lack one thing: sell all that you have and distribute it to the poor, and you will have treasure in heaven. Then come, follow Me."
>
> After he heard this, he became extremely sad, because he was very rich. (Luke 18:18–23)

I wonder what that rich young ruler would have been told by our churches today. While you may not have to sell everything you have in order to follow Christ, the underlying principle is that a follower of God must be willing to yield control of anything God desires in order to glorify and obey Him.

Obedience Quotient: Biblical Truth Compels Change

This greater understanding of the need to change can occur in many ways, but it most often results from intentional exposure to the Word of God. One of the questions we asked in our survey is:

How much do you agree or disagree with this statement: Reading and studying the Bible has not made significant changes in the way I live my life?

This question is stated in the negative, so the most positive response would be "strongly disagree." But only 37 percent gave the ideal response, indicating that reading and studying the Bible have made significant changes in the way they live.

James speaks of looking into the law of freedom, the Word, without changing.

> But be doers of the word and not hearers only, deceiving yourselves. Because if anyone is a hearer of the word and not a doer, he is like a man looking at his own face in a mirror; for he looks at himself, goes away, and right away forgets what kind of man he was. But the one who looks intently into the perfect law of freedom and perseveres in it, and is

> not a forgetful hearer but a doer who acts—this person will be blessed in what he does. (James 1:22–25)

Forgetting what one looks like. This is when we encounter the truth of God's Word yet remain unchanged. True spiritual transformation is synonymous with change, and biblical transformation is radical in nature. It is a deep change from within, not a mere face-lift. The gospel is at the heart of this transformation, taking enemies of God and making them His friends. The gospel empowers us to break free from slavery to sin to become bond servants of Christ. The gospel exposes our self-centeredness and creates in our hearts love for others. Many believers have been so transformed that they laid down their lives for others. The apostle Paul, for example, went from murdering Christians to dying in service to them.

Obedience Equals Submission

As Christian servants, we must follow the instructions we've been given by Jesus. Yet it's difficult because words like *submit* and *obey* unfortunately are countercultural today. Few seem to understand that submission to legitimate authority is ultimately in their best interest. Just as submitting to God's physical laws is in our best interest, so is submitting to God's spiritual laws.

My son learned a hard lesson about physical laws while driving toward Steamboat Springs, Colorado, for some snow skiing. As he rounded a corner on a snow-packed road, he learned about the laws of friction and the loss of it. His car began to slide, and the laws of velocity and momentum took over. A car coming from the opposite direction proved that two pieces of matter cannot occupy the same space at the same time. Thankfully the most serious injuries were to my son's ego and his bank account.

But What about Abuse?

The word *submit* is worrisome to many people because of the unfortunate reality of spiritual abuse. Christian counselors tell me they are amazed at how many people have been hurt by religious leaders who abuse their authority and influence. This same injury can be inflicted in the home by a marriage partner or a parent who selfishly abuses his position.

Think about it. If you were the enemy of God, wouldn't you seek to make inroads into the church and into the clergy? Sadly, it is a successful strategy.

Despite our cultural resistance to authority and despite the sad fact that some flawed leaders abuse overly submissive followers, submission to God and His Word is essential to spiritual trans-formation. True transformation cannot occur without submission.

Final Equation: Whose Way Will It Be?

In his first epistle, the apostle John wrote:

> If we say, "We have fellowship with Him," and walk in darkness, we are lying and are not practicing the truth. But if we walk in the light as He Himself is in the light, we have

> fellowship with one another, and the blood of Jesus His Son cleanses us from all sin. (1 John 1:6–7)

John uses the metaphors of darkness and light, the former representing sin and disobedience and the latter signifying walking according to truth. Spiritual transformation occurs when a believer pursues truth and submits to it. There is no other path. Truth leads to understanding, and understanding leads to change. Change is the fruit of repentance and submission.

Another way to analyze obedience is to look carefully at our track record when confronted with choices. In our survey we asked:

How much do you agree/disagree: When I realize that I have a choice between "my way" and "God's way," I usually choose my way?

This question is stated negatively, so ideally we were looking for "strongly disagree" responses. Unfortunately only 19 percent said they strongly disagreed with this statement. Another 31 percent "disagreed somewhat."

Most Christians feel uncomfortable with their level of obedience. I do not know anyone who claims he or she chooses God's way every day in every circumstance. Scripture acknowledges "we all stumble in many ways" (James 3:2). But consistently choosing God's way is the normal expectation and goal of the Christian life. I would certainly expect more than 19 percent of churchgoers to say they "usually" choose God's way.

Consider my current pursuit of good health. When I started

writing this book, I was at least twenty pounds overweight. (Some of my friends with the spiritual gift of trash-talking would suggest it was more like thirty pounds.) At the beginning of the year, I signed up for a six-month, peer-based weight-loss accountability group at the local YMCA. I paid a $25 entrance fee and determined how much weight I wanted to lose. Then I set monthly goals. I have to weigh in every four weeks with a witness. Every day I am out of compliance, I pay a $1 fine until I catch up to my goal for the month. At the end of six months, if I reach my ultimate goal, my entrance fee is returned along with a share of the fines collected from all of the participants.

Money is not my prime motivator. Bill, the captain of this peer-pressure group, sends out e-mails with updates that highlight in red anyone who is out of compliance, along with a tally of fines for each person. Without fail, when the updated spreadsheet is sent out, the out-of-compliance participants are harassed with trash-talking e-mails by the others in the group.

This peer pressure works! When the spreadsheet shows my name in red, I become much more motivated to lose weight.

So what is my point? No one expects to reach their weight-loss goals overnight or even in a month, but we expect one another to make progress over time. No one loses weight every day, and most people experience setbacks when they yield to temptation. But bad days and setbacks do not define the entire six months. The majority of the participants make progress. In other words, we *usually choose* the right things to eat.

Most Christians experience some failure in living up to biblical standards. The Lord does not expect perfection, but He does require a determination to pursue godliness. As the apostle Paul expressed:

> Not that I have already reached the goal or am already fully mature, but I make every effort to take hold of it because I also have been taken hold of by Christ Jesus. Brothers, I do not consider myself to have taken hold of it. But one thing I do: forgetting what is behind and reaching forward to what is ahead, I pursue as my goal the prize promised by God's heavenly call in Christ Jesus. (Phil. 3:12–14)

A clear sign of spiritual transformation is closing the gap between what one professes and how one lives. Maturation is a process. The New Testament describes spiritual transformation, much like physical development, as progressive. There should be clear and discernable progress in faith. The lack of progress caused some biblical authors to rebuke some churchgoers because more growth should have occurred in their lives, given the time since they became Christ followers.

> Brothers, I was not able to speak to you as spiritual people but as people of the flesh, as babies in Christ. I fed you milk, not solid food, because you were not yet able to receive it. In fact, you are still not able, because you are still fleshly. (1 Cor. 3:1–3)

> For though by this time you ought to be teachers, you need someone to teach you again the basic principles of God's revelation. You need milk, not solid food. (Heb. 5:12)

Persistent lack of growth is not an option for a Christian. We also need to stop rationalizing our failure to advance spiritually. In his important book on spiritual transformation, *The Pursuit of Holiness*, Jerry Bridges expresses it this way:

> It is time for us Christians to face up to our responsibility for holiness. Too often we say we are "defeated" by this or that sin. No, we are not defeated; we are simply disobedient! It might be good if we stopped using the terms "victory" and "defeat" to describe our progress in holiness. Rather we should use the terms "obedience" and "disobedience." When I say I am defeated by some sin, I am unconsciously slipping out from under my responsibility. I am saying something outside of me has defeated me. But when I say I am disobedient, that places the responsibility for my sin squarely on me. We may, in fact, be defeated, but the reason we are defeated is because we have chosen to disobey. We have chosen to entertain lustful thoughts, or to harbor resentment, or to shade the truth a little.[5]

Obedience Quotient: Integrity

In March 2007 news broke about Eliot Spitzer, the governor of New York. We learned that he was unfaithful to his wife through his involvement in an illegal prostitution ring. He resigned a few days later. Many politicians survive moral failure and remain in office. Not Mr. Spitzer. New York Assemblyman James Tedisco called on the governor to step down if the allegations were true. Tedisco said,

"The governor who was going to bring ethics back to New York State, if he was involved in something like this, he's got to leave. I don't think there's any question about that."[6]

Many news commentators showed no tolerance for Spitzer's moral failure because he was highly outspoken against prostitution. He lived a lie. He was one way in public and completely different in private.

There are far too many examples of people living a lie. Unfortunately this is too often the case within the church. If anyone should seek to live according to profession, it should be Christians, especially spiritual leaders.

The Bible frequently calls believers to integrity. Biblical integrity is more than simply telling the truth. It involves a holistic consistency of life. It means that what we say lines up with the way we live. Integrity is the opposite of dissonance. *Webster's Dictionary* defines *dissonance* as a "lack of agreement; esp. inconsistency between the beliefs one holds or between one's actions and one's beliefs."[7]

To get at this idea of integrity of life, we asked our sample of churchgoers this question:

How much do you agree/disagree: I am generally a different person in public than I am in private?

As this question was asked negatively, we wanted to see a high level of "strongly disagree." But only 31 percent "disagreed strongly" and 23 percent "disagreed somewhat," clearly showing significant dissonance between profession and behavior.

The Obedience Quotient in the Shape of Faith to Come

Christian faith is synonymous with following and honoring God, and we cannot do that without repentance, change, submission, and integrity. Following God is exciting, stretching, rewarding, sacrificial, and, at times, painful. Transformation is not a path of legalism, nor is it the opposite extreme of license. It is not exclusively a divine process, and it definitely is not merely a human endeavor. God is the source, and believers must submit to and cooperate with His established means of spiritual formation.

When the apostle Paul admonished the believers at Philippi to "work out" their salvation, he was not telling them to sustain their saving faith but was clearly referring to the process of spiritual transformation. It requires immense diligence, commitment, and effort to become more like Christ day by day. This process is beyond our own strength, but God never demands of us what He does not make possible. My favorite verse concerning spiritual transformation is Philippians 1:6, "I am sure of this, that He who started a good work in you will carry it on to completion until the day of Christ Jesus."

This passage encourages me when I seem to be facing a dead end. I try never to shirk responsibility for my lack of progress in spiritual maturity. If I am not growing, I know the responsibility lies with me, but what keeps me going is knowing that God's full intention is to perfect His transforming work in me. My failure or sin does not change God's intention toward me. What a promise! What a comfort!

When it comes to the Obedience Quotient, spiritual leaders can and must make a difference. We can do this in a number of ways, but here are some transferable concepts that can transform our churches. These principles begin in the heart and practice of spiritual leaders. Then they emanate from the pulpit. Eventually, they permeate the thinking and practices of the people.

Fear of God

When I notice trends of indifference in my own life, I find it helpful to ask myself if I have lost my fear of and reverence for God. I am not talking about an unhealthy kind of fear. I am talking about a sober, honest understanding that God is no respecter of persons. His standards are perfect, and He does not look the other way for anyone.

God is long-suffering, but He does not suspend His principles like, "You reap what you sow" (see Gal. 6:7). The path of obedience and self-denial begins with a proper concept of the holiness of God. God demands and deserves our obedience. He deserves our loyalty and respect. Acts of obedience are like bowing the knee before our holy God. Too many sermons have watered down the awesome and fearful nature of God.

Many spiritual leaders need to regain a deep reverence for God and pass that attitude on to the people of God.

It's in Our Best Interest

I stated this earlier: spiritual leaders need to create an understanding within the people of God that obeying God is in their best interest. God's love is perfect. His wisdom is unfathomable. His ways are the best ways. Aligning with the will and ways of God provides rewards in this life and in eternity. I am not speaking of the health, wealth, and prosperity heresy some preachers spout. I am talking about the joy, peace, freedom from enslaving sin, and clean conscience that come from obeying God. We do ourselves grave harm and injustice when we stupidly think our way is better than God's. How silly it is for us to place ourselves on the throne! How arrogant!

A Culture of Obedience

As we hold ourselves and those we influence to God's standards, we will see the culture of our churches change. Imagine what would happen in our churches if things like gossip and slander were lovingly but firmly confronted? What if fellow believers were gently to disallow such things as outbursts of anger, misrepresentations, or manipulation?

The immune systems of most churches are weak. Because we have lowered our view of God and set aside His standards, we have allowed sinful attitudes and practices to prevail. We have treated God's Word as if it were a collection of suggestions. This weak immune system allows sickness and disease to proceed unchecked. The culture of our churches will become much healthier when we simply begin to hold one another to God's clear standards.

Drawing Deep from Divine Resources

All of this sounds good, but it is difficult to practice. The path of obedience is impossible to travel in our own strength. I believe that prayer and the humble confession of dependence, coupled with immersion in God's Word, can unleash God's power of transformation. Heartfelt obedience, contrasted with mere external performance, is enabled by substantial time set apart for prayer and reflection upon God's Word.

I know from personal experience that my ability to obey God is substantially curtailed when I get too busy to spend time drawing on His resources. I know of no other way even to sustain a desire to obey, deny self, and submit to God. It is impossible and arrogant for any Christian to attempt the path of faith without doing it God's way.

---

1. Elisabeth Elliot, *Shadow of the Almighty* (San Francisco, CA: Harper & Row, 1958), 108.

2. The author of Hebrews, in writing what we call "the Hall of Faith," described Moses as a man who understood that faith would be rewarded in the age to come: "By faith Moses, after he was born, was hidden by his parents for three months, because they saw that the child was beautiful, and they didn't fear the king's edict. By faith Moses, when he had grown up, refused to be called the son of Pharaoh's daughter and chose to suffer with the people of God rather than to enjoy the short-lived pleasure of sin. For he considered reproach for the sake of the Messiah to be greater wealth than the treasures of Egypt, since his attention was on the reward" (Heb. 11:23–26).

Many other passages powerfully illustrate the truth that, in the end, faithful obedience, regardless of temporary sacrifice, is the path to abundant joy and reward. Yet the Bible does not mince words about the cost of following Christ. Obedience will create temporary hurt or sense of loss, especially in terms of relational pain. Many Christians have suffered deeply because following Christ brought confusion, distance, or even outright hostility from friends and family members.

3. J. Oswald Sanders, *Spiritual Leadership: Principles of Excellence for Every Believer* (Chicago, CO: Moody Press, 1886), 142.

4. Richard J. Foster, *Celebration of Discipline* (San Francisco, CA: Harper & Row, 1978), 148.

5. Jerry Bridges, *The Pursuit of Holiness* (Colorado Springs, CO: NavPress, 2006), 80.

6. See http://www.nytimes.com/2008/03/10/nyregion/10cnd spitzer.html?hp.

7. *Merriam-Webster's Collegiate Dictionary, Eleventh Edition.*

Chapter Five

Domain Three

Serving God and Others: The Service Quotient

"For even the Son of Man did not come to be served, but to serve, and to give His life—a ransom for many."

—MARK 10:45

Biblical Truth: Each of us is called to serve God and to serve others.

The Service Quotient: We grow spiritually when we serve God and serve others on His behalf.

Welcome to Shepherd's Gate, Mr. Mathētēs. We're so glad you've chosen to dine with us tonight. And I see you've brought your entire family. That's marvelous! We love families here at Shepherd's Gate; in fact, we pride ourselves on providing the best service in town.

Let me show you to your table. You know, you are so fortunate to be seated immediately; we've found that 47 percent of our patrons who make reservations still have to wait at least an hour to be seated. It's a disappointment for us and the customers, but then it's not like we can do anything about it. Sometimes you just have to accept these things.

Ah, here's your table. I think you'll find this location to be excellent. You're right next to the kitchen door, so your food will still be at least warm when someone remembers to bring it to you, and the cart of dirty dishes right behind you will allow you to clear your own table.

I'm afraid only 49 percent of our staff has been trained to provide good service, but the good news is your waiter tonight will be Edmund. There's a 51 percent chance he'll be here within the next two minutes and a 36 percent chance he'll bring you some of our famous complimentary breadsticks. The other 64 percent of the time he's likely to forget; but just remind him, and he'll get them to you about the time you finish dessert.

Why is it good news that Edmund is your waiter? Right, I see why you'd ask that question. Well, it's because Edmund is among 22 percent of our servers who believe his financial well-being is based upon his service to you. There's another 32 percent who are giving serious thought to possibly caring about your needs.

Would you believe that 53 percent of our customers still leave good tips for our waiters? Oh, but Mr. Mathētēs, I didn't say we provide *excellent* service. I simply said we provide the *best service in town*. Try the rest and you'll see we're the best.

The Service Quotient—Biblical Ideal

It's hard to argue that a commitment to service is unimportant when you consider the dining experience at the Shepherd's Gate restaurant. An experience like the one above may make you laugh or grit your teeth in frustration, but if service for one meal is important to us, how much more important is serving God and others through our obedience to Christ?

We measured Christian service in the study's third domain: Serving God and Others. Based on our survey sample, many believers look more like the waiters at Shepherd's Gate than Jesus. Our study shows the need consistently and continually to teach believers the biblical model of Christian service, but equally as important is pointing them to specific opportunities for service within our congregations, communities, and the world.

Our research questions were developed from the biblical model for service, where Christians are taught to be "doers" of the Word and not just "hearers." The apostle James says believers who are "hearers only" deceive themselves:

> But be doers of the word and not hearers only, deceiving yourselves. Because if anyone is a hearer of the word and not a doer, he is like a man looking at his own face in a mirror; for he looks at himself, goes away, and right away forgets what kind of man he was. But the one who looks intently

into the perfect law of freedom and perseveres in it, and is not a forgetful hearer but a doer who acts—this person will be blessed in what he does. (James 1:22–25)

An Inefficient Strategy?

Our perfect God chooses to use flawed humans to advance His kingdom. In our limited, human wisdom, it seems like an inefficient strategy, yet the Bible shows us that God routinely "calls out" and "raises up" ordinary men and women to serve Him.

This call to serve isn't limited to a select few; it includes all Christians. Paul explains this in his letter to the church at Ephesus: "For we are His creation—created in Christ Jesus for good works, which God prepared ahead of time so that we should walk in them" (Eph. 2:10).

Since we are created to produce good works, serving others simply isn't an option. For example, when Paul wrote to the church in Corinth, he explained the Holy Spirit had given each of them in the church spiritual gifts meant to be used in service to others (see 1 Cor. 12:4–7).

These gifts aren't mere accessories to the Christian life; they're necessary for our spiritual growth and essential to our work in advancing God's kingdom. God gave us these gifts so we will succeed at our mission, which means we're also accountable to use our gifts faithfully to serve God and others.

In my own spiritual journey, God used several Bible teachers to help me understand His plan of using ordinary people, just like me, to invest in matters that will last for eternity.

Obedience and self-denial are major steps into lifelong spiritual transformation, but they still are only the beginning of the journey. Salvation is not just a past-tense event and a future-tense reward; it is also a present-tense journey that takes us from one end of life's rugged, narrow path to the other.

A key dimension of our journey toward the "narrow gate" (Matt. 7:13–14) is a life of service in God's kingdom. No one reaches his destination without leaving his starting point. We only reach that point when we receive our reward by making our way, day by day, along the road of serving God and others.

James addresses this issue in a strong manner:

> Pure and undefiled religion before our God and Father is this: to look after orphans and widows in their distress and to keep oneself unstained by the world. (James 1:26–27)

This call to serve is not limited to a select few. The apostle Paul encouraged the church at Ephesus to understand that living out God's will is built into who we are as new creatures in Christ:

> "For we are His creation—created in Christ Jesus for good works, which God prepared ahead of time so that we should walk in them." (Eph. 2:10)

Every Christian is created to produce good works. Service to God and others is not an à la carte offering on a spiritual menu; it's part of the main course.

We see the same emphasis in Paul's letter to the Corinthians. How we serve differs from person to person, but all believers have been given gifts by the Holy Spirit, and all are expected to use them:

> Now there are different gifts, but the same Spirit. There are different ministries, but the same Lord. And there are different activities, but the same God is active in everyone and everything. A manifestation of the Spirit is given to each person to produce what is beneficial. (1 Cor. 12:4–7)

Notice the statements "God is active in everyone" and "given to each person." It could not be clearer. God bestows spiritual giftedness upon every Christian. These gifts are not mere accessories. We must exercise these gifts to advance God's kingdom. These gifts present us with wonderful opportunities, and every believer will account to God for his or her faithfulness in using them.

Your gifts have been given to you as part of God's unique creative work in you, and identifying the gifts you have been entrusted with is a key step toward discovering God's unique plan for your life. When a Christian discovers His kingdom mission, a mission of service no one else can fulfill, it changes his entire life.

As a senior in college, I had the opportunity to return home to work for, and eventually help lead, our family ranching business, which consisted of twelve thousand acres and a nationally known cattle herd. Yet during that senior year God began to show me that He had other plans for my life. He began to create a passion in me to invest in people and make disciples. He filled my heart with a vision for the Great Commission. As much as I loved working hard on the ranch, God redirected my passions.

I will never forget the event that altered the direction of my life. I was attending a weekend retreat led by Dave Dawson, who worked with the Navigators. He drew a time line on a chalkboard. The left end of the line represented our birth, and the right end signified heaven. He drew a cross on the left side to represent the point at which we became Christians. Just to the right of that, he made a mark for age twenty, the average age in the room. Everything to the right of that mark stood for the rest of our lives on earth. He labeled the unknown future "X."

Then Mr. Dawson said: "Life is brief. Life is precious. When you stand before God at the end of your life, what will you be able to point to that has eternal significance?" The question pierced my heart and altered the trajectory of my whole life. I knew I needed to devote my life to serving God and discipling others.

It's awesome to watch God redirect people's passions as they discover His design for their lives. I have seen it happen repeatedly. Excitement dawns in their eyes. Sometimes it is followed by a look of fear or even guilt. There are no neutral reactions when God confronts genuine believers with His plan to use them to advance His purposes.

Apart from the staggering thought that God has a mission in mind that only they can fulfill, they also have to come to terms with the amazing notion that the God of the universe, in all of His perfection, uses flawed humans to advance His kingdom. It could be considered an inefficient strategy. But even a cursory reading of the Bible reveals that the great heroes of the faith were ordinary men and women. What a humbling thought that Almighty God, in His providence, has chosen you to carry out His purposes and accomplish something that will last for eternity!

The Service Quotient—Real Numbers

In this third domain we asked our twenty-five hundred churchgoers nine questions seeking to evaluate their perceptions, beliefs, and practices related to *serving God and serving others*. The first four questions measured the degree to which each person agreed or disagreed with statements relating to Christian service. The remaining questions focused on behaviors and practices.

- Questions where "agree strongly" is considered the top or ideal response:
    - I believe everything I have belongs to God.
    - I regularly use my gifts and talents to serve/help people in need who are not part of my church.
    - It is necessary for a Christian's spiritual well-being to give time on a regular basis to some specific ministry within his/her church.

  - With reference to my values and priorities, I can honestly say that I try to put God first in my life.

- Questions related to frequency of certain behaviors or practices:
  - Pray for fellow Christians I know every day.
  - Pray for my church and/or church leaders every day.
  - Volunteer my time to serve in any capacity at my church.
  - Give 10 percent or more of my pre-tax income to charities, church, or ministries.
  - Have identified my primary spiritual gifts and am currently using them to serve God/others.

Of the twenty-five hundred respondents, only 2 percent provided the ideal response to every question in this domain. The number jumps to 11 percent when you add respondents who provided at least a positive response to every question. Since we're talking about basic Protestant perspectives and practices, it is surprising so few offered a strong affirmation of the nine statements above.

A Profit-Sharing Servant

God's Chosen Stewards

The term *profit-sharing servant* seems contradictory. If you're a servant, then you usually don't think of sharing in the rewards of a job well done. But Paul reminds us that we are more than servants; we are joint heirs. So we serve others on behalf of our Father, knowing we will share in the inheritance.

> Whatever you do, do it enthusiastically, as something done for the Lord and not for men, knowing that you will receive the reward of an inheritance from the Lord—you serve the Lord Christ. (Col. 3:23–24)

Paul says we're to serve others as if we're working for the Lord, and so we thought it was important to ask some questions related to motivation. Jesus calls us to do more than just project an outward image of godliness; we're called to live out what we profess to be true.

The foundation of Christian service is an understanding that God owns us and everything we have, including our time, talent, and treasures. God owns it all, and He trusts us to manage it. One of my favorite psalms states: "The earth and everything in it, the world and its inhabitants, belong to the LORD; for He laid its foundation on the seas and established it on the rivers" (Ps. 24:1–2). Knowing that all good things come from God changes the way we view our possessions and everything else in life. Cultural seepage tells us we are entitled to the best life has to offer, but biblical truth says God is the owner of all we have and all we are. We are to be good stewards of His gracious gifts.

Two of Jesus' parables, the parable of the talents (see Matt. 25:14–30) and the parable of the faithful servant (see Luke 12:41–48), illustrate this truth. God entrusts us with certain things and expects us to be good stewards of His generosity.

Biblical stewardship isn't just volunteerism. Many people feel good about doing things for others. There is nothing wrong with that, but serving to feel better about yourself misses the mark. God calls us to serve obediently in gratitude for what He has done for us, out of a sense of stewardship.

> And He died for all so that those who live should no longer live for themselves, but for the One who died for them and was raised. (2 Cor. 5:15)

Living for Christ certainly includes service. What husband can claim to love his wife and yet never do anything for her? In the same way our love for Christ is evident in our service.

In an attempt to measure the degree to which our sample of churchgoers understood and embraced God's ownership, we asked the following question:

How much do you agree or disagree with this statement: I believe everything I have belongs to God?

Of the twenty-five hundred people surveyed, 60 percent indicated they agreed strongly, while another 21 percent agreed somewhat. Some might be encouraged by the combined 81 percent positive response until you realize the question did not ask people to evaluate how well they live up to the implications of God's ownership. All any respondent had to do was affirm that God is Creator and Owner of everything.

A "God First" Servant

Our service to God should be based on the conviction that God always comes first: "But seek first the kingdom of God and His righteousness, and all these things will be provided for you" (Matt. 6:33). When we become believers, we acknowledge a transfer of ownership—a transfer of priorities—moving from self-centered to other-centered, where we place God at the top of the list. Submitting to God's ownership, to the lordship of Christ, provides the "why" of service. With this in mind, we asked the following question:

How much do you agree/disagree: With reference to my values and priorities, I can honestly say that I try to put God first in my life?

In response, 36 percent indicated they "agreed strongly," while another 35 percent said they "agreed somewhat." While no genuine Christian is completely content with his or her level of obedience to Jesus Christ, we ought to be concerned that 29 percent of these professing Christians hesitate even to attempt putting God first in their lives.

As pastors and church leaders, we've all had concerns about church members who come forward during a public invitation, prayed the "sinner's prayer," but then seem to display little evidence of the lordship of Christ in their lives. Repentance isn't merely apologizing to God for our sins and then continuing to live as if we control our own lives. Paul says we've been transferred "into the kingdom of the Son He loves, in whom we have redemption, the forgiveness of sins" (Col. 1:13–14).

This and many other passages tell us that the gospel transforms the believer's identity, ownership, and destiny, yet it appears many respondents either lack solid exposure to the essence of what it means to be a Christian, or they've chosen to ignore the truth that being a Christian means putting God first.

Service Is a Necessity

We wanted to measure the connection between spiritual maturity and being a full-service disciple, so we asked the following question:

How much do you agree/disagree:
It is necessary for a Christian's spiritual well being
to give time on a regular basis to some specific
ministry within his/her church?

Once again the response was less than encouraging. Only 22 percent indicated they "agreed strongly," and another 32 percent "agreed somewhat." We did not ask if they believed ministry within the church was essential or how diligently they applied that conviction to their lives. This particular question merely asked about their support for the concept of service.

Many factors contribute to this situation. Besides cultural seepage, "felt needs" preaching, and the lack of solid discipleship, we ought to add the failure of the Christian family. Service and ministry should be taught, modeled, and expected in the home.

A clear strategy to teach, train, and mobilize young people for ministry makes a significant difference in whether those young people will live meaningful Christian lives. One of our LifeWay Research studies revealed that 70 percent of twenty-three- to thirty-year-olds drop out of church for a least a year between the ages of eighteen and twenty-two. According to the survey, many stopped attending because they were not meaningfully involved in the church.

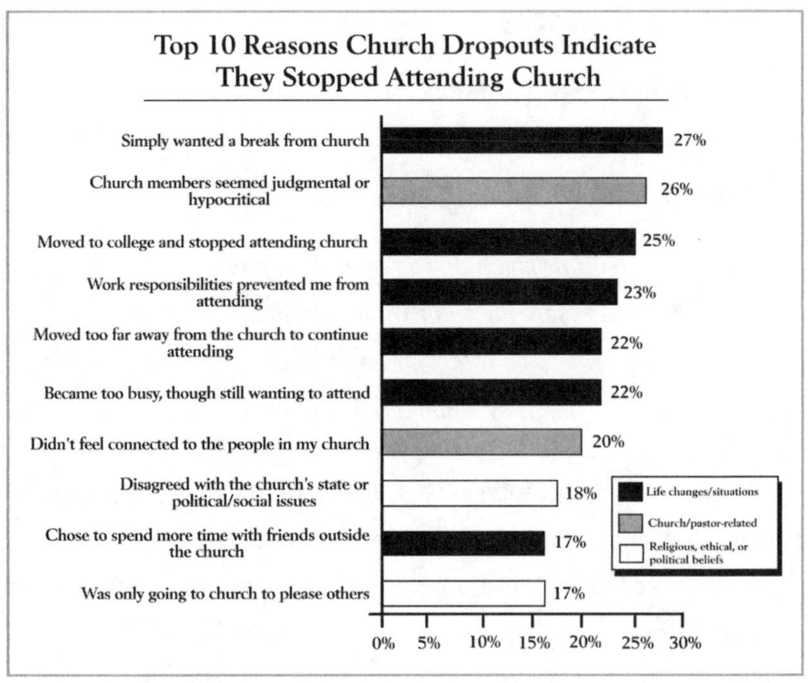

In this study we asked the 30 percent of teens who remained active in their church the following question:

Which of the following factors contributed to your continued regular attendance between the ages of eighteen and twenty-two?

Significantly 42 percent said they remained active because they were "committed to the purpose and work of the church."

Meaningful involvement is critical to avoiding young adult attrition. Those who work with children and youth must factor this into their thinking as they plan their programs. Leaders have to be focused on something other than just growing the church. Leaders should also try to instill a sense of obedience in their people.

The Service Quotient—Preparation

It is easy for people to say they want to get involved in service, but actions speak louder than words. You can tell if a church or an individual actually values service if the church offers training and if members take the training. With this in mind, one indicator of how committed people were to service was to measure how they'd trained for service. We asked our survey sample the following question:

Have you ever identified your primary spiritual gifts, as defined in the Bible? This might be done through a class, a spiritual gifts inventory, or another process.

We discovered that 49 percent of our participants had participated in some sort of class with the intention of identifying and learning about spiritual gifts. Among evangelicals that number rose to 70 percent.

Actually those numbers were higher than I expected. I am pleasantly surprised that nearly half of regular churchgoers and 70 percent of evangelicals have participated in a class dealing with spiritual gifts. Thinking back to the three churches where I served, I doubt the percentage would have been that high even though we regularly promoted such opportunities. This would seem to indicate more and more churches are offering training with the goal of service and involvement.

Church leaders need to develop clear strategies for promoting and facilitating the training of members.

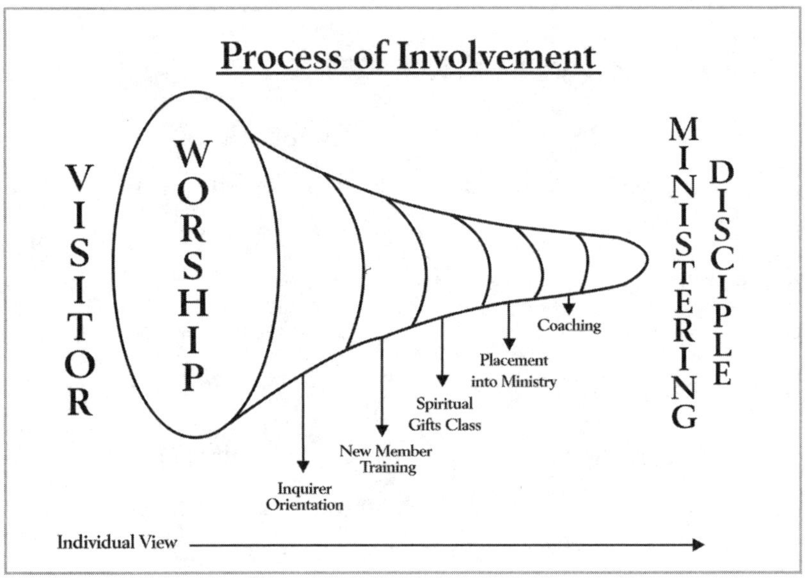

The 80/20 Service Quotient

You've probably heard of the Pareto Principle that states that 80 percent of the effects come from 20 percent of the causes. Relating this to the church, most people say that 20 percent of the people do 80 percent of the work. In my last full-time church, we had a comprehensive strategy for engaging members in ministry, and I was certain we had a huge percentage of the congregation involved in our ministries—music, children, youth, women, men, community—these all involved a lot of people. But when we actually counted, our ratio was only about 70/30.

Some time later I read the challenging book *The Church of Irresistible Influence* by Robert Lewis,[1] who at the time was pastor of the Fellowship Bible Church in Little Rock, Arkansas. In the book he explained how they mobilized large numbers of church members into serving God and others. I heard Johnny Hunt, pastor of Woodstock Baptist Church in Atlanta, proclaim his view that if the flock did not serve, the failure was his. My vision was renewed. If taught and led properly, the flock will follow their shepherd. We need to raise the bar of expectation. At the end of the day, leaders are responsible to teach and lead believers to serve God and others.

A few years ago I discovered a church where nearly 80 percent of the members were involved in service. The pastor was not content for Christians to sit and soak. He not only preached about involvement, but God used him to create a culture of engagement. It can and should be done. I love it when leaders accept responsibility for the condition of their flocks!

We need to help individual believers realize they must embrace their personal responsibility for service. With this in mind, we asked the following question:

Do you currently volunteer your time to serve in any capacity or role within your church?

I was surprised that 50 percent of the respondents answered "yes." I wouldn't have guessed so many regular churchgoers were involved in some type of service. It would be interesting to see how many of the "man hours" involved resulted in transformed lives.

God does not grade on a curve. The biblical standard is that every Christian should serve God and others. Church leaders need to analyze carefully both the qualitative and the quantitative nature of their flocks' ministry activities. The old "nickels and noses" metric won't cut it. It isn't enough for worship attendance, baptisms, and giving to be going up. We should want to see people transformed by Christ and serving Him in a ministry that fits how He uniquely made them.

One-on-One Discipleship

Many professions rely on mentoring in order to properly train its next generation of workers and leaders. The trainee learns from an experienced professional, so the one being trained can effectively serve others for years to come.

The principle is the same when we mentor or disciple young believers. Our training needs to be more than book work; we need to model service, encourage service, and work alongside other believers as they learn to serve.

My path to service began with one-on-one discipling by an older student named Dave Edwards. For two years Dave and I met for prayer, dialogue, Bible study, accountability, and guidance. He helped me navigate difficult waters I probably wouldn't have been able to manage on my own. He helped me establish some consistency in the disciplines of spiritual formation—prayer, daily Bible reading, in-depth Bible study, Scripture memorization, etc. He also focused on issues of character formation.

After a while, Dave pointed me toward service to God and others. For example, I began to share my faith with lost friends and acquaintances. We started a Bible study with some of my fraternity brothers, which Dave soon turned over to me. One of the guys in the study, an energetic freshman named Lynn Rundle, began to show interest in getting to know, love, and serve God. I began to do for him what Dave had done for me. It was not long before Lynn began to disciple a young man named Chan Gates. This is how the story goes. One person invests in another, who invests in another, one generation after another.

Billie Hanks Jr. calls this "multiplication discipleship." He illustrated the power of multiplication by asking how long it would take to reach the entire world for Christ if one person invested in another person for one whole year, and then they each discipled another person for a year, and so on. I was shocked to realize it would only take slightly more than thirty years to disciple the entire population of the world.

Of course, that is a theoretical illustration, but it does demonstrate the power of one person investing deeply in the life of another. For me personally, I doubt I would have progressed spiritually and grown toward service to God and others without the intentional encouragement of others.

The apostle Paul expresses this vision in a letter to one of his early disciples: "What you have heard from me in the presence of many witnesses, commit to faithful men who will be able to teach others also" (2 Tim. 2:2). I am not suggesting the apostle Paul was only envisioning one-on-one disciple making, but it is clear that faithful Christians are supposed to teach and equip faithful Christians to teach and equip other faithful Christians.

In order to determine the potential impact of one-on-one discipling upon our sample of churchgoers, we asked the following question:

Have you ever discipled or mentored a less spiritually mature person one-on-one, intentionally spending time with them on a regular basis (at least once a month), for the purpose of helping in that person's spiritual development?

Again the results were surprising: 38 percent of the respondents answered yes. This was encouraging! We do not know exactly what took place in these relationships or the theological content of what was taught. Nor do we know how solid the objectives were or what results occurred. What we do know, however, is that a large number of churchgoers have made themselves intentionally available to help others. We can take some encouragement from this.

Of course, mentoring is currently popular in our culture, especially in secular business circles. We are not, however, merely talking about the method of mentoring. Our focus is on establishing a disciple-making ministry patterned both methodologically and theologically after that of Jesus Christ and the apostles.

I had the privilege of being discipled by Dr. Robert Coleman while I was attending Trinity Evangelical Divinity School near Chicago. I enjoyed sitting in his missions and evangelism classes, where I absorbed the following principles of disciple making:

- *The Principle of Selection:* Jesus chose some men to train in an intense manner.
- *The Principle of Association:* Jesus called these men to be with Him, to be near Him, to spend time with Him in a variety of settings. While He ministered to the masses, He poured His life into a few.
- *The Principle of Demonstration:* Jesus modeled how to do ministry. The disciples were able to observe how He preached, how He dealt with the enemy, and how He ministered to the less fortunate and those who were spiritually hungry.
- *The Principle of Delegation:* Jesus sent them out to minister to others. He put them in on-the-job training.
- *The Principle of Supervision:* Jesus coached the disciples as they were learning to minister to others.

These and other principles are spelled out more thoroughly in his classic book, *The Master Plan of Evangelism.* Dr. Coleman makes the point that churches can be greatly strengthened by a robust strategy for creating a large number of disciple makers. The potential of mature Christians reproducing themselves in the lives of others is tremendous.[2]

The author of Hebrews makes this penetrating observation:

> We have a great deal to say about this, and it's difficult to explain, since you have become slow to understand. For though by this time you ought to be teachers, you need someone to teach you again the basic principles of God's revelation. You need milk, not solid food. Now everyone who lives on milk is inexperienced with the message about righteousness, because he is an infant. (Heb. 5:11–13)

Many of our church members could and should be ready to teach and disciple others but are sitting on the sidelines. We must give serious thought and prayer to developing a strategy of equipping church members to disciple others. When pastors begin multiplying their effectiveness by equipping others to in turn equip others, only the Lord knows what lies in store!

Prayer in the Service Quotient

Putting prayer on the list of ways we serve in ministry isn't as common as it should be. Prayer can be such a vital way in which we serve others. In fact, as I wrote this chapter, I received a phone call from a good friend in another state. A couple of weeks earlier, I'd told him I was dealing with a serious relational challenge, and he was calling back to check on how the situation was going. He said he had been praying about the concern every day. His display of support and concern warmed by heart. My friend was serving me in a significant way.

The apostle Paul believed the prayers of others made a powerful difference in his life and ministry. In his letters he said:

> Pray also for me, that the message may be given to me when I open my mouth to make known with boldness the mystery of the gospel. (Eph. 6:19)

> Because I know this will lead to my deliverance through your prayers and help from the Spirit of Jesus Christ. (Phil. 1:19)

> Brothers, pray for us also. (1 Thess. 5:25)

> Finally, pray for us, brothers, that the Lord's message may spread rapidly and be honored, just as it was with you. (2 Thess. 3:1)

> But meanwhile, also prepare a guest room for me, for I hope that through your prayers I will be restored to you. (Philem. 1:22)

Through prayer we minister to fellow believers as we seek their spiritual welfare—praying for guidance, strength, peace of mind, wisdom, opportunity to witness, effectiveness in ministry, victory over sin, physical safety, and many other things. When we say, "I am holding you up in prayer," it is truer than most of us realize. Prayer not only brings honor and glory to God, but it's also a great service to fellow believers.

With this in mind, we wanted to discover the degree to which Christians are praying for their leaders and fellow Christians. The first question we asked was *"How often do you pray for fellow Christians you know?"* The bar chart on the next page shows the response.

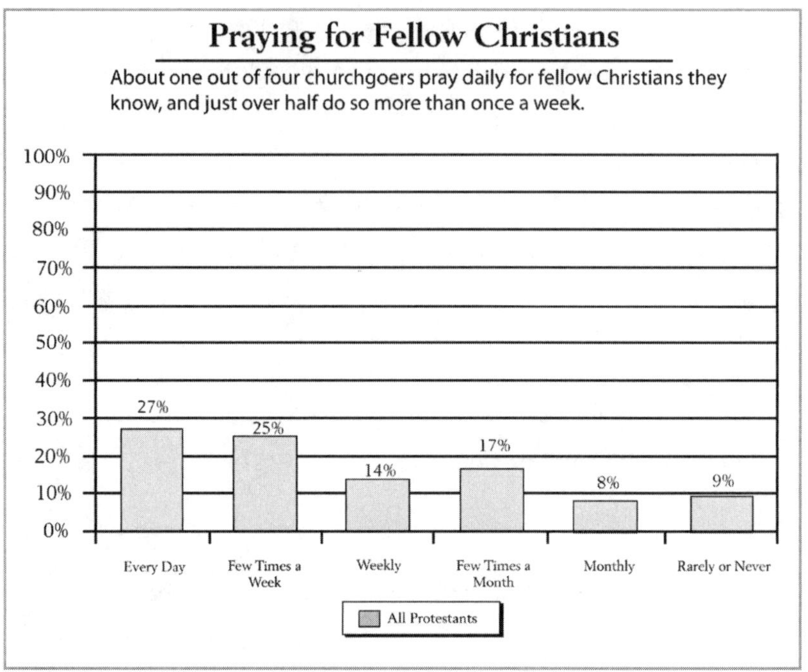

Once again the numbers were higher than I expected. While it was encouraging, it wasn't ultimately satisfying. I am grateful that many Christians believe in and practice prayer, but these numbers can and should increase.

We also asked a second question: *"How often do you pray for your church and church leaders?"* "Every day" drew 20 percent of the responses, another 18 percent said they prayed a few times a week, and 16 percent said they did so on a weekly basis.

The shape of faith to come must include vibrant, robust prayer, just as Luke records that prayer was a major characteristic of the early church: "And they devoted themselves to the apostles' teaching, to fellowship, to the breaking of bread, and to prayers" (Acts 2:42).

Several years ago I wanted the key prayer leaders of a church I served to grow in their vision of what a church committed to prayer looked like. We planned a road trip to spend a couple of days at Brooklyn Tabernacle Church, whose pastor, Jim Cymbala, wrote the book *Fresh Wind, Fresh Fire*.[3]

As I had hoped, the experience was life transforming. The spiritual dynamic of this church was amazing. Joy was abundant, the fellowship warm, ministry involvement high, conflict low. Much praise was being offered to God, and the members of the church prayed for one another with great fervency and consistency.

When Cymbala first came to the church, it was all but dead. He called the small, beleaguered membership to prayer, and over time spiritual renewal began to occur. The pastor preached and taught on prayer. He modeled prayer and raised the bar of expectation. He provided opportunities for people to pray for and with one another.

When leaders, especially the pastor, have a clear vision for what the church should be and then lead the way, people generally follow. To biblically shape the faith to come, leaders and the people will be committed to prayer, not merely as routine fixtures of church services but as a way of life. When leaders are committed to prayer, the people will begin to see prayer as a ministry to one another.

Giving as Part of the Service Quotient

As church leaders we talk a lot about servant leadership, but Scripture indicates that God wants us to express service more through action than words. For instance, when the rich, young ruler came to Jesus, he wanted to serve; but Jesus, in effect, said service included giving things that are tangible, such as money, to God and to others. The young man "went away grieving, because he had many possessions" (Matt. 19:21–24).

The rich, young ruler was a leader, but he struggled with being a servant. And like any of us today, you could see what was dear to the young ruler's heart by looking at his bank account or his daily schedule. We know most people give time and money only to those things they value, and when this wealthy man asked Jesus what must be done to inherit eternal life, the Lord replied:

> If you want to be perfect," Jesus said to him, "go, sell your belongings and give to the poor, and you will have treasure in heaven. Then come, follow Me."
>
> When the young man heard that command, he went away grieving, because he had many possessions.
>
> Then Jesus said to His disciples, "I assure you: It will be hard for a rich person to enter the kingdom of heaven! Again I tell you, it is easier for a camel to go through the eye of a needle than for a rich person to enter the kingdom of God."
> (Matt. 19:21–24)

Then in the parable of the soils, Jesus makes this comment:

> Others are sown among thorns; these are the ones who hear the word, but the worries of this age, the seduction of wealth, and the desires for other things enter in and choke the word, and it becomes unfruitful. (Mark 4:18–19)

And finally:

> Don't collect for yourselves treasures on earth, where moth and rust destroy and where thieves break in and steal. But collect for yourselves treasures in heaven, where neither moth nor rust destroys, and where thieves don't break in and steal. For where your treasure is, there your heart will be also. (Matt. 6:19–21)

In many churches the only time sermons about money are delivered is when the budget is not being made or a building program is in the works. And yet proper spiritual formation requires us to address seriously the issues of money and materialism. Jesus makes it clear that we cannot serve two masters (see Luke 16:13). The shape of faith to come will keep affections centered on honoring and pleasing Jesus with no trust or security placed in what this world can provide.

Another important component of disciple making is stewardship of the money God entrusts into our hands to advance His kingdom. The apostle Paul dedicates much of his second letter to the Corinthian church to this issue. At one point he says, "For the ministry of this service is not only supplying the needs of the saints, but is also overflowing in many acts of thanksgiving to God" (2 Cor. 9:12). The "ministry of service" was the raising of a financial gift for Christians in need.

A person's view of money, pattern of giving, and use of money in service will show their spiritual depth. With this in mind, we asked the following question:[4]

About what percentage of your total annual income do you contribute to charitable causes or organizations, including your local church and other nonprofit organizations?

The bar graph below shows what we found related to charitable giving.

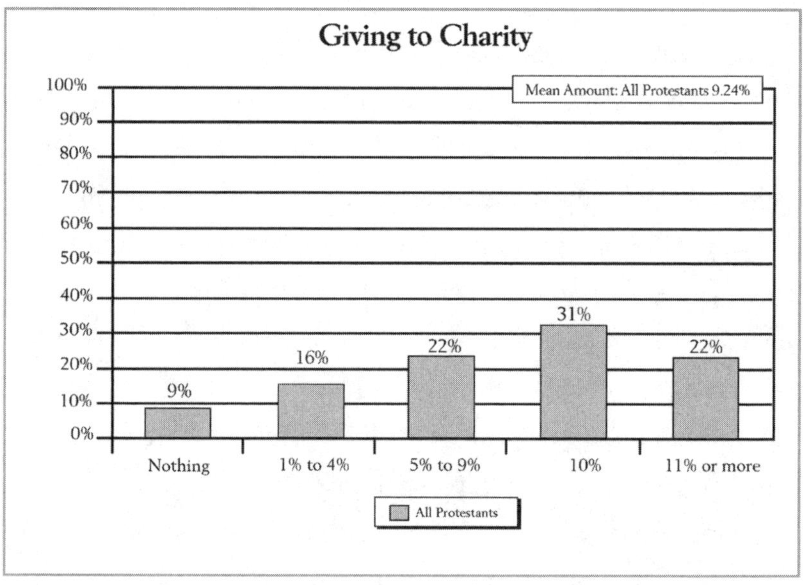

A full 53 percent of those surveyed report giving at least 10 percent to their church or other charitable organizations. This should encourage us. We will need additional studies to examine in depth the nature of this giving.

Most pastors I know say 20 percent of their people give 80 percent of the money. In my own twenty-plus years of local church service, the low level of giving always frustrated me. One of my most frustrating moments came during a building program we had launched because our church was completely out of parking and education space. We were closing in on two thousand people in worship each Sunday, but we only owned ten acres of land. The church decided to purchase land in another part of town and relocate.

We worked with architects to develop several approaches to the building program, depending upon the finances God brought our way. Consultants encouraged us to solicit widespread input about church members' desires and expectations. Initially, the first phase included a multipurpose gymnasium. When the initial pledges were gathered, however, the total would not cover the gym, and we had to move it to phase two. Several members of a Sunday school class for young couples with children were disappointed and became vocal in demanding the gym. I asked our business manager to look into the giving patterns of the couples class while keeping members' names confidential. I was shocked to discover that only three couples out of thirty or more gave more than $3,000 per year to the church, though the average annual income of the group was well over $50,000. No one in that large class even came close to practicing what is traditionally known as tithing.

Of course, the main issue here is not building programs and budgets. There are far more important spiritual issues at stake when it comes to money, possessions, and giving. This story, however, illustrates a connection between spiritual maturity and giving. As God changes us, He changes our perspective and practices related to possessions and money. In the shape of faith to come, followers of

Christ will honor God with their wealth. They will give generously and lay up treasures in heaven. They will think and live in a way that reflects true biblical stewardship. They will minister to others, in part, by giving.

Salt and Light as Service

I have always been impressed by Christians and churches characterized not only by vibrant service but also by aggressive ministry to the community. Jesus gives us insight into how our behavior can change the world around us. In the Sermon on the Mount, Jesus said:

> Let your light shine before men, so that they may see
> your good works and give glory to your Father in heaven.
> (Matt. 5:16)

Unchurched people and the lost do not understand Christians or the church. The apostle Paul said, "But the natural man does not welcome what comes from God's Spirit, because it is foolishness to him; he is not able to know it since it is evaluated spiritually" (1 Cor. 2:14). Lost people, however, still can see individual Christians and the church live out the love of Christ, a contagious witness the Holy Spirit uses to draw men to Christ. Jesus said, "I give you a new commandment: love one another. Just as I have loved you, you must also love one another. By this all people will know that you are My disciples, if you have love for one another" (John 13:34–35).

Many of the messages and images the lost world sees are not consistent with the love of God. Many of the "Christian" programs on television—everything from fake healings, to the lies of "health, wealth, and prosperity" preaching, to slick appeals for money—are a perversion of true Christianity. I can only imagine what non-Christians conclude about Christians and, consequently, Christianity.

LifeWay Research recently conducted a study of how unchurched people in America view God, the culture, and the church. While unbelievers are unable to understand truths about God, all Christian leaders should be concerned about how Christians are perceived by non-Christians.

We asked three questions. First, we asked about the degree to which unchurched people agreed or disagreed with this question:

How much do you agree/disagree: The church is full of hypocrites, people who criticize others for doing the same things they do themselves?

A full 72 percent indicated they agreed either somewhat or strongly. We also asked how much they agreed or disagreed with the statement, "Christians get on my nerves." Of those surveyed, 44 percent agreed either somewhat or strongly.

Then we asked our sample to respond to this statement:

I think Christianity today is more about organized religion than about loving God and loving people.

The bar graph for the response is below.

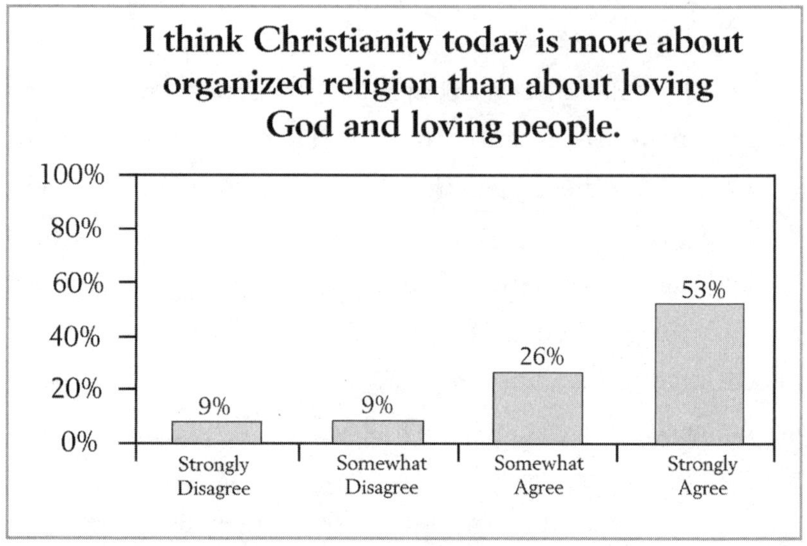

We do not want to overreact to these findings because some unchurched people have a natural prejudice against and even hostility toward Christianity. The Bible makes it clear that the gospel is a stone of stumbling to some (see Rom. 9:33) and foolishness to others (see 1 Cor. 1:18). We should not, however, add offense or a stumbling block by our attitudes and behavior. Sometimes we fail to live consistently with the Bible's clear moral and ethical standards. Sometimes we display a lack of love or take hard stands on issues not pertinent to the gospel.

One of the many things we can do to counteract these perceptions is to seek avenues of service in the community. In the aftermath of Hurricane Katrina, the Southern Baptist North American Mission Board set an admirable example by stepping in with effective relief, and the world took notice. Almost every time a disaster occurs these days, we hear many positive reports of Baptist disaster relief teams ministering to victims.

Some of my fondest church memories are of church members acting as salt and light in the community. I recall Nancy Caverlee displaying the love of Christ in pregnancy counseling centers. I watched Bob Hartman and Gene Carroll mobilize many of our members to build Habitat for Humanity homes. I remember Ray Paul gathering food and clothes for an inner-city relief center. My own father-in-law, Jim Thompson, has spent many nights sharing Christ and leading Bible studies in prisons. Jim Kilby started an outreach center for teens in trouble. One of my closest friends, Gary Gepfrey, has reached out to people struggling with addictions. In recent years Dr. Gary Palmer and his wife, Marilyn, have often traveled overseas to provide medical treatment to those in need.

Does the gospel need this kind of Christian love to give it authenticity? Absolutely not! The gospel is self-authenticating. But genuine Christianity will show itself in love and good deeds. To determine the degree to which our sample was active in serving those in need, we asked the following question:

How much do you agree/disagree:
I regularly use my gifts and talents to serve/help
people in need who are not part of my church?

Of those surveyed, 20 percent agreed strongly, and another 34 percent agreed somewhat. I would not have guessed that 54 percent of regular churchgoers spend some level of effort serving outside the church. We do not know the exact nature of their service, but we are encouraged by this insight.

In the shape of faith to come, I envision more and more church leaders guiding and equipping their people to minister in the community. While the entire spectrum of spiritual gifts is given to build up the body of Christ, this ministry of edification should be complemented by reaching into the community with the love of Christ. The Spirit of Christ compels us to demonstrate His love to others. The author of James puts it this way: "Pure and undefiled religion before our God and Father is this: to look after orphans and widows in their distress and to keep oneself unstained by the world" (James 1:27).

In the shape of faith to come, however, we will not fall prey to the heresy of the "social gospel." We won't rest content with meeting the physical needs of others without addressing the even more significant need for the gospel. If all we do is feed and clothe people, the fruit of our labor is merely temporal. The world's real need is redemption, which is available only through repentance and faith in the redemptive work of Christ on the cross. We will deal with this more fully in the next chapter.

Serving God and others is a mark of spiritual maturity. In fact, without service, spiritual transformation is impossible. One of my favorite passages sums it up this way:

> If then there is any encouragement in Christ, if any consolation of love, if any fellowship with the Spirit, if any affection and mercy, fulfill my joy by thinking the same way, having the same love, sharing the same feelings, focusing

> on one goal. Do nothing out of rivalry or conceit, but in humility consider others as more important than yourselves. Everyone should look out not only for his own interests, but also for the interests of others. (Phil. 2:1–5)

Looking out for the interests of others runs against our natural bent. We are selfish people in our old nature, but the path of self-sacrifice and obedience naturally leads us to serve God and others. And more importantly it brings honor and praise to God.

The Service Quotient—Conclusions

In the shape of faith to come, we will teach and model an excellence of service fueled by a servant's heart and compelled by our Father's love. We will be intentional in training our members for service and intentionally providing them opportunities to serve.

---

1. Robert Lewis, *The Church of Irresistible Influence* (Grand Rapids, MI: Zondervan, 2001).

2. Robert Coleman, *The Master Plan of Evangelism* (Grand Rapids, MI: Fleming H. Revell, 1994), 21, 38, 73, 82, 94.

3. Jim Cymbala, *Fresh Wind, Fresh Fire* (Grand Rapids, MI: Zondervan, 1997).

4. Before looking at the results of this inquiry, I want to offer an explanation regarding both the scope and specific wording of this inquiry. In our interaction with the professional firm that worked with us in this research project, it was determined that we should phrase the question to relate to the broad base of Protestants included

in the study. In my faith tradition we use and understand the terms *tithes* and *offerings*. Furthermore, most pastors in my denomination view a tithe as giving at least 10 percent of one's income to the local church. Offerings are viewed as gifts over and above the tithe to other organizations or causes. In many denominations, however, this is not the case. To avoid confusion we used broad terms related to charitable giving.

Chapter Six

Domain Four

Sharing Christ: The Evangelism Quotient

Therefore, we are ambassadors for Christ; certain that God is appealing through us, we plead on Christ's behalf, "Be reconciled to God."

—2 Corinthians 5:20

Biblical Truth: Jesus came to "seek and save the lost."

The Evangelism Quotient: God's strategy is to call, equip, and send His followers into the world with His love and message of redemption.

Identified as Ambassador

At a dinner sponsored by the State Department, dozens of ambassadors from countries all around the world gather to become better acquainted with their fellow diplomats. As each ambassador arrives, he or she is announced to the others:

"Presenting the ambassador from the Kingdom of 'God is with everyone, even on the golf course every Sunday morning.'"

"Presenting the ambassador from the Republic of 'I put a Bible verse in my Christmas card and that's my yearly plan for sharing Christ.'"

"Presenting the ambassador from the Affiliated States of 'I don't want to make anyone uncomfortable.'"

The next ambassador enters the banquet hall quietly. Looking up, the protocol official asks, "Sir, may I announce which kingdom you represent?" The anonymous diplomat answers, "I'd rather not tell you who I represent. I think that should remain a private matter."

"But how can you represent your king?" asks the protocol officer. "How can you make appeals on his behalf?"

"I am a private ambassador," says the unknown, unbranded ambassador. "I don't want anyone to know whose brand I wear. I'm a stealth ambassador, and there's no need for me to be identified with any specific kingdom."

An ambassador who remains unidentified cannot represent his country, or kingdom, or Lord. The apostle Paul said we are holy representatives of King Jesus, sent on His behalf to seek the lost (see 2 Cor. 5:20), just as Jesus came "to seek and to save the lost" (Luke 19:10). We serve Jesus when we tell others how He served us: "For even the Son of Man did not come to be served, but to serve, and to give His life—a ransom for many" (Mark 10:45).

What Is the Gospel?

God's plan for seeking and saving the lost stems from the beginning of time: "But when the completion of the time came, God sent His Son, born of a woman, born under the law, to redeem those under the law, so that we might receive adoption as sons" (Gal. 4:4–5). The beauty of the gospel is Jesus Christ, taking on the sins of the world, providing the wonderful gift of redemption. On the cross God's wrath was satisfied, making possible the atonement of sin. As Paul noted, "He made the One who did not know sin to be sin for us, so that we might become the righteousness of God in Him" (2 Cor. 5:21).

Theologians use the term *imputed righteousness*. Just as Adam's sin was imputed, or transferred to our legal record, so the righteousness of Christ is imputed to those who believe. We do not earn it, we do not deserve it, and we receive this new status joyfully by placing our faith in Christ's death on the cross.

We could say much more about this from Scripture, but this lays the theological foundation for Domain Four. Not everyone participating in this study agreed with this definition of the gospel; only those described as "born again" and those who affirm the seven doctrinal criteria of being "evangelical":

- God-inspired accuracy of the Bible
- Reality of Satan
- Personal responsibility to share Christ with others
- Importance of Christianity in their daily lives
- View of Jesus as sinless on earth
- View of God as all-knowing, all-powerful deity
- View of salvation as by grace alone[1]

The Biblical Basis of Evangelism

In addition to the doctrinal foundation of the gospel, we also need to understand the biblical basis of evangelism. Not only did Jesus come to "seek and save the lost," His strategy was to call, equip, and send His followers into the world with His love and message of redemption. Recall some of the biblical stories that cover this:

- Early in His public ministry, Jesus told His first disciples they were to become "fishers of men" (Matt. 4:19 NIV).
- He often sent those early disciples out to preach and minister (see Matt. 10:5; Luke 10:1).
- When John the Baptist asked if Jesus was the promised Messiah, Jesus responded in part by saying, "The poor have the good news preached to them" (Luke 7:22).
- After Jesus' resurrection, He gave His followers the most significant commission ever delivered, making it clear that God's redemptive plan was to evangelize the world through the verbal witness of His followers (see Matt. 28:16–20).

- Luke records that, prior to Pentecost, Jesus declared, "But you will receive power when the Holy Spirit has come upon you, and you will be My witnesses in Jerusalem, in all Judea and Samaria, and to the ends of the earth" (Acts 1:8).
- At Pentecost, God gave the Holy Spirit to His followers to empower them to take the gospel to the world (see Acts 2:1–41).
- The written account of the early church clearly records that evangelism was a dominant theme of church life (see Acts 3:12–26; 4:5–12, 29–32; 8:5, 26–38; 10:27–43; 17:22–32).
- Paul's various missionary journeys demonstrate that he picked up the mantle of taking the gospel to the gentile world.

Besides the evangelistic and mission narratives of Christ's public ministry and the outreach activities of the early church, certain passages in the Bible provide additional insight into God's intention for His people to witness verbally.

Paul's letter to the church in Rome explains the necessity of a verbal presentation of the gospel:

> How can they call on Him in whom they have not believed? And how can they believe without hearing about Him? And how can they hear without a preacher? And how can they preach unless they are sent? As it is written: How welcome are the feet of those who announce the gospel of good things! But all did not obey the gospel. For Isaiah says, Lord, who has believed our message? So faith comes from what is heard, and what is heard comes through the message about Christ. (Rom. 10:14–17)

Paul's letter to the church in Corinth uses the phrase "ministry of reconciliation" and the analogy of an ambassador to convey the nature of our witness:

> Now everything is from God, who reconciled us to Himself through Christ and gave us the ministry of reconciliation: that is, in Christ, God was reconciling the world to Himself, not counting their trespasses against them, and He has committed the message of reconciliation to us. Therefore, we are ambassadors for Christ; certain that God is appealing through us, we plead on Christ's behalf, "Be reconciled to God." (2 Cor. 5:18–20)

This means we have clear *description* related to evangelism (written accounts describing the evangelistic activities of the followers of Christ), and we also have clear *prescription* (commands to take the message of the gospel to the ends of the earth). Consequently, evaluating the spiritual maturity of either an individual Christian or a congregation as a whole requires us to factor in both commitment to and practice of evangelism.

The Evangelism Quotient—Real Numbers

In developing Domain Four, we designed seven agree/disagree questions and three questions related to the frequency of certain activities.

Questions Related to Agree or Disagree Responses

1. It is every Christian's responsibility to share the gospel with non-Christians.
2. I have a personal responsibility to share my religious beliefs about Jesus Christ with non-Christians.
3. I feel comfortable that I can share my belief in Christ with someone else effectively.
4. While interacting with others on a normal, daily basis, I seek opportunities to speak out about Jesus Christ.
5. I intentionally spend time building friendships with non-Christians for the purpose of sharing Christ with them.
6. I am hesitant to let others know that I am a Christian.
7. Many people who know me are not aware I am a Christian.

Frequency of Activities

8. Pray for the spiritual status of people I know who are not professing Christians (how often).
9. In the past six months shared with someone two or more times how to become a Christian.
10. In the past six months invited an unchurched person to attend a church service or some other program at my church two or more times.

Overall Scores

A mere 1 percent of the twenty-five hundred churchgoers provided an ideal response to all ten questions. When you consider the foundational nature of the questions, it is hard to fathom how only twenty-five out of twenty-five hundred regular churchgoers could fully affirm the principles involved.

Beyond that, only 5 percent of the respondents provided a positive response to all ten questions: "agree somewhat" and "agree strongly" for questions 1–5, "disagree somewhat" and "disagree strongly" for questions 6 and 7, and the highest frequency response for questions 8–10. Out of 2,500 people surveyed, only 125 provided a positive response to all ten questions.

Another way to analyze Domain Four is to convert the scores to a 100-point scale, like those used in a typical school system. From that perspective we find that 21 percent of the respondents scored 80 or above, meaning that only 525 of the 2,500 received a grade of C or higher.

Although these scores could have been even worse, I doubt many pastors and church leaders would be pleased to see such grades.

Evangelism: Is It Everyone's Responsibility?

When we become believers, we also become ambassadors of Christ, filled with the Holy Spirit (see Acts 2:1, 4). God places this Spirit-gift within us so we can be effective representatives on His behalf. Being identified as God's ambassadors, we become His "witnesses in Jerusalem, in all Judea and Samaria, and to the ends of the earth" (Acts 1:8). Our witness is not the result of a request by Jesus; He fully commissions us into a holy ambassadorship, expecting us to shoulder the responsibility of sharing the gospel with nonbelievers.

This view of evangelism was a prominent characteristic of the early church, and it is clear the passages commanding evangelism are meant for all Christians. But there is no doubt God's design for the church also includes calling some individuals to special offices. Paul makes this clear in his letter to the church at Ephesus:

> And He personally gave some to be apostles, some prophets, some evangelists, some pastors and teachers, for the training of the saints in the work of ministry, to build up the body of Christ, until we all reach unity in the faith and in the knowledge of God's Son, [growing] into a mature man with a stature measured by Christ's fullness. (Eph. 4:11–13)

This passage and others show clearly some Christians are called to special offices that entail certain functions. Historically, some individuals have carried out the task of evangelism with remarkable effectiveness. In our lifetime Billy Graham would be the most famous example. But in addition to evangelists, the Scripture is also clear that some are called to preach, to proclaim the gospel.

The question is, are all Christians responsible for sharing the gospel with the lost? Consider these observations from key texts.

In Christ's postresurrection appearances, He commissioned all of His followers to "make disciples of all nations." The phrase "make disciples" basically means to make followers, an activity that includes the task of evangelism. The maturing of disciples is contained in the phrase, "teaching them to observe everything" (Matt. 28:16–20).

The first chapter of Acts records that in one of Jesus' post-resurrection appearances He specifically commanded His followers to be His witnesses: "But you will receive power when the Holy Spirit has come upon you, and you will be My witnesses in Jerusalem, in all Judea and Samaria, and to the ends of the earth" (Acts 1:8).

In Acts 8, we find that persecution scattered the early Christians, and Luke observes: "So those who were scattered went on their way proclaiming the message of good news" (Acts 8:4).

In Paul's second letter to the church at Corinth, he asserts that God has given the church and, thus, all believers, the "ministry of reconciliation," which is another way of describing the task of evangelism. "Now everything is from God, who reconciled us to Himself through Christ and gave us the ministry of reconciliation: that is, in Christ, God was reconciling the world to Himself, not counting their trespasses against them, and He has committed the message of reconciliation to us. Therefore, we are ambassadors for Christ; certain that God is appealing through us, we plead on Christ's behalf, 'Be reconciled to God'" (2 Cor. 5:18–20).

In Paul's admonition to put on the full armor of God, he says, "Having shod your feet with the preparation of the gospel of peace," a clear reference to evangelism (Eph. 6:15 NASB).

In Philippians, Paul described the impact of his imprisonment on fellow Christians: "Most of the brothers in the Lord have gained confidence from my imprisonment and dare even more to speak the message fearlessly" (Phil. 1:14).

Paul's letter to the church at Colossae clearly referred to evangelism: "Your speech should always be gracious, seasoned with salt, so that you may know how you should answer each person" (Col. 4:6).

The apostle Peter's epistle underscores the importance of being ready to share the gospel: "But set apart the Messiah as Lord in your hearts, and always be ready to give a defense to anyone who asks you for a reason for the hope that is in you" (1 Pet. 3:15).

Based on the strong biblical evidence that evangelism is every Christian's responsibility, our study made this statement and asked for levels of agreement or disagreement:

How much do you agree/disagree: It is every Christian's responsibility to share the gospel with non-Christians?

Of twenty-five hundred respondents, 46 percent said they "agreed strongly," and another 26 percent said they "agreed somewhat," a positive response of 72 percent. Thus, the majority believes evangelism is every Christian's responsibility, but I expect most pastors would prefer more than 46 percent of their flock agree strongly that they are personally responsible for sharing the gospel.

For this particular issue we need to compare two belief systems: of those who identified themselves as "evangelicals," 88 percent "agreed strongly" with the above statement. Another 11 percent "agreed somewhat." So 99 percent of evangelicals gave a positive response about personal responsibility for evangelism. Compare that with those who do not consider themselves evangelical: only 32 percent "agreed strongly" and 31 percent "agreed somewhat."

Of those affiliated with mainline churches, just 28 percent "agreed strongly," while another 30 percent "agreed somewhat."

Another related study to draw on is LifeWay Research's longitudinal study, Teenagers' Views on Eternity and Religious Activities of Teens. In 2005 and 2007 LifeWay surveyed twelve- to nineteen-year-olds (1,030 in 2005 and 1,016 in 2007), seeking to understand how they view religious issues and practices. The bar chart shows how often American teenagers talk about their faith and invite their friends to attend church. Note the significant decline of outreach-related activities over the two years.

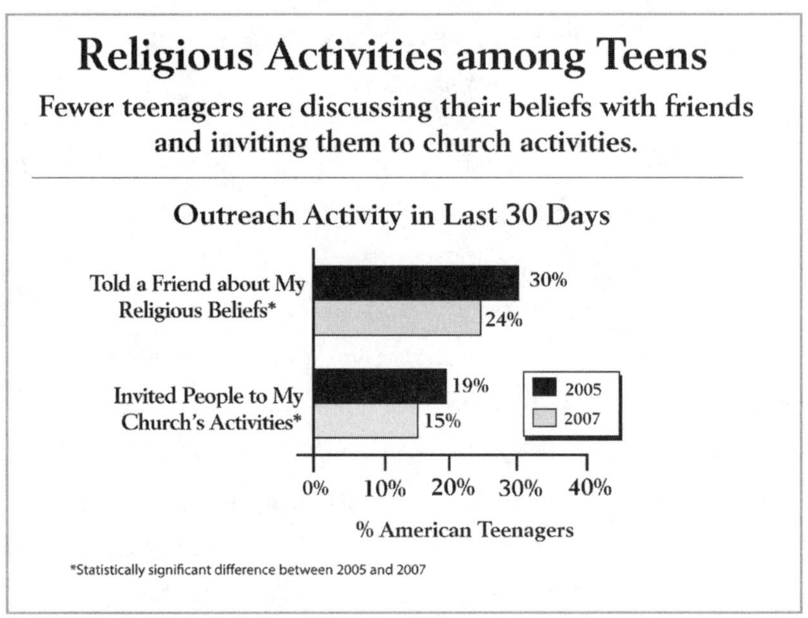

Divine Appointments for Ambassadors

It's lunchtime, and as he prays, the apostle Peter is starving, thinking about the food he'll soon eat. But before Peter can pop a morsel into his mouth, God shows him food forbidden to eat. Probably thinking his hunger is affecting his brain, Peter recoils, saying, "No, Lord! . . . For I have never eaten anything common and unclean!" (Acts 10:14).

In the meantime, while Peter sits perplexed by this vision, God is already working His plan to introduce Cornelius and his family to Jesus. God speaks personally to Peter, telling him the gospel is for all people, even the Gentiles. Peter, as an ambassador for Christ, is not to discriminate against anyone when he shares the good news.

To underscore this, God spoke to Cornelius, telling him where he could find an ambassador who represented Jesus—a man called Peter, who could introduce Cornelius to Christ, the Savior of the world (see Acts 10:22).

This divinely directed (see Acts 10:22) encounter reveals the personal nature of sharing the gospel, that the lost come to Christ one person at a time. Our role as ambassadors for Christ is critical as God seeks the lost. As with Peter, God will specifically direct His ambassadors to those who need to know about Jesus and, as with Cornelius, God will direct those searching for Jesus to His ambassadors in order to hear our witness.

In the story of Peter and Cornelius, God reveals the importance of understanding the personal responsibility involved in sharing Christ. God told Peter, specifically and personally, to share Christ with Cornelius; God arranged a specific meeting for the two men.

In order to measure how many among our sample shouldered the *personal responsibility* for sharing Christ, we asked this question:

How much do you agree/disagree with the following statement: I have a personal responsibility to share my religious beliefs about Jesus Christ with non-Christians?

Of those surveyed, 46 percent said they "agreed strongly"; another 24 percent said they "agreed somewhat." Notice these percentages are basically the same as for the previous question about evangelism being every Christian's responsibility. The respondents felt the same level of responsibility for themselves as they expected from others. Yet more than half of Protestant regular churchgoers feel no clear personal responsibility for sharing the gospel. No wonder most churches in America are either declining or not growing.

The rest of the questions in this domain are related to personal interest in, preparation for, and participation in sharing Christ. We wanted to know the degree to which our churchgoers prayed about, thought about, and actually took steps to reach the unchurched and unsaved. It seemed logical to begin with the subject of prayer.

Prayer Sandals

God's ambassadors help create a readiness for the gospel of peace by praying for the salvation of nonbelievers, asking God to prepare their hearts for hearing, and then receiving, the good news

(Eph. 6:15). Through prayer we become sensitive to the Holy Spirit's guidance as God directs us toward divine appointments.

Few things reflect a person's heart like their prayers. Visualize a friend or family member coming before the God of the universe to petition Him on your behalf. Wow! What more significant thing could one person do for another?

Knowing that prayer reflects a person's heart, we wanted to investigate the degree to which Christians in our study prayed for the salvation of acquaintances, friends, and loved ones. It seems reasonable to view prayer as a strong indicator of evangelistic concern.

Therefore, we asked this question:

How often do you do the following: Pray for the spiritual status of people I know who are not professing Christians?

Twenty percent said they prayed for lost people every day; another 20 percent said they prayed a few times a week; 12 percent said they prayed once a week; 9 percent said monthly.

Almost 60 percent of our sample pray at least weekly for acquaintances, friends, or family members they believe are not professing Christians. This would indicate the majority of churchgoers give some thought and concern to the spiritual condition of others. We should find hope and encouragement in these numbers.

Any church leader will, or should, be concerned about 42 percent of churchgoers who seldom, if ever, pray for those outside the household of faith. To biblically shape the faith to come, leaders must set the example in praying for the lost. Those who follow them will know their leaders are concerned for people outside the church. It is impossible to hide personal passion and concern.

Besides personal passion and leading by example, leaders of the future must preach, teach, and equip others to pray for the lost. To biblically shape the faith to come, most churches will need to rethink the traditional church prayer meeting some call an "organ recital." I do not want to minimize the importance of Christians praying for one another's physical needs, but there must be some balance. I have sat through many prayer meetings in which little or no concern was expressed for people outside the household of faith. Let's inject concern for the lost into the times we pray together.

Comfort with Sharing One's Faith

Paul never let his circumstances stop him from being an ambassador representing Jesus. Even when he was a prisoner in chains, his identity remained unchained, slipping through the prison bars like a sweet song carried down the streets and into the hearts and homes of those who hear it. Soon others began singing this unchained melody, carrying it with confidence wherever they would go.

"Because of my imprisonment, most of the believers here have gained confidence and boldly speak God's message without fear" (Phil. 1:14 NLT). We, too, should join Paul's unchained melody, sharing our beliefs under any circumstances at any time.

This boldness in telling others about Jesus was something we wanted to measure but not boldness as in working up the nerve to witness. Rather, we tried to measure the degree to which the people we surveyed saw themselves prepared to share the gospel when the opportunity arose. Toward that end we asked this question:

How much do you agree/disagree with the following statement: I feel comfortable that I can share my belief in Christ with someone else effectively?

Of those surveyed, 28 percent said they "agreed strongly," while another 40 percent said they "agreed somewhat." If you look at the combined numbers, which we have been calling a "positive response," I was surprised that 68 percent of the twenty-five hundred we surveyed were at least somewhat confident they were capable of sharing the gospel effectively.

Keep in mind that it was beyond the scope of this research to determine what the group thought "sharing the gospel" means. In other words, we do not know how holistic the respondents' understanding of the gospel is. For some, their understanding could be as simple as "I believe in Jesus." Still, our respondents viewed themselves as capable of effectively communicating their faith.

When we look at the "strongly agree" responses to the first three questions in this domain, we see that 46 percent of the sample believe it is every Christian's responsibility to share the gospel and that it is their personal responsibility to do so, and 28 percent feel comfortable they can share their faith effectively. Now let's take a look at the degree to which our respondents actually share Christ.

An Uninvited Guest

One afternoon two neighbors met while walking down a country road. One neighbor said to the other, "Why don't you ever come by the house for a visit? You know you're always a welcome guest."

The second neighbor responded, "Why haven't you ever invited me to your house? I didn't know I'd be welcomed as a guest."

The first neighbor thought for a moment, and then smiled: "Well, I guess you've been an uninvited guest, so let me invite you to be my guest."

There are "uninvited guests" all around us, and unless we act as ambassadors on Christ's behalf, how will they hear about Jesus? "How can they call on Him in whom they have not believed? And how can they believe without hearing about Him?" (Rom. 10:14).

Starting with this simple question about inviting others to church, we used seven questions to measure witnessing behaviors:

In the past six months, about how many times have you, personally, done any of the following: invited an unchurched person to attend a church service or some other program at your church?

Thirty-six percent said they had invited someone to church or a church-related activity at least twice in the past six months. Another 18 percent said they had done so once during the same period of time. Nearly half of the sample, 46 percent, had not attempted this at all.

Most people would likely agree that it is fairly easy to invite people to church; at least it is easier than probing into someone's view of Jesus and the implications of what Jesus said and did. Most pastors try to energize their flock to invite their relatives, friends, and neighbors to church.

The first church I served as a staff member scheduled a regular "Friend Day" designed to get every church member to bring a friend to Bible study or worship. Without fail, many of our members would do just that. Of course, from a leadership point of view, we were hoping to motivate them to invite others on a regular basis.

Andy Stanley probably has done more in recent years than any pastor to build this behavior into the culture of his church. He popularized the slogan, "Invest and Invite." In our Standout Church Study, we saw this behavior was common in the nineteen churches who participated in the study. The environment in each was warm and friendly. Without exception we found members were excited about their pastor, the worship services, and the preaching. They were confident unchurched friends would have a positive experience. These churches expected to have unchurched visitors, and they were ready for them.

Church members should be encouraged and instructed about investing in relationships with the unchurched and unsaved. *Investing* can take many forms—getting together socially, performing acts of service, and engaging in spiritual conversations one-on-one or in small groups. *Inviting* means asking them to visit church or some church-related event.

In my last full-time staff position, our church would host three or four major evangelistic events each year. The events were well planned and executed with excellence. Over time our members became excited about helping prepare for these events and, even more important, inviting their unchurched friends.

No church should rely solely on the *invest and invite* strategy. Christians should be prepared to share the gospel on their own. Fortunately this is not an either/or proposition. To biblically shape the faith to come, churches must put much energy into creating a culture of evangelism. Leaders will set the pace and lead by example. Church members will be equipped, guided, and encouraged to participate in the joy of personally sharing the gospel.

Public Identification

Another indicator of an interest in witnessing is willingness to identify publicly with Christ. For many Christians, "going on the record" as a believer is a big step. Sometimes it happens when you see an opening in a conversation and take it. It may be explaining why you do or do not do certain things or why you believe certain things. For some the first step may be as simple as praying prior to a meal at a restaurant.

The day I was writing this section of the book, I met some friends at a restaurant. I noticed the young waiter's name tag said "Josh." But what caught my attention was that he had altered his name tag to say "Josh and Jesus." That may seem corny, but the fact is that Josh displayed confidence in his faith by publicly identifying with Christ.

Anyone who has demonstrated public identity with Christ will attest it can lead to more faith. Stepping out in faith fosters more faith. Small steps can lead to bigger steps.

With this in mind, we asked about public awareness of one's faith. It was worded in the negative, so the ideal response was "strongly disagree." Here is the question:

How much do you agree/disagree: Many people who know me are not aware I am a Christian?

Only 29 percent said they "disagreed strongly" and another 27 percent "disagreed somewhat." As with most questions in this study, it is hard to imagine any pastor or spiritual leader who would be satisfied that less than one-third of their flock are known as Christians by those around them.

Intentional Relationship Building

One sign of a healthy church is that many members work hard at building relationships with people outside the church. The last church I served as a full-time staff member asked people to share their testimonies as they were baptized. I recall in particular the joint baptism of a married couple, both of whom were professors at a local university. As they shared their story, both mentioned the influence of one church member, a doctor who lived a consistent witness in front of his patients.

When it comes to relational evangelism, two mistakes must be avoided. The first is the unbiblical notion of "just walking the walk," implying a lack of emphasis on verbal witness. Living a consistently godly life in front of a watching world is important but not to the exclusion of a verbal witness. I believe the longer a Christian waits to bring up his or her faith to a friend, the harder it becomes.

A second important clarification is that the gospel is self-authenticating. Some advocates of relational evangelism seem to imply that the witness's character makes the content of the witness. Wrong. The gospel is authentic, regardless of the character and consistency of the witness. I am not suggesting the witness's lifestyle is irrelevant. It is very relevant. I am merely affirming that the gospel is true even if I am a hypocrite.

Realizing the importance of building bridges to people outside the household of faith, we asked this question:

How much do you agree/disagree: I intentionally spend time building friendships with non-Christians for the purpose of sharing Christ with them?

We were deeply disappointed to discover that only 7 percent of respondents said they "strongly agreed" with the statement, and another 18 percent "agreed somewhat." Of all the questions in Domain Four, the responses to this statement ranked lowest. To think only seven out of one hundred churchgoers can strongly affirm this statement is disturbing. No wonder most churches in America are declining or on a plateau.

When looking at responses related to personal responsibility and the survey responses, a huge discrepancy is apparent. While 46 percent "agreed strongly" that it is their responsibility to share Christ, only 7 percent actually work on building bridges to do so. We all may know it is true, but good intentions are not enough. Intellectual assent is not the same as actually putting feet to our intentions.

Perhaps we need to give more time to helping churchgoers understand the importance of relational evangelism. Maybe we need to share more success stories of one friend reaching another. Perhaps our worship services are too tightly planned to allow opportunities to share how God has used ordinary people to accomplish extraordinary things. Perhaps we could take some time during baptisms to allow our people to hear how God works and envision this happening in their lives as well.

The Ready Defense

With the big game just days away, a reporter asked the ol' ball coach: "What's your defensive strategy? Will you be playing them man to man, or will you put in more defensive backs to protect against their near-perfect passing game?"

The ol' ball coach leaned forward and said, "We're going to play the 'Ready Defense'."

"What is that, Coach? I've never heard of it," said the reporter.

"It means we prepare our players to be ready in any situation, to show the other team why we're hopefully certain of a victory," said the coach.

Peter instructs Jesus' ambassadors to "always be ready to give a defense to anyone who asks you for a reason for the hope that is in you" (1 Pet. 3:15).

In a sense we sought to measure this "ready defense" in our sample. Were they ready and proactive in evangelism? We asked:

How much do you agree/disagree: While interacting with others on a normal, daily basis, I seek opportunities to speak out about Jesus Christ?

The response to this question was only minimally better than the previous one: 10 percent said they "strongly agreed," while 25 percent "agreed somewhat." To state it another way, only ten out of one hundred regular churchgoers consistently seek opportunities to share Christ.

Our efforts in this area are far too limited. In the shape of faith to come, this must change. Christians must be taught, trained, and challenged to take the gospel to lost and unchurched people in their lives. Opportunities abound.

Before Jesus sent out seventy followers to share the good news, He explained:

> After this, the Lord appointed 70 others, and He sent them ahead of Him in pairs to every town and place where He Himself was about to go. He told them: "The harvest is abundant, but the workers are few. Therefore, pray to the Lord of the harvest to send out workers into His harvest." (Luke 10:1–2)

With so few Christians seeking opportunities, it is easy to conclude that we have lost our vision for the harvest God has prepared. We should be greatly encouraged that God always goes before us and our witness. He is the One who changes the human mind and heart. Our part is simply to testify faithfully to the gospel's truthfulness. Far too many Christians mistakenly believe people are not interested in spiritual things.

Our research shows people are more open to spiritual things than we think. Several years ago LifeWay President Thom Rainer discovered that 38 percent of unchurched people are receptive or very receptive to the gospel. In a recent LifeWay Research study, we asked for a response to this statement: *If someone wanted to tell me what she or he believed about Christianity, I would be willing to listen.* A full 50 percent of the respondents said they "strongly agreed," and another 28 percent "agreed somewhat."

These are high numbers. On top of that, our Church Dropout Study asked people not attending church, *What would prompt you to visit a church, with the idea that you might start regularly attending?* We found that 41 percent said they would consider returning to church if invited by a friend, and 25 percent said they would consider returning if a family member invited them.

On a trip a few years ago, I was reminded how the Holy Spirit works in the lives of lost people. As I boarded the plane and got situated in my seat, I introduced myself to a businessman named Ron. We engaged in the usual small talk. When he asked what I did, I told him I was a professor and pastor. He looked at me strangely, looked around to make sure no one was watching, and then carefully lifted the papers on his lap, revealing a Bible. He acted as if he had smuggled something illegal onto the plane.

When I asked what he was doing with a Bible, he explained that his wife had started attending a Bible Study Fellowship group and had some sort of religious experience that radically changed her. He liked the newfound joy and peace he saw in her and noticed significant changes in their home life. But it also scared him. He could not figure out what had happened to her. She tried to explain it to him, but he just did not get it. He had grown up Catholic and saw himself as a Christian, but he knew he did not have what she had.

The biggest stumbling block Ron was encountering was the idea of salvation by grace alone. He just could not accept the idea that a person did not have to earn a right relationship with God. He told me he brought the Bible to read during the four-hour flight, hoping to understand what had happened to his wife. He had no clue where to begin, but he was highly motivated to discover something in the Bible that would make sense to him.

I had the joy of walking him through Romans, explaining the gospel of Jesus Christ in detail. I explained why salvation could not result from any human merit. Using nontechnical language, I explained various concepts—the substitutionary death of Jesus, the atonement, and imputed righteousness. I explained that Jesus came to do for us what we cannot do for ourselves.

Time flew by (no pun intended). Although Ron did not pray to receive Christ on the plane, he promised he would seriously consider everything we had discussed. I was not sure if I would ever hear from him again, but to my delight he called a few days later to tell me he had committed himself to Christ. He was so grateful and full of joy. I encouraged Ron to find a Bible-based church. A few months later he sent me pictures of his whole family being baptized in the church they had joined. From time to time Ron still e-mails or calls with an update.

I wish I could say this happens every time I witness to someone, but that it not the case. Yet, as you can imagine, seeing the transforming power of the gospel in Ron's life motivates me even more to witness. Few things create a desire for sharing Christ like sharing Christ.

God is always at work. The Holy Spirit is drawing people to Himself. The fields are white unto harvest. As witnesses, we do not have to create spiritual desire or conviction in anyone's heart. God convicts and saves. Our job is to obey God, which includes praying for others, living a consistent life, building relationships, and seeking opportunities to witness. We sow the seed, and God produces the harvest.

Frequency of Witnessing

I saved this section for last because, when all is said and done, the real issue comes down to actually sharing Christ. This is, as the old saying goes, "where the rubber meets the road." It's as Paul stated, "How can they believe without hearing about Him?" (Rom. 10:14). Before the full transforming power of God is realized, one must hear the gospel.

With this in mind, we asked the following question:

In the past six months, about how many times have you, personally, done the following: shared with someone how to become a Christian?

As this bar graph shows, 29 percent of our sample said they had shared Christ at least twice in the past six months, 14 percent had done that once, and 57 percent said "not at all."

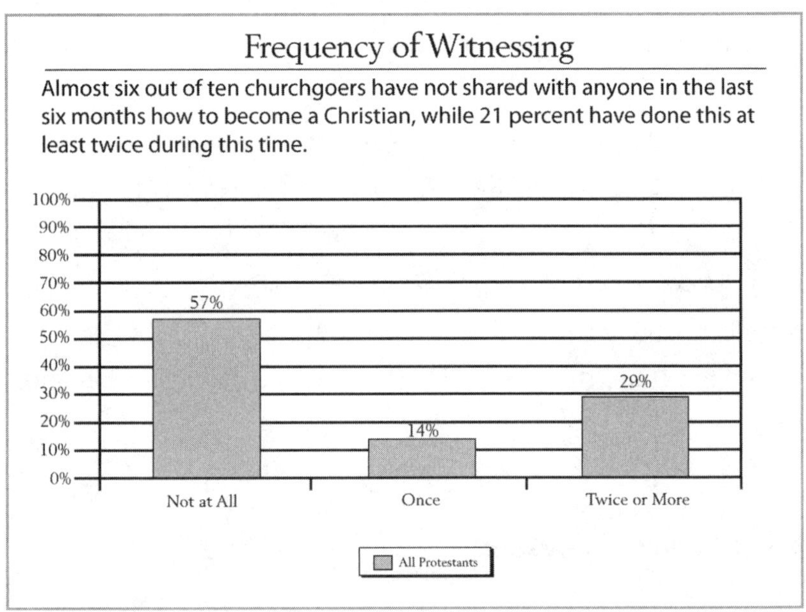

How do we evaluate these numbers? To be honest, I was surprised that 29 percent of our sample attempted to share Christ twice or more in a six-month period of time. Of course, we do not know how thoroughly the gospel was shared. Still, it is a little surprising that almost a third of our sample perceived themselves as sharing the gospel at least twice in six months.

As we have noted before, God does not grade on the curve. Think of the tremendous potential of a 57-percent majority motivated and equipped to share the gospel! Think about how many people could hear the gospel if the majority of Christians would just share Christ even once a month!

If you do the math, our twenty-five hundred churchgoers made eighteen hundred attempts to share Christ over the course of a year. That is good but not great. What if 80 percent of our sample had shared Christ at least once per month? It is hardly unreasonable to think Christians who are serious about their faith could find at least one witnessing opportunity per month. If our sample had done that, we would have seen twenty-four thousand attempts to share the gospel in a year, instead of eighteen hundred attempts. What a difference!

Years ago I worked on staff for the International Evangelism Association in Fort Worth, Texas. One thing I most remember from that time was how the president, Billie Hanks Jr., prayed every day that God would grant him an opportunity to share Christ with someone. I tried to follow that example. We know God encourages us to pray about all things (see Phil. 4:6). We also know Paul prayed for opportunities to advance the gospel. If we implemented this one practice, our outreach efforts would be multiplied beyond anything most of us can imagine. Surely we can do better than twenty-five hundred people making eighteen hundred attempts to share the life-transforming power of the gospel over the course of a year!

The Evangelism Quotient—Conclusions

When Jesus met the Samaritan woman at the well, He told her that, if she drank from the water He could provide, she'd never be thirsty again. He said the water would spring up within her like water from a well (see John 4:14).

Jesus wasn't saying she should simply let the water saturate her life, all in-take and no outflow. In fact, the complete story of the Samaritan woman teaches that the water from Jesus is to fill us to the brim and then overflow into the lives of others, drawing people to Christ.

> The Samaritan woman returned to her village, to bring back her neighbors to meet Jesus, and as they approached, Jesus pointed to them and told His disciples: "Don't you say, 'There are still four more months, then comes the harvest'? Listen to what I'm telling you: Open your eyes and look at the fields, for they are ready for harvest." (John 4:35)

Jesus gives so we can give. He gives His life so we can live, and with His life within us, we carry the news of eternal life to others. I love the words of Christ:

> "For whoever wants to save his life will lose it, but whoever loses his life because of Me will find it. What will it benefit a man if he gains the whole world yet loses his life? Or what will a man give in exchange for his life?" (Matt. 16:25–26)

Jesus said these words when Peter refused to believe the Lord's declaration that He would have to suffer at the hands of religious leaders in Jerusalem. Jesus used this teachable moment to help the disciples understand that God's will and ways often run counter to our mere human wisdom. Although Jesus was not addressing the specific issue of evangelism, it's a relevant point for our discussion because it explains that in giving we receive.

This principle holds true in sharing and serving Christ. By walking in faith, by taking risks, we gain. For most of us, sharing the gospel is not all that risky. For some believers, who live in hostile places, identifying with Christ is costly. Wherever we live, however, taking a stand for Christ requires faith and a willingness to pay a price, if necessary.

In the end sharing Christ is essential to true discipleship and spiritual formation. As leaders, we do our flock a major disservice if we do not invite them into the faith journey of witnessing. Testifying to the truth of the gospel brings life, life to those who respond with faith and repentance as well as to those who bear testimony to the redemptive work of Christ.

To biblically shape the faith to come, the church must be much more deliberate about sharing the good news of Jesus Christ. Many churches today, and the Christians who attend them, are far too timid about speaking the truth. We must train and equip followers of Christ to pray for the lost, build relationships with them, serve them, invite them to church, and most important witness to them!

"Open your eyes and look at the fields, for they are ready for harvest" (John 4:35).

---

1. See www.barna.org, Evangelical Christians, 2007.

Chapter Seven

Domain Five

Exercising Faith: The Faith Quotient

Now without faith it is impossible to please God, for the one who draws near to Him must believe that He exists and rewards those who seek Him.

—Hebrews 11:6

Biblical Truth: Without faith it is impossible to please God.

The Faith Quotient: Through faith God uses ordinary people to do extraordinary things.

His name was Faith and, as he stepped on the scales, he closed his eyes, hoping his months of inactivity wouldn't show up as extra pounds. But he knew no matter how tightly he kept his eyelids shut, it wouldn't change what the scale would reveal—Flabby Faith.

He opened his eyes and watched as the scale moved up, and up, and then up some more. No wonder he no longer had energy for the things of God! They made him sore and miserable because Faith hadn't exercised or even stretched in months. And he was paying the price for too many "I can do it without God" meals, not to mention all the "See first, then take a step" snacks. Faith had no one to blame but himself for his couch-potato condition.

Then the Trainer came by and said, "The problem when you don't exercise, Faith, is that you stop making progress toward the finish line. It's like you're running the race, but your eyes are no longer on the prize, or you're running aimlessly. You need to discipline your body so you can finish the race and keep the faith, Faith."

The story of Flabby Faith reminds me of lyrics by the Christian singer/songwriter Keith Green, which I'll paraphrase as, "Jesus rose from the dead, but we can't even get out of bed." God calls us to a life of faith, one where we're out of bed and on our feet, certain God "exists and rewards those who seek Him" (Heb. 11:6). When we live without faith, *we are living faithlessly.*

Friends, whom I'll call Don and Cindy because of the sensitive nature of their ministry, believed God was calling Don to leave a position serving a large church here in the United States. They moved their family, including three kids, to a difficult and unsafe part of the world to train leaders in countries hostile to Christianity. It has required enormous amounts of faith and inconvenience from all of them. They learned a new language and live with risk to their safety. They do not have access to quality medical care. They spend lonely nights missing family and friends.

Why would someone do this? Clearly it is the work of God in their lives. Don and Cindy understand their lives are not their own and have stepped out in faith, trusting God to guide them. They understand the importance of taking the gospel to all nations and know the desperate need for trained Christian leaders. They know life on earth is short, and one day they will give account for their response to God's call on their lives. They are exercising faith.

The Biblical Ideal

Hebrews 11 is the hall of fame for people who lived by faith. The author of Hebrews says of them, "The world was not worthy of them" (Heb. 11:38). But let's not make the mistake of thinking these people are the rare ones. Of the Old Testament prophet Elijah, James wrote:

> Elijah was a man with a nature like ours; yet he prayed earnestly that it would not rain, and for three years and six months it did not rain on the land. Then he prayed again, and the sky gave rain and the land produced its fruit. (James 5:17–18)

James makes sure we do not place Elijah on a pedestal beyond our grasp. As other great people of faith, he was a man "with a nature like ours." Yet, even though he was a mere human being, God still used him in miraculous ways. James expected Elijah's example to inspire us to believe that God can do extraordinary things through ordinary people.

Although most of us will not drop everything and go overseas to serve, God still expects us to walk by faith and not by sight. From the first day of the human race, God intended His kingdom to be an experience of faith, taking the risk of living out God's plan for our lives in spite of the unseen consequences it might entail.

In fact, what is unseen is at the center of the great definition of faith given to us in Hebrews: "Now faith is the reality of what is hoped for, the proof of what is not seen" (11:1).

"Not seen." Wow! That is difficult. Faith is not imagination, not hopeful thinking. Faith is not blind. God has designed the Christian life in such a manner that we must often act on His Word without physical manifestations from God.

God has, of course, provided an abundance of physical evidence that proves His existence. Theologians call it "general revelation." The apostle Paul put it this way:

> From the creation of the world His invisible attributes, that is, His eternal power and divine nature, have been clearly seen, being understood through what He has made. As a result, people are without excuse. (Rom. 1:20)

Day in and day out, however, spiritual formation happens by exercising faith, obeying God's Word even when we are not sure where it leads. Christians are to give time, energy, and money in service to God and others, based on obedience and the promise of reward in heaven. These Scripture verses give us a glimpse into this truth:

> Now without faith it is impossible to please God, for the one who draws near to Him must believe that He exists and rewards those who seek Him. (Heb. 11:6)

> So we do not focus on what is seen, but on what is unseen; for what is seen is temporary, but what is unseen is eternal. (2 Cor. 4:18)

Faith is related to the unseen, and acting on what is unseen results in eternal reward. We live out a Christian life with the understanding that, as Peter said, earth is not our home: "Beloved, I urge you as aliens and strangers to abstain from fleshly lusts which wage war against the soul" (1 Pet. 2:11 NASB). We are not to live this life as unbelievers do.

I recently watched the docudrama *Expelled*. In this movie Ben Stein interviews a number of atheistic Darwinists. Some are bold in admitting that eradicating God from the social consciousness means there is no basis for morality. In this terrible view of life, whatever you get is it. Remember that early computer phrase, "WYSIWYG" (What You See Is What You Get)? That's all; there is nothing else. When you are dead, you are gone. Forever.

What a sad worldview! The Christian worldview, on the other hand, is abundantly optimistic and hopeful. We invest in what is unseen, and yet it is very real. Our true reward awaits us. We can barely envision what eternity will be like.

> For now we see in a mirror dimly, but then face to face; now I know in part, but then I will know fully just as I also have been fully known. (1 Cor. 13:12 NASB)

"Face-to-face." Can you imagine that? Face-to-face with the God of the universe. Face-to-face with the Jesus we have so often reflected upon. This is where faith finally transcends the unseen.

We must also remember that faith is not just the preferred path; it is the *only* path. "Without faith it is impossible to please God" (Heb. 11:6). There is no other avenue to true spiritual formation. Any other strategy is merely an attempt at self-transformation. That may yield some degree of improvement, but it does not result in spiritual transformation.

Can I Trust the Ice?

Of our seven domains this may be the most difficult to measure. Faith has both subjective and objective elements, both attitudinal and behavioral aspects. The attitudinal aspect is confidence that everything God says is true. The behavioral aspect lies in the specific actions a person takes in obedience to God.

Some people are imbalanced in their understanding of faith. They place too much emphasis on emotion. Consequently they waver. Sometimes they feel like they believe; other times they feel doubt. Feelings vary.

Ron Dunn was one of my favorite preachers. He is now with the Lord, but when I first began to grow as a Christian, he was one of a handful of preachers who influenced my understanding of faith. Ron often illustrated faith with a story about two men who drove their vehicles up to the edge of a frozen lake. The first man stopped and got out of the car, cautiously stepping out onto the ice with great hesitation. He gradually moved farther out, trying to gain more confidence. I could almost see this man saying to himself, "I believe, I believe, I believe," trying to bolster his emotional strength.

The other man, however, drove his two-ton vehicle right out into the middle of the lake without hesitation or fear.

What made the difference? The second man knew the lake. He had grown up nearby and, over time, had learned that, after so many days of cold weather, the ice was thick enough to easily hold up a vehicle. This man knew objective truth and experiential knowledge about the strength of the ice and did not have to conjure up feelings of confidence.

So it is with biblical faith. A Christian begins to act on the objective truth of God's Word, and over time its truthfulness becomes apparent. Feelings of confidence arise from a pattern of acting on God's Word. God says it, we obey it, and we learn He is faithful to keep His promises.

A word of caution is needed here: I am not saying faith is based purely on experience. God's Word is true regardless of our personal interpretation of life events. Sometimes, due to a lack of understanding about God, we make false assumptions and set ourselves up for disillusionment. God never promises that life will always go the way we want it to. He does, however, stay true to His Word. As we experience His faithfulness, we grow in our ability to act on what God says. As we obey Him, we experience His faithfulness, and our ability to obey Him grows even more.

Before the great Old Testament leader Joshua died, he passed along some wisdom to God's people:

> I am now going the way of all the earth, and you know with all your heart and all your soul that none of the good promises the LORD your God made to you has failed. Everything was fulfilled for you; not one promise has failed. (Josh. 23:14)

These parting words were intended to remind the Israelites about God's nature and, thereby, bolster their faith. God is trustworthy, and our faith grows as we take Him at His word and obey Him.

The Faith Quotient—Real Numbers

In Domain Five: Exercising Faith we asked five questions testing levels of agreement, and one question related to frequency of activities, related to faith. As with the other domains, we looked at the ideal responses and the positive responses.

Only 2 percent of the sample, fifty out of twenty-five hundred churchgoers, provided an ideal response to all six questions. Sixteen percent provided positive responses to all of them.

- Levels of Agreement:
  - I believe that God has a purpose for all events in my life, regardless of whether I perceive each event as being good or bad.
  - I consistently give financially to God's purposes even if I am not sure I have enough money.
  - I express praise and gratitude to God even in difficult circumstances.

  - ✦ During difficult circumstances I sometimes doubt that God loves me and will provide for my life.
  - ✦ My life is often filled with anxiety and worry.
- In the past six months:
  - ✦ I made a decision two or more times to obey or follow God with an awareness that choosing His way might be costly to me in some way.

Faith in Sunshine and in Rain

We exercise our faith when we see God at work, regardless of whether things appear to be good or bad. It means we're thinking like Jesus when we keep walking in faith. We don't allow anyone or anything to cut us off or prevent us from obeying the truth. Just as the faith of a mere mustard seed can move mountains, the faithlessness of a little yeast can undermine your walk of faith (see Gal. 5:7–9).

This means faith does not and cannot exist in a vacuum. Faith development is linked to and flows out of a particular worldview. The theological foundation for any biblical understanding of faith is related to one's basic view of God.

Faith is often confused with a general sense of optimism or a vague sense that things will work out in the end. But this is not equivalent to biblical faith, which is rooted in the conviction that God is in full control of all things and that He has a purpose in every situation. With that in mind, we posed this statement to the sample:

I believe that God has a purpose for all events in my life, regardless of whether I perceive each event as being good or bad.

Of those surveyed, 63 percent indicated they "strongly agreed" and another 24 percent said they "agreed somewhat." Only 3 percent of the twenty-five hundred people we interviewed actually expressed disagreement.

The majority expressed confidence in God's purposeful guidance of their lives. The word *control* is not stated but is clearly implied. What is also strongly implied is that God brings good out of both positive and negative events.

I am confident that most pastors want all their members to affirm God's control of life's events and that such a belief adds purpose and meaning to events, both good and bad. This biblical worldview is essential for personal spiritual growth.

Think how often the Bible describes Satan as casting doubt on the goodness and power of God. The Bible's first description of Satan shows him questioning God's nature:

> "No! You will not die," the serpent said to the woman. "In fact, God knows that when you eat it your eyes will be opened and you will be like God." (Gen. 3:4–5)

If the enemy can cast doubt in anyone's mind about the nature and character of God, the prospect for faith development is dealt a death blow. Casting doubt about God's control has been the enemy's tactic since the beginning.

Recently we have seen this tactic used by those who propagate the concept of open theism, which suggests that God experiences time with us and changes in some respects, not entirely knowing the future because He allows human freedom to help create it. This new twist on an old heresy has the same timeless objective: If the enemy can cast doubt on God's control of events and circumstances, then faith is either prevented or eroded. If we cannot fully trust God, then we cannot trust His Word. Life is merely a roll of the dice.

To biblically shape the faith to come, leaders will model, uplift, and teach walking by faith. Faith stories will be celebrated. We will learn from one another as people share their victories and struggles. Sermons will consistently highlight the fact that "without faith it is impossible to please God" (Heb. 11:6). Christians will hold one another accountable to clear biblical standards in the context of love and encouragement.

Faith stories, those recorded in the Bible and those we share out of our lives, help all of us connect the dots. And by connecting the dots, I mean gaining the conviction that God has a purpose for all the events in our lives.

Unbelieving Faith

God is not shocked by our unbelief in His ability to handle the challenges we face in life. The whole process of redemption reveals His understanding of our situation and His willingness to help us. We can be honest and admit where our belief ends and our unbelief begins.

We can admit that we often, like the father in Mark 9, approach Jesus from the faith position of "Lord, if you can . . ." Jesus replies, "'If You can?' Everything is possible to the one who believes." We can cry out, "I do believe! Help my unbelief" (see Mark 9:21–24). I am not speaking of a pattern of disbelief. I am describing the reality that most believers struggle with feelings of doubt and confusion. The crucial issue is the degree and frequency of the doubt and our reaction to it. This passage from the Gospel of Mark is instructive:

> Out of the crowd, one man answered Him, "Teacher, I brought my son to You. He has a spirit that makes him unable to speak. Wherever it seizes him, it throws him down, and he foams at the mouth, grinds his teeth, and becomes rigid."
>
> "How long has this been happening to him?" Jesus asked his father.
>
> "From childhood," he said. "And many times it has thrown him into fire or water to destroy him. But if You can do anything, have compassion on us and help us."
>
> Then Jesus said to him, "If You can? Everything is possible to the one who believes."
>
> Immediately the father of the boy cried out, "I do believe! Help my unbelief." (Mark 9:17–18, 21–24)

This father provides a good example for us. He clearly displayed faith by seeking Jesus' help. When he appeared to express some uncertainty, Jesus used the teachable moment to highlight the nature of faith. The father revealed his teachable heart and asked for help with his unbelief. His faith is not seen in absence of doubt but in his desire to learn to trust God.

To determine the level of doubt within the lives of our churchgoers, we asked the following question:

How much do you agree/disagree: During difficult circumstances, I sometimes doubt that God loves me and will provide for my life?

Forty-four percent of our sample of churchgoers said they "disagree strongly" with our statement about experiencing doubt, an ideal response since this statement was worded in the negative. Another 21 percent responded "somewhat disagree."

If you are responsible for the spiritual development of others, these results are instructive. We need to remember that fewer than 50 percent of the sample are completely confident in God's love and provision. And more than a third have significant faith issues. We must focus on this as we prepare to preach and teach and decide what kind of content to offer our people in spiritual formation. If a significant number of our people are incapacitated by doubt, the church as a whole will be weak and ineffective.

Informed or Transformed?

A word of caution: when it comes to our preaching, we must remember that it takes more than mere intellectual knowledge to spur faith development. I have known a number of theologically informed people who still seemed to lack robust faith. Preaching that fills the head with a lot of biblical facts is vastly different from preaching that focuses on putting truth into practice. We must call the people of God to action, and they must see that we are practicing what we preach. I am not suggesting we lessen our emphasis on doctrine, but we must validate what we say with how we live. Are we authentic? Are we satisfied with informed people rather than transformed ones?

Exercising faith requires that we run in such a way that we win—that is, win in doing the will of God and running with a faith that abandons any option but God's. In reality anxiety and faith cannot coexist, just as we cannot run the race in such a way that we win while running aimlessly. Instead, we discipline our faith, exercise our faith, bringing it under strict control (see 1 Cor. 9:24–27).

Can Anxiety and Faith Coexist?

The Bible makes a clear connection between genuine spirituality and peace, or the absence of anxiety.

> May the Lord of peace Himself give you peace always in every way. The Lord be with all of you. (2 Thess. 3:16)

> You will keep in perfect peace the mind that is dependent on You, for it is trusting in You. Trust in the LORD forever, because in Yah, the LORD, is an everlasting rock! (Isa. 26:3–4)

> "Peace I leave with you. My peace I give to you. I do not give to you as the world gives. Your heart must not be troubled or fearful." (John 14:27)

> The fruit of the Spirit is love, joy, peace, patience, kindness, goodness, faith, gentleness, self-control. (Gal. 5:22–23)

> And the peace of God, which surpasses every thought, will guard your hearts and your minds in Christ Jesus. (Phil. 4:7)

> And let the peace of the Messiah, to which you were also called in one body, control your hearts. Be thankful. (Col. 3:15)

The word *peace* has different meanings in the Bible. Often it is used to describe reconciliation between believers and God through Christ. Sometimes it has to do with relationships between fellow Christians. And on other occasions it has to do with internal peace.

The last meaning is the one used for our survey. We assumed there is an inverse relationship between faith and persistent anxiety—the more faith, the less anxiety, and vice versa.

The statement we posed was:

My life is often filled with anxiety and worry.

Any leader would want to see a high percentage of "strongly disagree" responses to this statement. But as you can see from the following table, the responses were diverse.

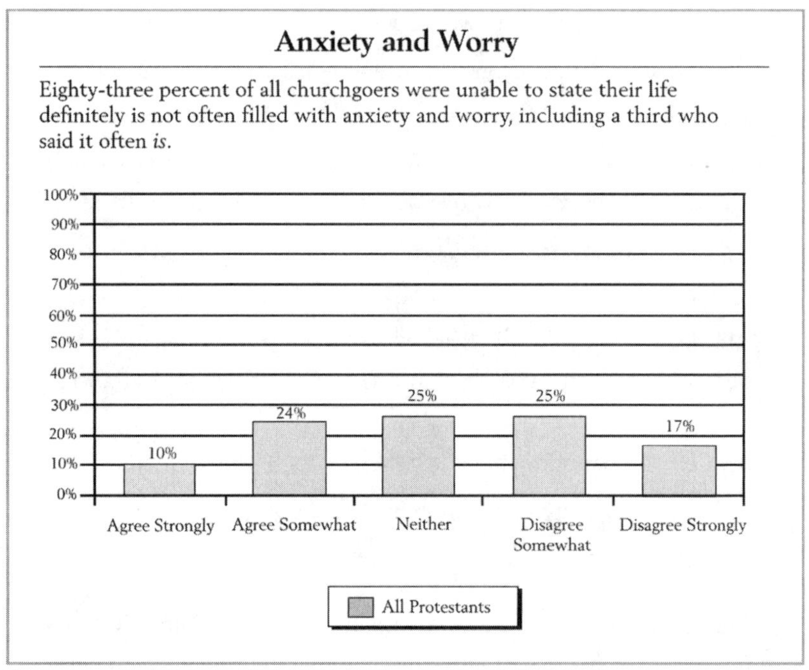

Nearly one in every five churchgoers perceives himself as relatively free from anxiety and worry; one in ten is filled with negative emotions and patterns of thinking. Another 24 percent "agreed somewhat," meaning they struggle a bit with worry and anxiety; 25 percent perceive themselves relatively free from worry and anxiety.

As an individual believer, or as a spiritual leader, how do you interpret these numbers? Is the glass half full or half empty? Clearly more than one-third of our sample struggles with unhealthy patterns of worry and anxiety.

We certainly ought to strive toward the goal of all believers experiencing a life of joy and peace. A worry-free life is God's desire for us.

> Rejoice in the Lord always. I will say it again: Rejoice! Let your graciousness be known to everyone. The Lord is near. Don't worry about anything, but in everything, through prayer and petition with thanksgiving, let your requests be made known to God. And the peace of God, which surpasses every thought, will guard your hearts and your minds in Christ Jesus. (Phil. 4:4–7)

We must strive to make this biblical challenge a reality in all of our churches. What should be our strategy?

- Live as an example. Paul said, "Be imitators of me, as I also am of Christ" (1 Cor. 11:1). We cannot pass along what we do not possess. We have to realize that living a life characterized by rejoicing and peacefulness is not optional. This is what God asks, even demands, of us.
- Teach what God's Word says. Every aspect of spiritual formation begins with God's revealed wisdom. Spiritual leaders need to pursue truths related to living by faith and overcoming worry and passionately teach them to others.
- Encourage and facilitate relationships. Holistic spiritual formation cannot be facilitated just from the pulpit. Attitudes and practices like rejoicing and peacefulness occur in the context of the community of faith. All Christians need opportunities to interact with and relate to fellow believers.
- Provide special help for those who need it. It is beyond the scope of this book to unravel the complicated issue of counseling. Suffice it to say that some people need more intense

input and encouragement. We must provide biblically solid, emotionally helpful guidance for those who experience patterns of anxiety and worry.

Praise, the Ultimate Expression of Faith

God granted the evil one's request; he could sift Job in an attempt to prove that Job followed God only because of the blessings the Father bestowed. God knew this wasn't true, so He allowed the evil one's test, with the solitary restriction that the devil could not kill Job.

Job, devastated by the losses in his life and fighting sickness in his body, sat scraping the sores on his skin with pieces from a broken clay pot. His wife said, in effect, "Have integrity enough to admit this God of yours doesn't care about you, and then curse God before you die!"

Job replied, "Should we accept only good from God and not adversity?" (Job 2:10).

By faith we praise God in times both good and bad. God often refines our faith in the crucible as we learn to praise Him in the midst of difficulty. You cannot truly praise God if you do not believe in Him and His Word. Praise is an expression of faith. By faith we acknowledge the attributes and actions of God.

To measure this connection between praise and faith, we asked our sample this question:

How much do you agree/disagree: I express praise and gratitude to God even in difficult circumstances?

Forty percent said they "strongly agreed" and another 36 percent said they "agreed somewhat." Only 5 percent expressed any level of disagreement with the statement.

I am greatly encouraged to see so many respond with high levels of affirmation for praise and gratitude toward God even in difficult circumstances. In the next chapter we will look more carefully at what the Bible says about praise. In this domain we are looking at the aspect of praise in difficult times.

Perhaps the classic example of praising God in spite of difficult circumstances is the previously mentioned Old Testament character of Job. God allowed extreme adversity to engulf Job's life, whose attitudes and thoughts in the midst of great distress are an example to us all:

- "Should we accept only good from God and not adversity?" (Job 2:10)
- "Wisdom and strength belong to God; counsel and understanding are His." (Job 12:13)
- "Even if He kills me, I will hope in Him." (Job 13:15)
- "But I know my living Redeemer, and He will stand on the dust at last." (Job 19:25)
- "I have not departed from the commands of His lips; I have treasured the words of His mouth more than my daily food." (Job 23:12)

When Jesus delivered the Sermon on the Mount, He expressed the positive side of persecution:

> "Blessed are you when they insult you and persecute you and falsely say every kind of evil against you because of Me. Be glad and rejoice, because your reward is great in heaven." (Matt. 5:11–12)

James explains that trials should lead to joy because God uses them to perfect His work in us:

> Consider it a great joy, my brothers, whenever you experience various trials, knowing that the testing of your faith produces endurance. But endurance must do its complete work, so that you may be mature and complete, lacking nothing. (James 1:2–4)

Peter adds insight into the connection between suffering, praise, and faith development:

> You rejoice in this, though now for a short time you have had to be distressed by various trials so that the genuineness of your faith—more valuable than gold, which perishes though refined by fire—may result in praise, glory, and honor at the revelation of Jesus Christ. (1 Pet. 1:6–7)

In difficult times our attitudes can be straightened out and our perspectives renewed. We remember what is really important. We can become more grateful for God's goodness and provision and be reminded that we need one another.

Checkbooks and Calendars

I consistently give financially to God's purposes even if I am not sure I have enough money.

I have heard it said, "Show me someone's daily planner and checkbook, and I will tell you where his heart is." For many, trusting God is most difficult when it comes to their time and money. In my years of church work, I found the majority of churchgoers fail to demonstrate significant faith when it comes to giving.

The Bible offers many negative examples, and some positive ones, about handling money or possessions. In chapter 5 we looked at the story of the rich young ruler. Here are some additional insights from Scripture:

- "Don't collect for yourselves treasures on earth, where moth and rust destroy and where thieves break in and steal. But collect for yourselves treasures in heaven, where neither moth nor rust destroys, and where thieves don't break in and steal. For where your treasure is, there your heart will be also" (Matt. 6:19–21).
- Jesus often confronted religious leaders for their lack of pure hearts and genuine faith. In this passage, Jesus pointed out that these phonies were "lovers of money" (Luke 16:14).
- Jesus noted the genuine faith of a widow who gave proportionately more than many rich people. Jesus said, "I tell you the truth, . . . this poor widow has put in more than all of

them. For all these people have put in gifts out of their surplus, but she out of her poverty has put in all she had to live on" (Luke 21:1–4).

- Here we find the story of a married couple, Ananias and Sapphira, who lied to the Lord and the church about their giving and lost their lives as a result. They loved their money more than the Lord and their integrity (Acts 5:1–11).
- Paul listed qualifications for pastors and specifically included the words "not greedy" (1 Tim. 3:3).
- Paul offered this insight: "But godliness with contentment is a great gain. For we brought nothing into the world, and we can take nothing out. But if we have food and clothing, we will be content with these. But those who want to be rich fall into temptation, a trap, and many foolish and harmful desires, which plunge people into ruin and destruction. For the love of money is a root of all kinds of evil, and by craving it, some have wandered away from the faith and pierced themselves with many pains" (1 Tim. 6:6–10).
- Talking about the end times, Paul stated, "For people will be lovers of self, lovers of money" (2 Tim. 3:2).
- This wisdom is offered: "Your life should be free from the love of money. Be satisfied with what you have, for He Himself has said, I will never leave you or forsake you. Therefore, we may boldly say: The Lord is my helper; I will not be afraid. What can man do to me?" (Heb. 13:5–6).

Probing the Depths of Faith

For many new believers, giving is one of the early challenges of faith development. God's economy is contrary to the world's ways. The world often tells us that it is in taking that we receive; but God says we receive in *giving*.

In God's hands money is a great tool for spiritual formation. How believers handle money is an excellent indicator of spiritual health. God has chosen to finance His kingdom largely through the gifts of His people. With every paycheck, we have the marvelous opportunity to worship God and trust Him through giving. God's requirement for us to give is actually a gift from Him. He has no need for our money, but we need the opportunity to be good stewards of His blessings.

I have probably heard more faith stories related to trusting God with finances than any other issue. I am moved by testimonies from Christians who, out of conviction from God's Word, began to give to their local church. It is particularly moving when the person lives on a limited income. Sacrificial giving is impressive. A close friend of mine recently told me he had discovered that his parents, who are not wealthy, give nearly 40 percent of their income to ministry. A rare story indeed!

With this biblical understanding of the nature and purpose of giving, we believe it necessary to inquire about "sacrificial" giving. We have already analyzed giving patterns in chapter 5. In an attempt to tie giving to faith, we asked about giving in circumstances of financial uncertainty. We wanted to know how people gave when they knew it might hurt financially. So we asked this question:

How much do you agree/disagree: I consistently give financially to God's purposes even if I am not sure I have enough money?

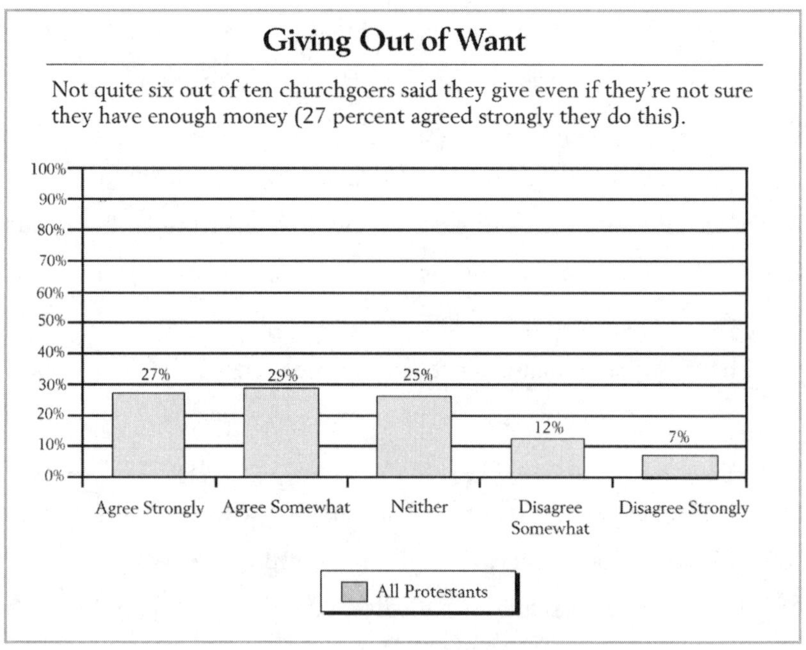

As you can see, 27 percent said they gave even when they were not sure they had enough money. Another 29 percent agreed somewhat. Nearly two-thirds gave with the awareness that they may not, from a human perspective, have enough money left to cover all of their needs or desires.

To biblically shape the faith to come, believers must be taught that giving is an essential aspect of walking by faith and is a form of worship. God is pleased with the heartfelt sacrifices of His people. Those who preach, teach, and disciple must explain the proper motive for giving.

> Remember this: the person who sows sparingly will also reap sparingly, and the person who sows generously will also reap generously. Each person should do as he has decided in his heart—not out of regret or out of necessity, for God loves a cheerful giver. And God is able to make every grace overflow to you, so that in every way, always having everything you need, you may excel in every good work. As it is written: **He has scattered; He has given to the poor; His righteousness endures forever.** Now the One who provides seed for the sower and bread for food will provide and multiply your seed and increase the harvest of your righteousness, as you are enriched in every way for all generosity, which produces thanksgiving to God through us. For the ministry of this service is not only supplying the needs of the saints, but is also overflowing in many acts of thanksgiving to God.
> (2 Cor. 9:6–12)

We must stop treating the subject of giving merely as a means for meeting the church budget. Assuming the budget is biblically aligned, using the gifts from God's people for the budget is legitimate. This, however, is not the highest motive. We ought to give out of a sense of stewardship, out of faith. We should give cheerfully as a form of worship. We give so our faith can grow because we have been the recipients of God's immense mercy. We give out of gratitude for God's goodness.

Win-Win or Win-Lose? Nevertheless Faith

Shadrach, Meshach, and Abednego told King Nebuchadnezzar they would not worship his statue as if he were a god. "If the God we serve exists, then He can rescue us from the furnace of blazing fire, and He can rescue us from the power of you, the king. But even if He does not rescue us, we want you as king to know that we will not serve your gods or worship the gold statue you set up." In effect, they were saying, "God may rescue us; He may not rescue us; nevertheless, we still have faith in our God" (adapted from Dan. 3:16–36).

We tried to measure this "nevertheless faith" by asking our survey group how much they saw themselves as obeying God even when doing so would likely cost them something. It is easy to follow God in a "win-win" situation, but what about when it looks like we will lose in the process?

Another biblical example of this "nevertheless faith" is when God told Abraham to sacrifice his only son, Isaac. This is found in Genesis 22:1–19, and Hebrews 11 and James 2 give us additional insight into this faith-stretching moment. Look at what James says about this unique event!

> Wasn't Abraham our father justified by works when he offered Isaac his son on the altar? You see that faith was active together with his works, and by works, faith

was perfected. So the Scripture was fulfilled that says,
Abraham believed God, and it was credited to him for righteousness, and he was called God's friend.
(James 2:21–23)

Notice the sentence, "Faith was active together with his works." Abraham acted in a profoundly sacrificial spirit. James calls that "works." Abraham put action to his beliefs, and James describes his faith as "active." Abraham's faith grew through this sacrificial act of obedience.

With this sacrificial idea in mind, we asked our sample this question:

In the past six months, about how many times have you, personally, done the following: made a decision to obey or follow God with an awareness that choosing His way might be costly to you in some way?

Of those we surveyed, 36 percent could not recall a single time in six months where they made a choice to obey God that might be costly. Another 20 percent said they could recall one such decision, and 44 percent said they had done so at least twice or more.

When you consider the religious freedom we enjoy in America, it is difficult to imagine many instances where following God would be costly, especially compared to some places in the world where such a choice can cost you your life or family. A few years ago I led a group of students on a mission trip to Kenya, where we met a missionary family who had taken in a sixteen-year-old girl. She had been disowned by her family because she gave her life to Christ. Now that is costly faith!

Even though most of us will never face this situation, we will still be faced with decisions that can be sacrificial:

- Refusing to cave in to pressure at work could cost you a promotion.
- Choosing not to join in on some activities could cost you socially.
- Sharing your faith in Christ may invite some strong opposition from others.
- Distancing yourself from gossip may cost you friendships.
- Choosing not to push the envelope on tax deductions will cost you financially.
- If you watched the Ben Stein movie *Expelled*, you heard testimonies of university professors who lost their jobs because they expressed belief in intelligent design.

In the end these are not real sacrifices because nothing is better than obeying God. The Lord rewards those who choose to honor Him and follow His ways. At the time such choices can be painful. Faith enables us to push through these uncomfortable situations. Making choices like these is one way faith is developed. If all our choices were easy, our faith would be weak. We can be grateful that God gives us opportunities to face opposition. Few meaningful things in life come without a cost.

The Faith Quotient—Conclusions

If we average the responses to all six items about exercising faith in Domain Five, we find that 39 percent of the twenty-five hundred people we surveyed provided a top or ideal response. And, as we stated at the beginning of the chapter, just 2 percent gave a top response to all six questions.

Clearly there is much room for growth. All Christians who read this book should use these results to examine their faith. We must remember that "without faith it is impossible to please God, for the one who draws near to Him must believe that He exists and rewards those who seek Him" (Heb. 11:6).

The final chapter of this book offers a variety of prescriptions for the future, but for now ask yourself, *How often do I step out in faith? Do I honor God with my finances and time? Do I take a stand for biblical values? Do I do the right thing, even though I know it will cost me financially or limit my social or professional advancement?*

If you are a leader in the church, it is important to evaluate the degree to which your teaching and equipping ministries are intentionally focused on creating a culture of faith in action. How often do you celebrate individuals or the church as a whole stepping out in faith? We need to help our flock see others who step out in faith and take notice of the fruit of such faith.

To biblically shape the faith to come leaders will model, uplift, and teach that:

- Faith is not just the preferred path; it is the *only* path. Any other strategy is merely an attempt at self-transformation.
- Faith stories are something to be celebrated, helping believers to learn from one another as they share their victories and struggles with one another.
- Faith is possible even for those overwhelmed by doubt. God is not surprised by their doubt, and He will guide them to a place of faith.
- Faith is reflected in the way we worship and in the way we give.

Chapter Eight

Domain Six

Seeking God: The Worship Quotient

But from there, you will search for the LORD *your God, and you will find Him when you seek Him with all your heart and all your soul.*

—DEUTERONOMY 4:29

Biblical Truth: We worship God when we seek Him.

The Worship Quotient: Our pursuit of God must be active not passive.

The Biblical Ideal

The book of Psalms is filled with passion to know God:

> As a deer longs for streams of water, so I long for You, God. I thirst for God, the living God. When can I come and appear before God? (Ps. 42:1–2)

> Whom do I have in heaven but You? And I desire nothing on earth but You. My flesh and my heart may fail, but God is the strength of my heart, my portion forever. (Ps. 73:25–26)

As a college sophomore I heard a conference speaker talk about seeking God. His topic was "Seeking God's Face and Not His Hands." I was moved by the speaker's passion. Here was a man who had sought and found God. I was drawn to the invitation by God to seek, know, and love Him. Imagine, the God of the universe has invited and called us to know Him.

Service without Seeking

It is easy to serve God without passionately seeking Him. Many leaders become lost on this dry path. If we are not careful, we think because we once sought and worshipped God with fervor, we are still OK. In reality we are running on fumes.

God deserves a lot more than service without seeking. He deserves our prayers, praises, and worship. It reeks of ingratitude when we serve without worship.

Within our various communities of faith, we sense a lack of

genuine worship. The culture in many of our churches can be described by words like *dry*, *shallow*, and *passionless*. The apostle Paul warned us:

> But know this: difficult times will come in the last days. For people will be lovers of self, lovers of money, boastful, proud, blasphemers, disobedient to parents, ungrateful, unholy, unloving, irreconcilable, slanderers, without self-control, brutal, without love for what is good, traitors, reckless, conceited, lovers of pleasure rather than lovers of God, holding to the form of religion but denying its power. Avoid these people! (2 Tim. 3:1–5)

Scripture often tells us "with all of your heart." Moses, in his final charge to the people of God before they moved into the promised land, made this comment: "But from there, you will search for the LORD your God, and you will find Him when you seek Him with all your heart and all your soul" (Deut. 4:29).

There is similar emphasis in the Gospels where Jesus gave the primary commandments: "Love the Lord your God with all your heart, with all your soul, with all your mind, and with all your strength" (Mark 12:30).

Scripture has many examples of men and women who sought God above all else, but the expectation to seek God is not limited to a few spiritual saints. This is God's expectation of all believers.

Part of living as a disciple is the consistent pursuit and worship of God. The Bible is filled with the stories of those who pursued

God and worshipped Him with passion. Every Christmas season we recall the wise men seeking the newborn Messiah.

> After Jesus was born in Bethlehem of Judea in the days of King Herod, wise men from the east arrived unexpectedly in Jerusalem, saying, "Where is He who has been born King of the Jews? For we saw His star in the east and have come to worship Him." (Matt. 2:1–2)

Notice what they did when they found Jesus. They worshipped Him.

Domain Six represents the pursuit of the Triune God and the practice of worshipping Him. We asked our sample of churchgoers these questions:

1. Questions involving levels of agreement or disagreement:
    - ✦ When I sing at church, my thoughts are usually focused right on God.
    - ✦ I often express praise and thanksgiving to God for who He is and for what He has done.
    - ✦ One of the main reasons I live my life the way I do is to please and honor God.
    - ✦ The fruit of the Spirit (love, joy, peace, patience, kindness, goodness, faith, gentleness, and self-control) is evidence of a genuine relationship with God.
    - ✦ My Christian faith is important in my life today.
    - ✦ I have made a personal commitment to Jesus Christ that is still important in my life today.

- Often during the worship part of the church service (singing or prayer), I find myself just "going through the motions."

2. Questions about frequency of certain activities:

    - Set aside time for prayer every day.
    - Memorize Scripture once a week or more.
    - Set aside time for private worship, praise, or thanksgiving to God every day.
    - In the past six months: fasted two or more times.

Domain Six was one of the lowest scoring domains, meaning the Worship Quotient is weak for our sample of churchgoers. Only 1 percent of those surveyed provided an ideal response to all the questions in this domain, and just 5 percent gave positive responses to all the questions.

Praise: A True Sign of Seeking God

The Bible emphasizes praise and thanksgiving:

> You who fear the LORD, praise Him! All you descendants of Jacob, honor Him! (Ps. 22:23)

> Shout triumphantly to the LORD, all the earth. Serve the LORD with gladness; come before Him with joyful songs. Acknowledge that the LORD is God. He made us, and we are His—His people, the sheep of His pasture. Enter His gates with thanksgiving and His courts with praise. Give thanks to

> Him and praise His name. For the LORD is good, and His love is eternal; His faithfulness endures through all generations. (Ps. 100:1–5)

> Let the message about the Messiah dwell richly among you, teaching and admonishing one another in all wisdom, and singing psalms, hymns, and spiritual songs, with gratitude in your hearts to God. And whatever you do, in word or in deed, do everything in the name of the Lord Jesus, giving thanks to God the Father through Him. (Col. 3:16–17)

> Therefore, through Him let us continually offer up to God a sacrifice of praise, that is, the fruit of our lips that confess His name. (Heb. 13:15)

Since praise and thanksgiving are essential to seeking God and growing as a Christian, we asked the sample of churchgoers to respond to this question:

How much do you agree/disagree:
How often do I express praise and thanksgiving to God for who He is and for what He has done?

Within our sample, 48 percent said they "agreed strongly" with this statement. Another 30 percent said they "agreed somewhat." Again, is the glass half empty or half full?

Nearly half of those surveyed strongly affirmed they often express praise and thanksgiving to God. But more than 50 percent do not.

This limited praise and thanksgiving reflect widespread ingratitude. Can you imagine any parent being happy with half of his children being grateful for what they have? No way! We want all of our children to be grateful not only for what we have done for them but for all the blessings of God.

Being grateful should be easy for most American Christians since we enjoy so many blessings. This became clear to my wife, Patti, and me early in 2008. On February 5, while watching the TV news, we heard a report about strong thunderstorms headed toward Jackson, Tennessee. Serious damage from high winds and tornadoes had already struck Memphis, about an hour west of Jackson. I called my son, Blake, a senior at Union University in Jackson, to warn him. He sent back a text message that he was aware of the weather.

About twenty minutes later I received a call that a tornado had hit Union University and several students were buried beneath rubble. To our joy, Blake called to let us know he was injured but not seriously. He said there was massive devastation on the campus and several students were buried in the rubble of the building right next to his dorm.

Patti and I immediately drove to Jackson to see Blake. The next morning we walked around the campus to see the damage. It was a miracle that not a single student died. Many people showed up to help. First were the emergency crews, firefighters, and emergency medical teams. By the second day FEMA, the Red Cross, the National Guard, insurance adjusters, engineers, and many other leaders and volunteers were there to help. Companies such as Chick-fil-A and Wal-Mart donated food and water. Many professors, school administrators, and local residents took displaced students into their homes.

After the tornado I reflected on how grateful I was that God spared my son and that so many people had expressed concern. In the aftermath of that F-4 tornado, I saw America at its best. I was proud of the medical personnel, the firefighters, the insurance companies, and the administration and faculty of Union University. Then there were the church and denominational leaders who gave money and recruited volunteers to help clean up the campus and salvage students' belongings. I had to admit that prior to the tornado I had become spoiled and ungrateful.

In good times and in bad, we have significant opportunities to praise, adore, worship, and thank God. "Let us continually offer up to God a sacrifice of praise" (Heb. 13:15). Notice the word "continually." Those who seek God will do so continually.

Who Is the Audience?

Seeking God is a daily activity for those who believe in God and follow Him. For thousands of years, the people of God have gathered regularly to worship Him. Those who seek God find joy joining with others who seek Him. Heaven will be like that, with multitudes of people from all nations worshipping God.

Under the old covenant, the people of God gathered and worshipped in the tabernacle, then the temple, and then the synagogue, depending on the time in history.

The New Testament church was launched at Pentecost (see Acts 2:1–47). While there have been differences in the context and style of worship through the ages, the focus has always been on God. The people of God express adoration and thanksgiving for the person and work of God.

Genuine worship is a good indicator of spiritual health and maturity. I say, "genuine," because it is easy just to go through the motions of worship. Some of our research shows a significant number of people who attend church are unable to tell us what it means to be a Christian. Seemingly many lost people attend church. This is not what we have in mind when we talk about worship.

True Christian worship can occur only when those offering it are regenerated by the power of the Holy Spirit. Paul explains the key difference between a regenerate and unregenerate person.

> Now God has revealed them to us by the Spirit, for the Spirit searches everything, even the deep things of God. For who among men knows the concerns of a man except the spirit of the man that is in him? In the same way, no one knows the concerns of God except the Spirit of God. Now we have not received the spirit of the world, but the Spirit who is from God, in order to know what has been freely given to us by God. We also speak these things, not in words taught by human wisdom, but in those taught by the Spirit, explaining spiritual things to spiritual people. But the natural man does not welcome what comes from God's Spirit, because it is foolishness to him; he is not able to know it since it

> is evaluated spiritually. The spiritual person, however, can evaluate everything, yet he himself cannot be evaluated by anyone. For: who has known the Lord's mind, that he may instruct Him? But we have the mind of Christ.
> (1 Cor. 2:10–16)

The essential reality for true worship is the regenerating work of the Holy Spirit. This occurs at the point of salvation. But this is not the end of the work of the Holy Spirit. Believers are true worshippers when they come before God with genuine spiritual vitality. Sometimes "worship" is just going through the motions of singing songs, praying prayers, and listening to sermons while showing little genuine interest. We have all seen and done this.

In true worship God is the only audience. While worship includes the element of fellowship, God should remain the focus. When we stay focused on God, we become strong and fruitful (see Matt. 13:22).

Because worship is vital to living as a disciple, we asked our sample of churchgoers two questions about the focus of their worship. We worded one in the positive and one in the negative. Here's the positive question:

How much do you agree/disagree: When I sing at church, my thoughts are usually focused right on God?

When we seek God, we must remain focused on Him. This may seem self-evident, but we've all experienced times in worship when we had to fight to keep our focus on God and not on the worries of the world. When we lose focus, we become like plants growing among the thorns and thistles; we focus on our worry instead of our God, and that hinders our growth toward Christlikeness. When we stay focused on God, we become strong and fruitful (see Matt. 13:22).

From our sample 31 percent responded with "strongly agreed," another 39 percent "agreed somewhat." Less than a third of our sample strongly affirms a consistent focus on God during the singing portion of worship. Everyone gets distracted at times so we included the word "usually." That still leaves 30 percent who obviously focus little or not at all on God during worship.

The Bible teaches that God isn't looking for an inflexible ritual or going through the motions of worship. He wants a contrite heart, flexible and obedient, wholly and totally surrendered to Him.

A second question deals with focus.

How much do you agree/disagree: Often during the worship part of the church service (singing or prayer), I find myself just "going through the motions"?

One-fourth, 25 percent, "strongly disagreed" with this statement, affirming they are genuinely engaged in worship; another 28 percent said they "disagreed somewhat" with the statement. But this leaves nearly half of our sample, 47 percent, admitting they just "go through the motions" of worship.

The Bible makes it clear that God should be the focus of every Christian when gathered for worship. Here's what Paul says:

> And don't get drunk with wine, which leads to reckless actions, but be filled with the Spirit: speaking to one another in psalms, hymns, and spiritual songs, singing and making music to the Lord in your heart, giving thanks always for everything to God the Father in the name of our Lord Jesus Christ, submitting to one another in the fear of Christ. (Eph. 5:18–21)

> Let the message about the Messiah dwell richly among you, teaching and admonishing one another in all wisdom, and singing psalms, hymns, and spiritual songs, with gratitude in your hearts to God. And whatever you do, in word or in deed, do everything in the name of the Lord Jesus, giving thanks to God the Father through Him. (Col. 3:16–17)

Notice the wording: "*to the Lord*," "*to God* the Father," "in your hearts *to God*," "giving thanks *to God*." It could not be clearer. God must be our object of worship. We must remember that God is a jealous God (see Exod. 20:5). God is worthy of our undivided attention. He is worthy of our purest devotion. Nothing should distract us from thinking about, singing, and praying to Him, both privately and in corporate worship.

On this issue of spiritual formation, spiritual leaders must take primary responsibility. Many pastors and worship leaders no longer make a strong effort to plan and direct a Christ-centered approach to worship. Many churchgoers want to be entertained, and music at some churches has become a concert instead of worship.

I have seen services where congregations repeatedly award singers with standing ovations. Is this the proper focus? Instead of God being the audience, the congregation has become the audience.

Church leaders must teach the community of faith the nature and importance of worship, and they must set the tone for worship. We must plan and conduct worship so it centers on the person and work of God.

I have served in church staff positions for more than twenty years, and I know how difficult it can be for pastoral staff to keep a focus on God within the context of worship. It is easy for responsibilities and interactions with people to take our focus off God. But worshipping God must be our main focus.

Fertile Soil

Throughout the generations of Christian faith, many godly men and women have testified to God's role and the individual believer's role in sanctification. *Sanctification* is the term many biblical scholars use to describe the process of spiritual development or the process of becoming more like Christ. At the core of sanctification is the transforming work of the Holy Spirit. Only God can transform a person's mind, heart, and character; but God also places significant responsibility on each of us to take part in this spiritual formation process.

Although we asked a few questions related to spiritual discipline in Domain One: Learning Truth, for this domain we added four more questions related to the practice of spiritual disciplines.

Quiet Time or Cluttered Life?

While in seminary, I read about and researched "Christian spirituality," studying a branch of church history called "pietism." Much of this literature inspires a passionate pursuit of God. John Wesley, the founder of the Methodist movement and a major figure in church history, was deeply impacted by pietism. And, in part, this influence led Wesley to place strong emphasis on many of the classic spiritual disciplines.

One of those disciplines is what many today call a "devotional" or quiet time. Typically a devotional is time when one withdraws from the busyness of life to pray, read the Bible, and seek God. It is often portrayed as an essential discipline for spiritual formation.

Attending to the Word of God, prayer, praise, and confession, coupled with a teachable heart and a repentant attitude, leads to spiritual transformation. Christians for generations testify to the need of withdrawing from the activities of life to spend time alone with God.

With this in mind, we asked our sample of churchgoers this question:

How often do you set aside time for private worship, praise, or thanksgiving to God?

One-quarter of the sample set aside time daily. Another 21 percent said they did it a few times a week, and 13 percent said weekly. Thus, a majority (59 percent) of our sample spends time alone with God at least weekly, and this is encouraging. Any leader will want to see these numbers grow, but it is a good start. Obviously we don't know for certain the quantity or the quality of these devotions, but it is a good thing that so many churchgoers are trying to worship God.

Dining with Jesus

A man once planned a special dinner for his closest and dearest friend. He loved this friend as one would love a brother, and he looked forward to this private time when the two of them could talk and enjoy their friendship.

As the day for the dinner approached, the man's friend said he'd be unable to come because he was swamped at work. They agreed on another date, but again the friend canceled saying he'd been invited somewhere else by some other friends. Once again they agreed to a new night for the dinner, and once again the friend sent a message saying he was overcommitted with his family, and, as a result, he'd be unable to dine with his friend. Eventually it became apparent the one friend did not really value the other.

When we miss our private times with God, we are like the friend who is too busy to converse and dine with the most important person in our lives. Jesus said, "The one who will eat bread in the kingdom of God is blessed!" (Luke 14:15).

With this in mind, we wanted to know how much time our sample spends in prayer. There is much evidence in the Bible on the importance of prayer in spiritual formation. The psalms are filled with various expressions of prayer. When Nehemiah heard about the condition of Jerusalem, he said: "When I heard these words, I sat down and wept. I mourned for a number of days, fasting and praying before the God of heaven" (Neh. 1:4).

Our most important example is Jesus Himself. Here are some of His practices and teachings.

- Jesus taught His followers how to pray (see Matt. 6:5–13).
- Jesus taught His followers how to fast (see Matt. 6:16–18).
- Jesus withdrew to pray (see Mark 1:35).
- Jesus prayed in the garden with His disciples (see Mark 14:32–42).

Elsewhere in the Bible we find emphasis on praying and teaching about prayer:

- Peter and John prayed for boldness as they faced hostility from religious leaders (see Acts 4:13–24).
- Here we see one of the many examples of Paul's prayers for fellow believers (see Col. 1:9–14).
- Paul teaches that Christians should constantly pray (see 1 Thess. 5:17).
- The disciples were devoted to prayer after the ascension of Jesus (see Acts 1:12–14).

To quantify the level of commitment to and frequency of prayer, we asked the following question:

How often do you set aside time for prayer?

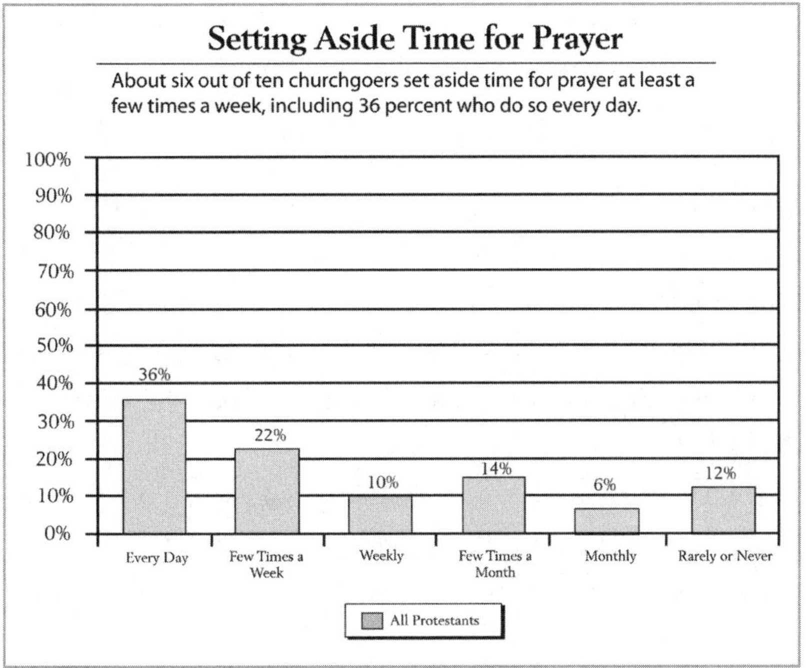

So 36 percent of our sample said they pray every day. Another 22 percent pray a few times a week, and 10 percent pray weekly, while the remaining 32 percent of our sample prays irregularly or seldom.

Making Time for What Is Important

When Patti and I were looking for a home to purchase in Nashville, she wanted one with a large kitchen and a bedroom on the main level. I wanted a large garage and lots of storage space for all of my "stuff." I like hunting, fishing, various other sports, and home improvement—all of which require space. Patti prioritizes what she enjoys and values, and I do the same.

When it comes to times of gift-giving (birthdays, Christmas, etc.), I ask my family to forgo the normal routines and just allow me to do guilt-free shopping one day each year. That day is Black Friday. Those in the retail business know Black Friday is the Friday after Thanksgiving when many people begin Christmas shopping. It is called "black" because, for many stores, this is the first day in the calendar year they start to make a profit and are in the black.

I get up early the day after Thanksgiving and go to places like Home Depot, Lowe's, and Sears to buy tools for my boys, my father-in-law, and myself. I love their door-buster sales. Then I go home and invent home improvement projects to justify the purchase of the tools. Ha! Then I will make time in my schedule for various projects. Why? Because I love doing it. It is my hobby. I spend time and money on the things I value.

What does this have to do with prayer? We find time and money for what we really like and enjoy. It comes down to priorities. If you understand the importance of prayer, you will make time for it. Praying yourself or getting others to pray is not rocket science, but it must take priority. We don't often admit it, but we usually find time for what is important to us. Take a look at your calendar, your to-do lists, and your checkbook or credit card accounts. You'll see what I mean.

As Christians we must simply block out time each day for prayer. When I began to do this, I used a devotional tool that had a prayer section in it. I use an acronym, ACTS, to help me: Adoration, Confession, Thanksgiving, and Supplication. *Adoration* is praising God for who He is; *Confession* is admitting sin to God; *Thanksgiving* is expressing gratitude to God for what He has done; and *Supplication* is an old-fashioned word that means praying for others.

Many churches have organized prayer ministries with designated prayer rooms, prayer lists, and schedules. Others just ask people to commit to pray one hour a week on their own. Churches effectively mobilize people to pray by starting prayer groups that meet weekly in homes, the workplace, at the church, or wherever there is a good place.

Many churches have a weekly prayer meeting open to all members, but unfortunately some of these weekly events lack leadership. Few people actually pray, and the prayer time rarely consists of genuine adoration, thanksgiving, or praise.

When it comes to prayer, leaders set the tone. What is important to them becomes important to the people. Prayer begins in the leader's private prayer closet. Then it moves out to the people of God. Spiritual leaders must teach about prayer, model prayer, and lead others to pray. There is no one right way to do this; there are many right ways. Leaders must choose a strategy and follow it.

Memorization: An Agent of Transformation

Another spiritual discipline that has been important to believers over the centuries is Scripture memorization. For spiritual transformation, it may be one of the most neglected opportunities. In a way memorization is like reprogramming our brains. We're running a self-centered program, but through memorization God's Word reprograms our brains into the other-centered mind of Christ.

Long before computers the Jewish educational system was based on memorizing the Torah, the first five books of the Old Testament. Today students barely know the names of the first five books of the Bible!

Hebrew children were expected to be diligent students of God's Word, studying the Law and the Prophets. Here's how Moses addressed the Israelites:

> Listen, Israel: The LORD our God, the LORD is One. Love the LORD your God with all your heart, with all your soul, and with all your strength. These words that I am giving you today are to be in your heart. Repeat them to your children. Talk about them when you sit in your house and when you walk along the road, when you lie down and when you get up. Bind them as a sign on your hand and let them be a symbol on your forehead. Write them on the doorposts of your house and on your gates. (Deut. 6:4–9)

Despite the image some people carry, Scripture memorization need not be complicated. While in college, I was around godly men and women committed to memorizing God's Word and teaching and encouraging others. I got a copy of the Topical Memory System[1] developed and distributed by the Navigators Ministry. It's an easy system to learn and follow. Passages I memorized back then still come into my thinking and conversation today.

Memorization can, if you let it, become dry and routine. Or worse, it can become a sense of pride. Approached in the right spirit, with the proper motive, it is life changing. Transforming one's character comes from the renewal of the mind (see Rom. 12:1–2). Renewing the mind can only happen when the Holy Spirit uses the Word of God.

When we asked our sample how often they memorized Scripture, 4 percent said "every day," 9 percent said "four times a week," 9 percent said "weekly," 14 percent said "a few times a month," 13 percent said "monthly," and 51 percent said "rarely or never."

Fasting: Who Does This?

Fasting, abstaining from food for a spiritual purpose, is seldom discussed in churches today. Yet it has a clear focus throughout the Bible. In the Old Testament we see examples of the people of God seeking Him through fasting (Judg. 20:26; 1 Sam. 1:11–12; 1 Kings 21:27–29; 2 Chron. 20:3–4; Ezra 8:23; Esther 4:16; Neh. 1:3–4; Ps. 35:13; Dan. 9:3; Jon. 3:5–8).

The prophet Joel records this word from God: "Even now—this is the LORD's declaration—turn to Me with all your heart, with fasting, weeping, and mourning" (Joel 2:12).

We see fasting in the ministry of Christ. In Matthew, Jesus provides instruction about fasting. Twice Jesus said, "Whenever you fast," implying fasting was expected (Matt. 6:16–17). Later Jesus explained that after His ascension His disciples would fast: "The days will come when the groom will be taken away from them, and then they will fast" (Matt. 9:15–16).

So we asked our sample how many fast and how often:

In the past six months, about how many times have you, personally, done the following: fasted (going without eating for a certain period of time, to concentrate on prayer or meditation)?

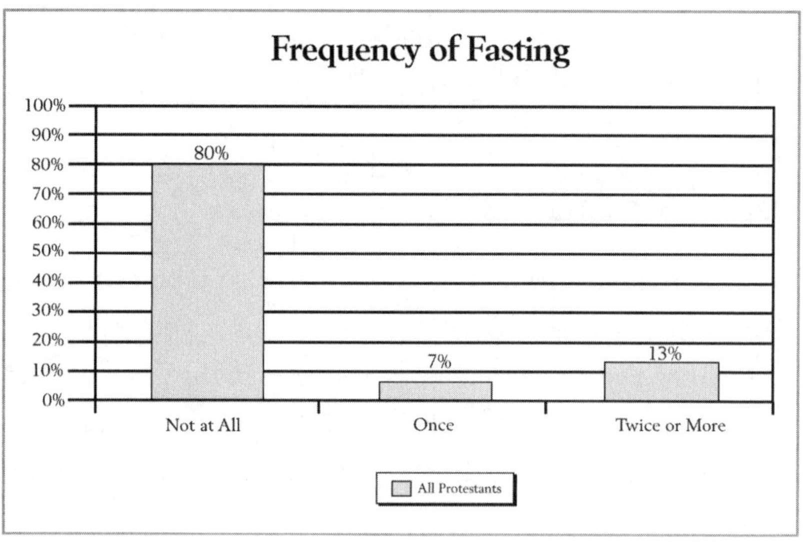

The graph shows most of those we surveyed never fast, or at least have not fasted in the six months leading up to the survey. Seven percent said they fasted once in six months, and 13 percent fasted twice in that period.

There is room for growth in teaching about and encouraging the spiritual discipline of fasting. Seemingly most churchgoers know little about fasting. Wouldn't it be exciting for leaders to pass along this historic practice of seeking God by fasting?

The All-Important Issue of Motivation

The last issue related to Domain Six: Seeking God is motivation; why people do what they do. Why do people attend church or pursue spiritual disciplines? Some churchgoers may be active in their church because it makes them feel good about themselves. There is nothing wrong with feeling positive about oneself as long as it is not based on a self-serving, self-loving motivation.

Motivation for religious pursuits is a major issue in the Bible. Jesus strongly confronted religious people He met because their motivation was self-serving. He spoke of godly motives so focused that we should be like a merchant who gives up everything else in order to buy the one priceless pearl (see Matt. 13:45–46).

To gain clarity about motivation, we asked this question:

How much do you agree/disagree: One of the main reasons I live my life the way I do is to please and honor God?

Surprisingly only 37 percent were able to "agree strongly" with this motivation for living the Christian life. Another 32 percent said they "agreed somewhat." But a third of our sample could not affirm this motivation to any degree. Now I find it difficult to imagine any Christian who would not express some desire to please and honor God!

Here is evidence of shallowness among many churchgoers as to why they are active in their churches. But before criticizing them, let's consider if their church leaders are encouraging a self-serving motive. "Come to our comfortable church. We accept you just as you are and will not impose any change that you do not feel good about. We can help you enjoy life more fully, worry less, and make friends in the process. We want you to feel better about yourself."

It is time for church leaders to look at the statistic that only 37 percent of Protestant churchgoers in America affirm they live their lives to please and honor God.

The Worship Quotient—Conclusions

The wonderful news of the Bible is that God promises to make Himself known to those who seek Him. He makes it possible to seek Him. Through the redemptive work of Christ, the opportunity to "know" God becomes real. Paul put it this way: "God is faithful; by Him you were called into fellowship with His Son, Jesus Christ our Lord" (1 Cor. 1:9). Then in Philippians we find this wonderful truth:

> More than that, I also consider everything to be a loss in view of the surpassing value of knowing Christ Jesus my Lord. . . . My goal is to know Him and the power of His resurrection and the fellowship of His sufferings, being conformed to His death. (Phil. 3:8, 10)

Seeking God is a daily activity for those who believe in God and follow Him. To biblically shape the faith to come:

- Leaders will consistently teach that we have the incredible opportunity to know the Creator of the universe, the Everlasting One, the only true God. How can we not seek Him with our whole heart?
- Leaders will model seeking God every day. With the pressures of church leadership, it's easy for responsibilities and interactions with people to take our focus off God. Worshipping God must be our main focus.
- Leaders will teach the nature and importance of worship, and we must set the tone for worship.
- Leaders will develop strategies that teach how to pray fervently and how to pray with fasting.

---

1. Navigators, *Topical Memory System* (Colorado Springs, CO: NavPress, 2006).

Chapter Nine

Domain Seven

Building Relationships: The Relational Quotient

I give you a new commandment: love one another. Just as I have loved you, you must also love one another. By this all people will know that you are My disciples, if you have love for one another.

—JOHN 13:34–35

Biblical Truth: We are designed by God to be in relationship with Him and in relationship with other believers.

The Relational Quotient: Jesus is the primary relationship in our lives, and through Him we build relationships with one another.

One another. First one, then another. One, another. We mature as Christians as we build relationships with other believers. First, we enter the cornerstone relationship, an intimate dependence on Jesus Christ. The Bible teaches us to become one with Jesus, so in tune with His will and wishes that we do not act independently of Him. Next, build significant, intimate relationships with other believers, loving, supporting, and encouraging one another.

Our faith strengthens as we walk with other believers, and their faith strengthens as they walk with us. This interdependence creates accountability, and it lightens the load of our service to God and others. One serves, another joins in serving, and soon many are serving.

The Bible is filled with stories and teaching that connect our spiritual formation to relationships. This connection is seen in the "one another" passages. The New Testament has at least fifty specific commands regarding interacting with "one another." Below is a sample:

- "Love one another" (John 13:34).
- Speak the truth to one another (see Eph. 4:25).
- "Accept one another" (Rom. 15:7).
- "Be at peace with one another" (Mark 9:50).
- Show compassion to one another (see Eph. 4:32).
- Forgive one another (see Col. 3:13).
- "Encourage one another" (1 Thess. 4:18).
- "Serve one another" (Gal. 5:13).
- Submit to one another (see Eph. 5:21).

- Show concern for one another (see Heb. 10:24).
- "Pray for one another" (James 5:16).
- Show humility toward one another (see 1 Pet. 5:5).
- "Act justly toward one another" (Jer. 7:5).
- Do not lie to one another (see Lev. 19:11).

The Old Testament reveals the connection between relationships and spirituality in the Ten Commandments. Six of the ten commands are tied directly to relationships. We cannot separate loving God from loving others.

The apostle John directly connects our relationship with one another to our relationship with God:

> If anyone says, "I love God," yet hates his brother, he is a liar. For the person who does not love his brother whom he has seen cannot love God whom he has not seen. And we have this command from Him: the one who loves God must also love his brother. (1 John 4:20–21)

Willing to Die for the Truth but Not Willing to Live by It

From what I see, many Christian leaders today need to reexamine what it means to love God. I see notable theologians and prominent leaders willing to die for essential doctrines such as the inerrancy of Scripture, yet they ignore the most basic teachings of the Bible: love one another, honor one another, and show compassion for one another.

How and why is this happening? Clearly one reason is that intellectual assent to doctrinal statements requires little effort. We can wrap our brains around a lot of truths without any sacrifice—dying to self, putting others first, and forgiving when hurt. While it is vitally important that all Christians think through and embrace biblical truths at the intellectual level, this falls short of all God expects and demands. Embracing the truth includes the life-transforming elements of repentance and obedience. We cannot claim to embrace the integrity of the Bible while blatantly ignoring its clear commands about how we should relate to others.

This problem is not limited to leaders. Many Christians live daily with dissonance, a great gap between what they profess and how they treat others. Gossip, backbiting, rudeness, prejudice, jealousy, misrepresentation, breaking confidentiality, withholding support and encouragement, and taking advantage of others—these are just a few of the destructive attitudes and behaviors displayed by many professing Christians.

Relationship Quotient Test

In seeking to measure the health of our churchgoing sample, we asked eleven questions, seven of which sought levels of agreement or disagreement with statements about relationships. Four of the questions were aimed at the frequency of certain behaviors.

Levels of Agreement/Disagreement

- I have developed significant relationships with people at my church.
- When I become aware that I have wronged someone, I go to that person to admit and correct my wrongdoing.
- I intentionally make time in my schedule to fellowship and interact with other believers.
- I am careful in my closest relationships to avoid people or situations that may negatively impact my Christian values and principles.
- I generally do not share personal things, such as feelings, joys, struggles, and needs, with my Christian friends.
- When I am wronged by others, I often have trouble responding with a forgiving attitude.
- Spiritual matters do not tend to come up as a normal part of my daily conversations with other Christians.

Frequency of Activities

- Pray in a group with other Christians once a week or more.
- In a typical month how often do you:
    - ✦ attend a worship service at your church four or more times?
    - ✦ attend Sunday school or Christian education classes at your church?
    - ✦ attend a small-group Bible study, study group, or cell group?

Domain Seven was the lowest-scoring domain with almost no one from any demographic group giving the top response on all elements of the domain. Only 4 percent gave a positive response on every element. Our churchgoers do not appear to be all that strong when it comes to relating well with others. Let's look at some of the particulars.

Building Significant Relationships

We wanted to know if our sample of churchgoers perceived themselves to be involved in significant relationships. We did not define the word *significant* but assumed respondents were capable of determining significance. We simply asked the following question:

How much do you agree/disagree: I have developed significant relationships with people at my church?

In our sample 27 percent "strongly agree" they have developed significant relationships in their church; another 33 percent "agreed somewhat." Less than a third of our churchgoers could confidently affirm they have high-quality relationships with fellow church members.

I can't imagine any pastor or leader being satisfied with these results. Some pastors and leaders have strong convictions about the relational health of the body of Christ. They model and teach godly relationships. They establish high standards for their churches.

The result is that, over time, positive relationships are encouraged and celebrated, while unbiblical practices are confronted.

Unbiblical relational patterns are one of the main reasons the majority of churchgoers are unable to strongly affirm their relational experience in their own churches. Cultural seepage is once again at work. Most Americans have adapted so easily to unhealthy relationships that they now appear normal to us. Many of our TV sitcoms play off this sick cultural reality. Popular shows like *Sex and the City* and *Desperate Housewives* provide excellent examples of our cultural sickness. We are so desensitized to our cultural dysfunction that it should not surprise us when we find it in our churches.

Allowing this cultural seepage into our churches causes conflict, pain, and superficial involvement. Many of us keep our distance from people who inflict pain and discomfort.

I am not speaking theoretically. One church I served had a fair amount of unhealthy DNA. Several families had been members of the church for many generations, and children and grandchildren had intermarried.

These deep generational ties offered some benefits, but they also created some serious flaws in the congregation. Some of these long-standing members saw the church as an extension of their family history and had a sense of ownership and entitlement. One member in particular enjoyed positioning himself as the "church boss." He openly displayed disrespect for the pastoral staff and took pride in driving off more than one pastor. His attitude was, "I was here before this pastor came, and I will be here when he leaves." He was rude, offensive, manipulative, and intimidating.

I will never forget one Wednesday night business meeting at which the new pastoral staff was to present the budget for the upcoming calendar year. This self-appointed "church boss" stood outside beforehand and distributed a lengthy addendum to the budget the pastor and church finance committee were putting forward to the church. Then during the business meeting he stood and presented his version of the budget, concluding his remarks, "And I would appreciate your support." He sounded like a politician campaigning before a public vote. Fortunately a majority rejected his efforts although he still had significant support from a core group that had grown accustomed to his abuse.

Such sinful patterns are common in many of our churches, destroying the ability of church members to develop significant and positive relationships. To biblically shape the faith to come, leaders will lovingly but firmly confront this destructive behavior. Leaders will teach and model healthy relationships. They will exemplify integrity, respect, humility, and brotherly love and will lead others in learning these same values and practices. They will lead their congregations into relational health.

For the past couple of years, I have served as a consultant for a church devastated by the moral failure of the pastor who divided his church rather than resign. Leading up to this tragedy, the pastor displayed a dictatorial leadership style. A common comment he made to members who questioned or had concerns was, "There are other churches, join one." The damage this pastor caused the church created all kinds of relational problems. Close friends and even family members are no longer speaking to one another due to this man's polarizing impact.

In the aftermath of the church split and all of the relational damage, I recommended the key lay leaders read the book *Making Peace* by Jim Van Yperen.[1] This insightful book identifies common sinful patterns in our churches and provides solid biblical solutions for regaining church health.

Eventually several of the leaders developed a deliberate, church-wide process for becoming healthy. While it took time, the church found itself in a much better position to call a new pastor and get on with being a church that is biblically focused not only on mission but also on relationships.

I know of another church that has sought to foster relational health by equipping its leaders to deal with conflict resolution through a study of the book *The Peacemaker* by Ken Sande, along with the training the Peacemaker Ministry offers.[2] These leaders are now spread throughout the church like leaven in bread, dealing with conflict before it becomes major. Buddy Gray, pastor of Hunter Street Baptist Church in Birmingham, Alabama, says this one initiative has transformed not only the deacon ministry but also the entire church atmosphere.

While a church can work together to improve the quality of relationships in many ways, setting high standards for how believers treat one another is crucial. Just as infections in the body must be fought to maintain good physical health, so addressing sinful relational patterns within the community of faith is essential for spiritual health. Pursued consistently, this will lead to a culture and environment conducive to godly relationships.

People, Work, Things, or Activities?

Our cultural patterns keep us from developing deep relationships. Many of us are too busy. Family members each go in their own direction without regard for one another. I enjoy a close relationship with my sister, Brenda. We often compare the lifestyle of our childhood to what families endure today. Brenda has three school-aged children and is constantly on the run between school, church, sports, and recreational activities. Not all of this is bad. She says she is glad her kids are active and not sitting around watching television. But for many families, the harried and hurried lifestyle can make it difficult to live in such a way that deep and meaningful relationships within the church can be developed and sustained.

Beyond families being so busy, many of us wrestle with the challenge of balancing work and relationships. Work schedules allow many to avoid spending significant time together. There is no shortcut to significant relationships; developing them takes time and energy. It must be a priority.

The other day my wife, Patti, and I were out in our yard when a neighbor came over and introduced herself. We were embarrassed to learn we had lived near each other for eighteen months and had not yet met. As we talked, she expressed interest in spiritual things, so we invited her to attend church with us. It is sad that so much time went by without our reaching out to our neighbor.

Just a few days ago, Patti heard another neighbor weeping. She went over to see what was wrong and learned the husband was leaving his wife and their two young children to take up with his former secretary. This neighbor has opened her heart and allowed Patti to pray for her.

What a reminder of how important relationships really are! Our priorities need constant scrutiny.

A foundational assumption of spiritual formation and maturity is that people matter. You cannot be mature spiritually without significant relationships. We asked our sample of churchgoers this question:

To what degree do you agree/disagree: I intentionally make time in my schedule to fellowship and interact with other believers?

Only 18 percent of our sample said they "strongly agreed," while another 29 percent "agreed somewhat." More than half of these churchgoers do not intentionally make time for fellowship and relationship building.

While significant relationships cannot be forced, opportunities for fellowship and relationship building can be fostered.

Maintaining a Culture of Fellowship

What a church does reflects its real values, just as what a family or individual does reflects core values. With most of us, when important things are neglected, we make excuses. I try to cut through this mental baloney by reminding myself that I do what is important to me. Practices usually reflect the heart.

Church practices vary. No congregation is exactly like another. Facilitating fellowship, however, does not have to be hard. We must get past the idea of a "friendly church" to the concept of a "church of friends." Many churches follow the practice of taking a few seconds in each worship service to greet one another. That's fine, but it amounts no more to friendship or true fellowship than eating an apple a week constitutes good dietary practices. Just as it takes a lot more than an occasional apple for healthy eating, it requires more than a few moments of polite greeting to create genuine Christian fellowship.[3]

Most healthy churches use a combination of four practices to facilitate fellowship and relationship building:

- **Assimilation Strategy.** Every church needs a strategy for introducing, orienting, and assimilating new believers and new members. This usually takes the form of a class designed to teach the basic beliefs and characteristics of the church.
- **Small Group Experience.** Most churches rely on either Sunday school classes or home groups to provide a setting for fellowship. These strategies have pros and cons, but each church must find a way to provide opportunities for members to enter into meaningful fellowship. The groups must be properly led and organized for true relationships to develop.
- **Ministry Involvement.** Deep, meaningful relationships are developed in the context of ministry teams. Few things are more helpful in developing significant relationships than serving side by side. Churches need an intentional strategy to enlist, equip, guide, and place people in ministry.

- **Prayer Groups.** While this could be included in the category of ministry involvement, the important practice of prayer deserves separate attention. Many homes have a plaque that says, "The family that prays together stays together." While fellowship is not the main motivation for getting believers together for prayer, it is a wonderful by-product. Nothing else compares to fellow believers coming together before a holy God for praise, adoration, confession, and petition. Biblical prayer binds our hearts to God and to one another.

Significant Relationships Include Prayer

In light of the above comments about prayer and its connection to meaningful relationships, we asked our sample this question:

How often do you pray in a group with other Christians?

In our sample 5 percent indicated they pray with other Christians every day. Thirteen percent said "a few days a week"; 27 percent said "weekly"; 16 percent, a few times a month; 10 percent, monthly; and 28 percent, rarely or never. Nearly half (45 percent) of regular churchgoers pray regularly with other Christians. These numbers are higher than I would have expected. In the churches I have served, all of which placed some emphasis upon prayer, I doubt 50 percent of the regular attendees or members prayed with other believers on a weekly basis.

Despite this discouraging news our study uncovered, there is evidence here to give church leaders hope. Many churchgoers have a solid interest in prayer. While we may not have insight as to the quality and nature of their prayer efforts, the fact that so many churchgoers engage in some sort of prayer is good. This, coupled with biblical teaching about prayer, could transform lives and churches.

Biblically informed church leaders know spiritual formation is impossible without prayer. Like all the other characteristics of biblical discipleship, leaders must model and teach prayer. Otherwise, it will not happen. Here are a few suggestions:

- Prayer needs to be part of regular worship.
- The small group/Sunday school strategy needs to include prayer.
- From time to time, the church's teaching and preaching ministry should give solid attention to prayer.
- Prayer groups should be formed throughout the community of faith.
- Churches should consider some type of regular, corporate prayer service.
- Individual members can sign up to pray one hour per week as part of a 24/7 prayer effort.

Significant Relationships Include Transparency

The nature of fellowship implies two or more people are spending substantial time together and are open enough to get to know one another. People are like onions, with multiple layers of complexity. When most of us encounter new people, we are cautious about revealing much of ourselves. But over time, if we feel confident in ourselves and if we begin to trust others, we will expose deeper and deeper layers—our personal history, ideas, and opinions about safe topics. As trust deepens, we move to more intimate levels of friendship, exposing our inner feelings, opinions, core values, and even struggles or hurts.

When Patti and I met our neighbor Cathy, she asked where we attended church. As we talked, she said her family had been looking four years for a church where they could build meaningful relationships. They liked the worship and preaching in the past two churches they attended but had not been able to break into the realm of fellowship. I believe most people are hungry to know others beyond a superficial level. Cathy was looking for something more than a friendly church. She was looking for true friends and was hungry for Christian fellowship.

Biblical fellowship requires certain levels of transparency and openness. Review the biblical "one anothers" at the beginning of this chapter. The content and context of those passages clearly depict Christians experiencing deep, meaningful, mutual fellowship. That kind of fellowship is not optional for a disciple of Christ. God expects and demands the pursuit of meaningful relationships.

We asked our sample of churchgoers this question:

To what degree do you agree/disagree: I generally do not share personal things, such as feelings, joys, struggles, and needs, with my Christian friends?

Since this question is worded negatively, we were looking for a high percentage of disagreement. We found that 22 percent of our churchgoers indicated they "disagreed strongly" with the statement and 27 percent "disagreed somewhat." Nearly half our sample responded in a healthy way. One in every two churchgoers shares life at some meaningful level with fellow believers.

As with many of our other findings, I do not know a pastor or church staff member who would be satisfied with only 49 percent of the congregation enjoying meaningful Christian relationships.

But it begins with the leaders. What kind of environment do we create? Do we model transparency? Do we reveal our true feelings, joys, needs, and struggles?

This is another example of cultural seepage. Secular society portrays leaders as always having on their "game face." Always confident. Always tough. Always armed with the answers. Never revealing need or vulnerability. On the one hand, you understand that people like to follow confident leaders, but confidence does not have to exclude transparency. In fact, certain levels of transparency and vulnerability can foster confidence because they lead to trust. I never put a lot of trust in someone who shows only his "game face."

Significant Relationships Include a Spiritual Tone

When measuring the quality of relationships between believers, factor in the "spiritual tone" of interaction. It is one thing to spend time with other believers but another to edify one another. We need to stop and evaluate the depth and content of our conversations.

This can be a little tricky to convey as I do not want to perpetuate the notion that Christians must always be quoting Scripture and shouting, "Hallelujah!" I suspect the opposite is far more common. It is easy to slip into a pattern of having Christian friends with whom you seldom engage in a biblically substantive manner. We need to ask ourselves how often we talk with one another about God and His Word. How often do we interact about matters of prayer and faith? How often do we quote Scripture, not in a Bible-thumping way but to encourage and edify one another? How often do we express praise and adoration of Jesus in conversation with one another?

We asked our sample of churchgoers to express their level of agreement or disagreement with this question:

To what degree do you agree/disagree: Spiritual matters do not tend to come up as a normal part of my daily conversations with other Christians?

As this question was worded in the negative, we hoped for high levels of disagreement. Of our sample 17 percent indicated they "disagreed strongly" and another 26 percent "disagreed somewhat," resulting in an overall positive score of 43 percent. So less than half of our sample responded in a spiritually healthy way to this inquiry.

One of the times Jesus confronted the Pharisees, He declared, "For the mouth speaks from the overflow of the heart. A good man produces good things from his storeroom of good, and an evil man produces evil things from his storeroom of evil" (Matt. 12:34–35).

The mouth reflects the heart. When it comes to assessing our people's spiritual maturity, listen to their conversations.

Significant Relationships Include Forgiveness

Several years ago a couple of good friends invited me to join them on a hiking and fishing trip to Montana. I love the outdoors, so I was quick to sign up. We spent weeks getting ready. When the day finally came, we flew to Billings, loaded our gear, and drove to the trail head. We enthusiastically threw on sixty-pound backpacks that soon felt as though they weighed more like two hundred pounds.

On the first day we ascended several thousand feet while covering about eight miles. Around the six-mile point I was ready to jettison gear that only hours before I had valued highly. But I resisted the temptation and plodded on. Finally, after four hours, we reached our first campsite. I will never forget how good it felt to drop that backpack. What a relief!

Many Christians carry a heavy burden of unforgiveness. Pride, fear, or plain old resentment keeps them from putting it down. It steals their joy, energy, and capacity to love others. At first the load might feel good, just like when I put on my new backpack. But eventually this burden of unforgiveness becomes nearly unbearable.

I have seen unforgiveness destroy entire families. I know a woman whose son has refused to speak with his two brothers for more than a decade. This mother is filled with pain as she watches her own flesh and blood refuse even to be in the same room with one another. She must plan separate holiday celebrations and special events to avoid the hatred. What a heavy burden to carry.

One of the best measurements of relational health and commitment is keeping short accounts and being quick to give and receive forgiveness. One of the tremendous joys of being a Christian is the God-infused ability to forgive. We are liberated when we make things right, forgive those who have offended us, and receive the forgiveness of others. It feels even better than dropping a heavy backpack after a long, steep hike!

Forgiveness is founded in the nature and character of God. Nehemiah and Isaiah make some important observations about God's nature:

> But You are a forgiving God, gracious and compassionate,
> slow to anger and rich in faithful love. (Neh. 9:17)

> Let the wicked one abandon his way, and the sinful one his thoughts; let him return to the LORD, so He may have compassion on him, and to our God, for He will freely forgive. (Isa. 55:7)

We find many similar descriptions of God throughout the Bible. The life and teachings of Jesus also teach us much about the topic of forgiveness.

- In His model prayer Jesus included the phrase, "Forgive us our debts, as we also have forgiven our debtors" (Matt. 6:12).

- Following His model prayer, Jesus said, "For if you forgive people their wrongdoing, your heavenly Father will forgive you as well. But if you don't forgive people, your Father will not forgive your wrongdoing" (Matt. 6:14–15).
- The apostle Mark recorded this comment from Jesus: "Whenever you stand praying, if you have anything against anyone, forgive him, so that your Father in heaven will also forgive you your wrongdoing" (Mark 11:25).
- One of Jesus' strongest statements on forgiveness is found in the parable of the unforgiving slave:

> "Then, after he had summoned him, his master said to him, 'You wicked slave! I forgave you all that debt because you begged me. Shouldn't you also have had mercy on your fellow slave, as I had mercy on you?' And his master got angry and handed him over to the jailers until he could pay everything that was owed. So My heavenly Father will also do to you if each of you does not forgive his brother from his heart." (Matt. 18:32–35)

- Jesus emphasized the scope of our forgiveness when He stated, "Be on your guard. If your brother sins, rebuke him, and if he repents, forgive him. And if he sins against you seven times in a day, and comes back to you seven times, saying, 'I repent,' you must forgive him" (Luke 17:3–4).
- The apostle Paul continued this important emphasis upon forgiveness:

> Be kind and compassionate to one another, forgiving one another, just as God also forgave you in Christ. (Eph. 4:32)

> Therefore, God's chosen ones, holy and loved, put on heartfelt compassion, kindness, humility, gentleness, and patience, accepting one another and forgiving one another if anyone has a complaint against another. Just as the Lord has forgiven you, so also you must forgive. (Col. 3:12–13)

God's expectation is clear. Forgiveness is a hallmark of Christianity. With this in mind, we asked our churchgoers to respond to two questions related to forgiveness. Our findings were mixed.

To what degree do you agree/disagree: When I become aware that I have wronged someone, I go to that person to admit and correct my wrongdoing?

Of our sample, 27 percent responded "agreed strongly" and another 43 percent "agreed somewhat", for a combined 70-percent positive response. This was more positive than the responses to the majority of our other items.

The second question we asked was:

To what degree do you agree/disagree: When I am wronged by others, I often have trouble responding with a forgiving attitude?

While the first statement approached the issue of forgiveness from the positive side, this statement was cast in the negative. We were hoping for a high level of disagreement.

What we actually found was that 15 percent of our sample indicated they "disagreed strongly," while another 27 percent "disagreed somewhat," giving us a 42 percent positive response—and a 58 percent negative response. Most of our churchgoers admit they struggle forgiving those who have offended or wronged them.

The fact that the first question received a 70 percent positive response, compared to a 42 percent positive response to the second one, is more than statistically significant. One possible explanation is that the first question was asked from the perspective of the offender, the one who has wronged others, while the second was asked from the view of the person offended. Perhaps our churchgoers felt more compelled to *receive* forgiveness when they know they have wronged someone than they are compelled to *give* forgiveness when wronged by others.

The Bible speaks directly to the person who has been offended. All Christians need to be ready to forgive others. Either our churchgoers are not adequately informed about God's expectations or, worse, they are indifferent toward God's expressed will.

Two major deficiencies related to forgiveness can be seen in many congregations. First, there is a lack of consistent and clear teaching on this biblical truth, which can be seen in the widespread confusion and misunderstanding that exists.

For example, many Christians confuse forgiveness and reconciliation. The Bible makes it clear that forgiveness is unconditional.

Believers must forgive, whether the perpetrator seeks forgiveness or not. We are not allowed to nurse bitterness or unforgiveness. We must relinquish the right to get even. We fail to understand that forgiveness is not tied to emotions or to the other person's behavior.

Another point of confusion has to do with how various leaders handle passages like this: "It is I who sweep away your transgressions for My own sake and remember your sins no more" (Isa. 43:25).

Some convey that if the offended party experiences any hurt or fear in the company of the offender, then they are guilty of unforgiveness. This is both theologically and psychologically flawed. Understood in context, this passage is about God's redemptive work with His people, not about humans forgiving other humans.

Most people are not going to forget offenses, and some will still feel uncomfortable around people they consider unsafe, even those they have forgiven. Why? Because forgiveness is not the same as reconciliation. Forgiveness is unconditional, while reconciliation is conditional. Reconciliation is possible only when both parties agree to the truth about the situation and follow with a new pattern of behavior that allows trust to be rebuilt. Many well-intended sermons about forgiveness have created confusion and false guilt in the hearts of sincere believers.

The second evidence of deficiency in our understanding of forgiveness is the failure of many leaders and churches to uphold high standards of respectful and godly behavior between fellow Christians. It is not uncommon for leaders to overlook a member's harmful behavior, especially when the person wields financial or political influence in the church. Some leaders are unwilling to pay the price of holding all members accountable to the same standards. Many leaders do not have thick enough skin to handle the conflict that comes from holding anyone to high standards.

If we expect spiritual formation to occur in the lives of our church members, we must model forgiveness, teach biblical truth about forgiveness, and hold one another to high relational standards.

Significant Relationships Avoid Negative Influences

Most of what we have been discussing so far in this chapter pertains to the pursuit of positive influences. Our Lord expects us to work at getting to know others and to pursue peace, love, and forgiveness with one another. The Bible, however, speaks also about our need to avoid negative influences:

> Do not be deceived: "Bad company corrupts good morals." Become right-minded and stop sinning, because some people are ignorant about God. I say this to your shame. (1 Cor. 15:33–34)

> Discretion will watch over you, and understanding will guard you, rescuing you from the way of evil—from the one who says perverse things, from those who abandon the right paths to walk in ways of darkness, from those who enjoy doing evil and celebrate perversity, whose paths are crooked, and whose ways are devious. It will rescue you from a

> forbidden woman, from a stranger with her flattering talk, who abandons the companion of her youth and forgets the covenant of her God; for her house sinks down to death and her ways to the land of the departed spirits. None return who go to her; none reach the paths of life. So follow the way of good people, and keep to the paths of the righteous. (Prov. 2:11–20)

> How happy is the man who does not follow the advice of the wicked, or take the path of sinners, or join a group of mockers! (Ps. 1:1)

> Do not be mismatched with unbelievers. For what partnership is there between righteousness and lawlessness? Or what fellowship does light have with darkness? What agreement does Christ have with Belial? Or what does a believer have in common with an unbeliever? And what agreement does God's sanctuary have with idols? (2 Cor. 6:14–16)

None of these passages call for us to shun unbelievers. To the contrary we are called to be salt and light to unbelievers. We must, however, guard our hearts and keep a safe distance from those who are not pursuing God. This doesn't mean we are to cease all interaction, but we must not allow unbelievers, or even misguided believers, to have access to our hearts. Preserving the Christian faith and community requires us to protect ourselves from the dangerous influences of those who promote perspectives and practices contrary to the will and ways of God.

With this in mind, we asked our sample of churchgoers this question:

To what degree do you agree/disagree: I am careful in my closest relationships to avoid people or situations that may negatively impact my Christian values and principles?

In our sample 20 percent responded "agree strongly" while another 32 percent "agreed somewhat." So slightly more than half our sample provided a positive response.

We can celebrate that half of our churchgoers display wisdom in relating to people who, in one way or another, to one degree or another, pose a threat to their spiritual health. We can also see that the other half of our sample does not consciously, carefully, and intentionally monitor or regulate the way they relate to negative influences.

Since all godly practices begin with God's Word, leaders must intentionally teach what the Bible says about how we are to relate to a lost world. Many years ago I read *Life-Style Evangelism* by Joseph C. Aldrich, an important and powerful explanation of how believers need to be *in* the world but not *of* the world. Aldrich says believers must avoid two extremes: radical difference and radical identification. The former he called "unbalanced rejectionism," where the Christian becomes so isolated from the world that the opportunity to witness is lost. The latter he called "unbalanced immersionism," where the believer lives so much like the world that any credible witness is lost.[4]

Spiritual leaders, whether speaking from the pulpit or in any other intentional training context, must teach fellow believers to be salt and light to a lost world. Our people need to know how to interact in their culture in a winsome way without compromise. We spend too little time equipping believers with a Christian worldview that prepares them to engage effectively our culture with a thoroughly biblical message.

Just Showing Up Contributes to the Relational Quotient

The Bible makes it clear that Christianity is not a solo journey. While there is indeed a private aspect to spiritual formation, there also is a communal necessity. The author of Hebrews put it this way:

> And let us be concerned about one another in order to promote love and good works, not staying away from our meetings, as some habitually do, but encouraging each other, and all the more as you see the day drawing near.
> (Heb. 10:24–25)

A Christian who claims to have a strong faith yet neglects gathering with other believers on a regular basis for worship, fellowship, and service is deceived. You cannot separate spiritual formation from living faithfully within the Christian community, a local body of believers that demonstrates all the essential biblical characteristics of a true church.

Since living in community is an essential aspect of biblical formation, we felt it necessary to determine the degree to which our churchgoers were committed to gathering together on a regular basis. We asked three questions related to participation in worship, Christian education, and small-group interaction.

Related to attendance in worship, we asked:

In a typical month, about how many times (if any) do you attend a worship service at your church?

Our sample was thus screened on the criteria of attending church at least once a month, so the entire sample attends church at least that often. We found that 14 percent of our sample attend church no more than once a month, 24 percent attend two to three times a month, 44 percent attend at least four times a month, and 18 percent attend five or more times a month. (Attendance more than four times a month is possible if opportunities such as midweek services are counted.)

We also asked about involvement in Christian education activities:

In a typical month, about how many times (if any) do you attend Sunday school or Christian education classes at your church?

Not all churches refer to their educational opportunity as Sunday school, so we added the wording "Christian education classes." We found that 28 percent of our churchgoers attend such a class four or more times a month, 9 percent attend two to three times a month, and 9 percent attend once a month, while 54 percent do not participate at any level.

Since many churches refer to their education or discipleship strategy as "small groups," we asked this question:

In a typical month, about how many times (if any) do you attend a small group Bible study, study group, or cell group?

We found that 18 percent said they attend a small group or cell group four or more times a month, 10 percent attend two or three times a month, and 12 percent attend once a month. That leaves 60 percent who do not participate at all.

To help evaluate these numbers, we looked at my own denomination, which has historically emphasized Sunday school. We discovered that, on average, 67 percent of those who attend worship also participate in Sunday school or its equivalent on Sunday mornings.

Some of the churches in our study likely offer both Sunday school (or its equivalent) and some sort of small-group Bible study or fellowship group. In churches that offer both, we may assume that a small percentage of those who do not attend Sunday school do participate in a small group and vice versa. Regardless of the exact percentage, a sizable number of churchgoers are not involved beyond worship attendance.

During most of my years of pastoral or church staff experience, I was responsible for the disciple-making strategies of the churches I served. I discovered it is essential to provide believers with some type of small-group experience that will take them deeper into biblical truth, relationships, and service. Weekly corporate worship is without a doubt the most important hour in the life of the church. It is mandatory. However, contrary to what some pastors think, corporate worship is not all that is needed for spiritual formation. Leaders must envision and implement a context for building relationships and fostering spiritual growth.

In my last full-time staff position, I led a strategy that involved both on-campus Sunday morning classes and midweek, off-campus small groups. In fact, for many years I both taught a Sunday school class and led a small group in my home. I loved both. I was committed to the Sunday morning on-campus strategy because I believe it is the most efficient way to assimilate large numbers of people, regardless of age and stage of life, into Bible study, fellowship, and service. I do not personally know of a church with a pure off-campus, small-group model that involves anywhere near the 67 percent noted above.

I also understand some of the limitations of a typical Sunday school or Sunday morning Bible study. The informal and hospitable environment of a person's home can foster a strong sense of community. Both strategies have advantages and disadvantages. A detailed analysis of various small-group and educational methodologies is beyond the scope of this book. Much research still needs to be done. Regardless of the context or structure you choose, moving people into meaningful fellowship must be led with intentionality, excellence, and consistency. True biblical community will not occur solely in the context of worship. We must provide more.

The Relational Quotient in the Shape of Faith to Come

We should be deeply concerned that of the seven domains of spiritual formation measured in this study, "Building Relationships" received the lowest score. Spiritual leaders must pray, think, and strategize to provide an environment and process that will facilitate the "one anothers" mentioned at the beginning of this chapter.

It is not enough to have a lot of bodies in the pews on Sunday morning. It is not enough to have growing budgets, buildings, and programs. People must be experiencing biblical community. Life together is vital and essential to God's plan for spiritual transformation.

A Culture of Fellowship

If leaders are biblically to shape the faith to come, we must move past the idea of a "friendly church" to the concept of a "church of friends." We must get past our superficial smiles and handshakes to build significant relationships and create a fellowship of friends within our congregations. A culture of fellowship includes these elements:

People over Programs. The things we value in our congregations are revealed in our priorities. We tend to do what we consider to be important, yet we often let overloaded schedules and busyness get in the way of developing significant, time-enriching relationships. To biblically shape the faith to come, we will constantly scrutinize our priorities, making sure religious activity never supplants the priority of building relationships.

Showing Up. We will teach our members that building quality relationships with one another and with God requires that we be part of a Christian community. We must consistently encourage our churchgoers to show up, gathering together on a regular basis.

Transparency. We will model a culture of fellowship through appropriate levels of transparency, teaching our members that a loving, safe environment creates an openness that allows them to experience deep, meaningful friendships.

Spiritual Tone. We will teach our members that what they say reflects their hearts, encouraging a fellowship of friends that helps steer one another toward wholesome, helpful conversations. We will routinely emphasize the biblical admonition to guard our hearts and keep a safe distance from those who are not pursuing God. This doesn't mean we tell our members to stop interacting with unbelievers; on the contrary, Jesus taught us to be the friends of sinners. The point is that we cannot allow unbelievers, or even misguided believers, to have access to our hearts.

Forgiveness. In a culture of fellowship, we will teach members about God's ever-present grace, encouraging them to release the heavy burden of unforgiveness. We will show members the spiritually practical need to let go of pride, fear, or old resentments. Living in a state of unforgiveness steals our joy and diminishes our capacity to love others.

Prayer. We will consistently remind our congregations that biblical prayer binds our hearts to God and to one another. We will teach our people how to pray and then give them many, many opportunities to pray together.

---

1. Jim Van Yperen, *Making Peace* (Grand Rapids, MI: Zondervan, 2002).

2. Ken Sande, *The Peacemaker* (Grand Rapids, MI: Baker, 2004).

3. I have said many times, "Speed of the leader; speed of the team." While this may not be true every time and everywhere, generally, if leaders stay in place long enough and are biblically healthy, the church eventually will take on their personality and values. What the leader values, most of the people eventually will value. When a church embraces these values, they usually are celebrated and supported. Such is the nature of leadership.

The tenure of key leaders, especially the pastor, is a crucial factor in changing the culture of a church. I've found it takes a couple of years for a new pastor to develop a relationship, collectively, with the congregation. After about five years a church begins to reflect the pastor's leadership.

In the LifeWay Research Standout Church Study, we analyzed nineteen evangelistically healthy congregations. Without exception these churches were led by pastors who were loved and respected. Interestingly, we discovered the average tenure was fifteen years. It takes time and consistent leadership to transform a church's culture.

4. Joseph C. Aldrich, *Life-Style Evangelism: Crossing Traditional Boundaries to Reach the Unbelieving World* (Portland, OR: Multnomah, 1983), 64.

Chapter Ten

Did One Year Make a Difference?

Who Grew and Why

Finally! I have been anxious to obtain the findings from our second survey and the individual phone interviews we conducted. The data is in and I have just finished pouring over the results. I have been eager to know how many of our twenty-five hundred participants in this yearlong longitudinal study have grown spiritually, in what ways, and for what reasons.

Good New or Bad News?

For review, in May 2007 LifeWay Research surveyed twenty-five hundred Protestant churchgoers using the Spiritual Formation

Inventory (SFI). The preceding chapters contain the analysis and summary of what we learned. Then in May of 2008 we re-surveyed the same people, obtaining responses from 1,044 of them. Finally we conducted phone and e-mail interviews.

So what did we learn? Here is an overview of some of the most significant insights.

View from Thirty Thousand Feet

Overall, the findings in this study are like a placid sea with a strong undertow. On top, there appears to be calmness and stability, with little movement. Underneath, there is turbidity and sometimes even chaos. This beneath the surface volatility is one of the major stories coming out of this study.

When looking at the total SFI scores, 3.5 percent of all respondents saw a positive net increase and 3 percent demonstrated a net decrease. When it came to the specific spiritual growth issues we measured (like frequency of witnessing, or faithfulness to prayer, etc.), 28 percent of these specific issues, when averaged all together, showed improvement and 26 percent showed decline.

The result, when everything is totaled up, is a change for the positive among a small number of people, which is largely offset by a decline in almost an equal number of people. Discipleship, or spiritual formation, changed very little in our churches over a twelve-month period of time. However, there were some incremental changes, and if these changes are consistent over time, it will lead to significant changes in the level of discipleship and spiritual formation in our churchgoers.

Some Specific Findings

Volatility

While there is little overall change in the total SFI scores, when you look at specific individuals, or subgroups, a lot of fluctuation and instability can be seen. It is like a plane full of people flying from New York to London. The same group takes off and lands, but on the way, half of the people change their seat assignments. This is not a perfect analogy, but it illustrates the point of change and unpredictability. Here are some examples of this volatility.

Fluctuating Beliefs

When comparing the 2007 and 2008 surveys, there appears to be little change in the total number of people who identified themselves as "born again" or as "evangelical." However, when looking beneath the surface, there are changes. Seventeen percent of our sample changed into or out of the "born again" category and 13 percent changed into or out of the "evangelical" category.

Half of this change is good. We are glad to see those who moved into the "born again" and "evangelical" categories. Praise God for this. However, what about those who only twelve months ago said they were "born again" and/or "evangelical," and now they say otherwise? This shows significant confusion or inconsistency among American Protestants.

Young Adults

Perhaps the biggest takeaway of this study is the volatility of those below the age of thirty. When looking at the total SFI scores, we see a small net positive in that 6 percent increased in their total spiritual formation scores while 4 percent decreased.

However, underneath the surface we see turbulence. Here are some examples:

- *Church attendance:* 34 percent attended church as often in 2007 as they did in 2008. 29 percent attended more often and 37 percent attended less often, for a net decrease in frequency of attendance of 8 percent.
- *Significant relationships:* 38 percent remained the same in how they answered this question. 39 percent saw improvement in their relationships with others, while 31 percent experienced decline, for a net improvement of 8 percent.
- *Responding with forgiveness:* 37 percent remained the same on this issue. 26 percent saw improvement, and 37 percent felt they had regressed, for a net decline of 9 percent.
- *Jesus as sinless:* 54 percent continued to hold the correct view of Jesus. 14 percent became more doctrinally sound, and 32 percent became more heretical, for a net decline of 18 percent. This represents a dramatic shift in the beliefs of young adults.

Once again we see both positive and negative changes in our sample. But the dramatic shifts, especially among young adults, show significant instability in beliefs and practices.

Church Dropouts and Church Switchers

I was surprised to discover that 13 percent of our overall sample completely dropped out of church within the twelve-month period of time. Another 9 percent switched to a different church, and the remaining 78 percent remained in the same church.

When we analyzed the specifics about those who dropped out of church, we discovered the following:

- There is a strong correlation between the belief system and the dropout rate. Four percent of those who identify themselves as evangelical dropped out of church while 16 percent of nonevangelicals dropped out. Five percent of those identified as "born again" dropped out, but 23 percent of those who are not "born again" dropped out.
- Those who dropped out of church are twelve times as likely to see a net decrease in their SFI scores. (We do not know whether dropping out of church caused SFI scores to drop, or whether changes in belief caused some to drop out of church, or a combination of the two, but we do know that a decreased SFI and leaving church are related.)
- We observed a small net positive in SFI scores for those who switched churches.

I don't know any pastor who would be happy with so many people dropping out of church. This is not a good sign. In most churches there is a front door and a back door. This study only reflects the backdoor problem because our entire sample was attending at least once per month when we surveyed them at the beginning of the study. Since we have been studying individuals, we do not have access to information related to the representative churches. Consequently we do not know if there was a net gain or net loss of members in these churches. What we do know is that there is significant "churn." Twenty-two percent of our sample was either in a different church than they were a year ago, or out of church altogether.

Perceptions of Growth

We asked our sample of churchgoers if they thought they grew spiritually over the past year, and then compared their perceptions to their survey scores. Here is the question we asked.

Think about your own spiritual life today and compare it to how things were one year ago. Which of the following is true for you?

Here is how they responded:

- 22 percent said they had "grown a lot"
- 33 percent said they had "grown a little"
- 31 percent said "no change"
- 9 percent said they "declined a little"
- 4 percent said they "declined a lot"

We discovered a problem with these self-perceptions of growth or decline. Fifty-five percent of our respondents believed they had grown spiritually in the last year. However, based on the SFI scores, only 3.5 percent showed a statistically significant level of growth.

On the other hand, only 8 percent of those who said they had declined spiritually actually showed significantly lower SFI scores.

This is not surprising since it is human nature to evaluate ourselves in subjective ways. It's like the couple going to a marriage counselor. The husband or wife may at first rate their marriage in a positive way, but when exposed to a careful analysis of their actual marriage practices, there is a large gap between their perception and reality.

Also, analyzing the respondents' comments about what they believe is evidence of their spiritual growth is instructive.

- "I'm much calmer."
- "I'm a better friend."
- "I'm a better person and more caring."
- "My marriage is better."
- "I am better at running my household to care for my family; I made some changes to facilitate hospitality in our home."
- "I am more tolerant of people."
- "There aren't many outward 'signs.' The growth I experienced is manifested more on a personal level."

These comments may or may not show spiritual growth, but they do show that these respondents did not have the same definition of spiritual growth as measured by our SFI.

Importance of Involvement

We observed a statistically significant correlation between overall spiritual growth and level of church involvement. We measured various kinds of church involvement including worship attendance, participation in Sunday school or small groups, and serving in some lay leadership position.

- Those who attend church less than weekly are substantially more likely to experience decline in spiritual growth as those who attend weekly.
- Those who are not involved in some type of lay leadership are substantially more likely to experience decline as those who are.
- Those who do not participate in Sunday school or some type of Christian education class are substantially more likely to experience decline as those who do.
- Those who do not participate in a small group are more likely to experience decline as those who do.

Life Change Events

We discovered that almost three out of ten of those we surveyed experienced a significant life change between 2007 and 2008: marital status: 8 percent; children in or out of the home: 12 percent; place of residence: 17 percent; education level: 7 percent. This doesn't even include those who went through a job change or loss, the death of a loved one or friend, illness, etc. Furthermore, as I read the transcripts from our phone interviews, I noticed a significant trend in how often individuals attributed their spiritual growth to some life event that God used to get their attention or spur them on. Some of these stories will be highlighted later in this chapter.

Activities and Spiritual Growth

In our second survey, we asked our sample the following question:

Which of the following (if any) have you done in the past year?

Then we listed several activities.

The table below shows the percentage of people who participated in each activity within the past year. We also wanted to show the level of involvement by those who believed they had grown significantly. Lastly, we wanted to show possible differences in the level of involvement between "evangelicals" and "nonevangelicals."

Type of Activity	Percent of the Entire Sample	Percent of High Growth	Percent of Evangelicals	Percent of Non-evangelicals
Participated in a New Believer's Class	6	6	6	6
Participated in a Spiritual Gifts Class	25	37	28	24
Was discipled by a more mature person	16	16	16	16
Discipled another Christian	20	27	25	18
Read a spiritual growth book	48	60	60	44
Read a book about the Bible	47	60	60	43
*Attended a conference or seminar	21	26	30	18
Participated in an international missions trip	3	3	2	3
Participated in a domestic missions trip	6	7	6	6
Participated in a class with homework	32	47	47	27
Reached out to help a person in need	72	76	82	68

*The conference or seminar had to relate to some aspect of spiriutal development

I noted earlier that we found a significant correlation between overall spiritual maturity and involvement in spiritual growth and service activities, and there are a few other specific things regarding the table above that deserves comment.

- One fifth of our sample indicated they had been discipled one-on-one by a more mature Christian. This is a surprisingly high percentage. We do not know about the quality or substance of the discipling process, but so many of our churchgoers perceiving themselves to have been discipled within the past year is unexpected.
- Nearly half of our sample invested time reading either books related to spiritual growth or knowledge of the Bible. This is a very encouraging statistic.
- A third of our sample participated in some type of spiritual growth class that was substantive enough to require outside homework.
- More than two thirds of our sample made efforts to help someone in need within the past year. This is a positive finding.
- Evangelicals were more involved in most of these activities.
- I was surprised that nonevangelicals edged out evangelicals when it came to involvement in international missions trips.

Perceptions of Impact

On our second survey, we asked our sample the following question:

How much positive impact has each of the following had on your personal spiritual growth over the past year?

Then we listed several activities.

The table below provides a summary of these perceptions of impact upon those who perceived themselves to have high levels of growth during the past year.

Type of Activity	Major Impact
Personal prayer life	85 percent
The prayers of others on your behalf	71 percent
Church attendance	87 percent
Bible reading	91 percent
Reading books	59 percent
Participating in outreach to others	50 percent
Participating in a small group	76 percent
Participating in Sunday school	65 percent
Mentoring someone	55 percent
Watching videos or listening to CDs	38 percent
Programs on radio or television	35 percent
Attending a conference, seminar, or retreat	41 percent
Being mentored by another mature believer	81 percent
Involvement in lay leadership in the church	58 percent

Note: When possible to determine, we only included the evaluation of impact for those who actually participated in the activity in question.

As with our analysis of much of the information provided by our churchgoers throughout this book, these results provoke mixed reactions. On the one hand, it is encouraging that the most fundamental aspects of normal Christian practices are having an impact on the lives of many Christians. Prayer, church involvement, reading the Bible, participating in outreach, etc., . . . are perceived as valuable. Another way of wording this is that these activities are "effectual" and valued by churchgoers.

The downside is that even though the majority of those believing they were growing spiritually believed these common practices had an impact, I would like to see close to 100 percent of them seeing these activities having an impact on their lives.

One More Look at the Seven Domains

As indicated earlier, when comparing the SFI responses from 2007 with those from 2008, there is little evidence of overall spiritual development in our sample of churchgoers. When analyzing the results by domains, the responses to the majority of the questions were similar from year to year. Below I will provide some examples within each domain where we saw evidence of minor, yet noteworthy change. After each question I will provide the percentage of net change. For instance, if 30 percent of our sample improved on any given issue, and 20 percent regressed, then the net positive change is 10 percent.

Domain One: The Learning Quotient

- "I tend to accept the constructive criticism and correction of other Christians." (While nearly half of our sample did not change in the way they replied to this question, we did observe a 9 percent net improvement in the answers.)
- "How often do you read your Bible?" (We saw a net increase of 6 percent increase in the frequency of Bible reading.)

Domain Two: The Obedience Quotient

- "I try to avoid situations in which I might be tempted to think or do immoral things." (5 percent improvement)
- "When I realize that I have a choice between 'my way' and 'God's way,' I usually choose my way. (6 percent improvement)

Domain Three: The Serving Quotient

- "How often do you pray for fellow Christians you know?" (9 percent improvement)
- "About what percentage of your total annual income do you contribute to charitable causes or organizations, including your local church and other nonprofit organizations?" (6 percent decrease)

Domain Four: The Evangelism Quotient

- There was a 4 percent improvement in the number of those we surveyed who shared the gospel with someone at least twice in the past six months.
- "While interacting with others on a normal basis, I seek opportunities to speak out about Jesus Christ." (Net improvement of 8 percent)
- "You have a personal responsibility to share your religious beliefs about Jesus Christ with non-Christians." (Net improvement of 8 percent)

- On a negative note, our respondents were less likely in 2008 than in 2007 to have invited someone to church in the past six months. (47 percent said "not at all" in 2007 compared to 52 percent in 2008)

Although the amount of improvement is small, it is encouraging to see some positive movement related to evangelism. As our culture continues to move further away from biblical truth, it is encouraging to see churchgoers moving, if even slightly, toward more intentional evangelism. The unfortunate trend toward less effort to get the unchurched to attend church should be met with positive encouragement toward the "invest and invite" strategy discussed earlier in this book. People are open to attending church if invited by a friend or family member.

Domain Five: The Faith Quotient

- "During difficult circumstances I sometimes doubt that God loves me and will provide for my life." (Net decline of 6 percent)
- "My life is often filled with anxiety and worry." (Net decline of 8 percent)
- "I express praise and gratitude to God even in difficult circumstances." (Net improvement of 8 percent)

Domain Six: Seeking God

- "Often during the worship part of the church service I find myself just going through the motions." (Net decline of 8 percent)

- "How often do you set aside time for prayer?" (Net improvement of 8 percent)

Domain Seven: The Relational Quotient

- "I generally do not share personal things such as feelings, joys, struggles, and needs with my Christian friends." (Net decline of 8 percent)
- "In a typical month, about how many times (if any) do you attend a worship service at your church?" (In 2008 we found that 12 percent of our sample selected "none" as their response compared to only 3 percent in 2007.)
- "Spiritual matters do not tend to come up as a normal part of my daily conversations with other Christians." (Net decline of 10 percent)
- "When I am wronged by others, I often have trouble responding with a forgiving attitude." (Net decline of 10 percent)

Biblical Beliefs

I dedicated an entire chapter to the doctrinal and theological beliefs, or lack thereof, of our sample of churchgoers. When comparing the results from 2007 and 2008, there was little change when lumping all of the doctrinal scores together. Four percent of the entire sample demonstrated improvement in doctrinal soundness and 3 percent showed erosion in these beliefs.

We already documented the volatility of beliefs, especially when looking at those below the age of thirty. We also observed some fluctuation and instability of beliefs within the category of those who dropped out of church. When looking at each doctrine separately, we found a few noteworthy changes.

- "The Bible teaches that participation in a local church is a necessity of any believer who desires to be truly obedient to God." We found that 31 percent of our sample grew in affirmation of the necessity of church involvement and 24 percent decreased in their affirmation of this belief. (Net positive of 7 percent)
- "Every person is born a sinner due to the sin of Adam being passed on to all persons." We determined that 20 percent of the sample moved toward a biblical perspective on the doctrine of original sin. Fourteen percent moved away from this belief. (Net positive of 6 percent)
- "The Bible is the written Word of God and is totally accurate in all that it teaches." Twenty-one percent of our sample moved toward a higher view of the integrity and inerrancy of Scripture. Fifteen percent experienced an erosion of conviction about God's Word. (Net positive of 6 percent)
- "Jesus may have committed sins while in human form on earth." Surprisingly, this is the only doctrinal question where there was a net decline in biblical perspective. Fourteen percent of the sample moved toward a view that Jesus was sinless. However, 21 percent regressed on this issue. (Net decline of 7 percent)

Personal Testimonies of Growth

Quantitative studies are extremely helpful in identifying trends in various fields of inquiry. I hope that this book has captured some important insights pertaining to the status of Protestantism in America. However, there are limits to what a survey can provide. Reading the results of a survey can leave you wondering about the real person on the other side of the data.

With this in mind, we added a third phase to our study. When we conducted the second survey, we asked for permission to follow-up in person, by either phone or e-mail, with some of the people who grew spiritually over the course of a year. Approximately 700 out of the 1,044 who took the second survey gave us permission to follow up with them. Of this group, we identified nearly 100 who experienced significant spiritual growth over the past year. We were able to make contact with about one third of these individuals.

In our phone and e-mail interviews, we sought to capture their personal stories of spiritual formation. We asked them to identify what they believe contributed the most to their recent growth. Here is a summary of the responses.

Life Events

The most frequently mentioned issue related to their spiritual growth had to do with some sort of unexpected life event that God used to draw them to deeper conviction and pursuit of Him.

- Tara has been going through a painful divorce and custody battle and her father is terminally ill. She specifically mentioned the impact of the book *Beloved Disciple* by Beth Moore that in part deals with not living in defeat.

- Herb referenced the death of a relative and the way God used that to spur him toward faith.
- Caty said this about a local church ministering to her after the death of a loved one: "Well, the church was there. I mean they supported us. They helped us and they prayed for us and with us."
- Diana told us the painful story of her husband leaving her after eighteen years of marriage, but how God sustained her. "There is a lesson in this. And I always try to get a lesson out of what I go through. So it doesn't make me get discouraged to the point where I would leave serving God. No. I mean, because I believe that once you fall in love with Jesus, you cannot . . . you just can go through anything. You can make it through anything. But you have to fall in love with God in order to be able to do that."
- David explained how his wife's unexpected pregnancy was used by God. "Nearly a year ago my wife and I had a baby girl. It was not a planned pregnancy, but it was not unwelcome. We went through a major 'shock to the system' when we found out and it presented opportunity for growth in many ways. I have never been one to fear the unknown, primarily due to my faith and acceptance of the will of God in my life. That being said, I was tested during the same time frame. I eventually wore down and had to ask God for help."

- Kim told us how her fight with breast cancer brought her closer to God.
- Susan told the story of her sister's death.
- Bobbi recounted her coming close to death due to cancer.
- Joanne's unmarried teenage daughter who lived with her became pregnant and then their house was ruined in a flood.
- Sandy is struggling to take care of her mother who was debilitated by a stroke and then she (Sandy) was diagnosed with multiple sclerosis.

These and other stories point out the fact that life is often filled with unexpected and tragic events. God is at work in the midst of these difficult times. He brings good out of bad situations. He is close to those who are hurting and who seek Him. Suffering provides a unique opportunity to seek God and deepen relationships with fellow believers.

Exposure to God's Word

Almost everyone we interviewed referred to the powerful impact of God's Word upon his or her life. We heard many stories of people who began to read and study God's Word. Others spoke of the impact of their pastor's sermons, or of some Christian book. Others mentioned a Sunday school class, or a small group Bible study centered on learning the Bible. Here are a few quotes related to the impact of God's Word on those with whom we spoke.

"I guess being able to read the Bible. Well, see, I'm reading it and possibly when I get to work early I sit in the car and read some passages." (Dan)

"Every morning I spend a half hour reading the Bible and in prayer. Then once I get on the computer, I've got about another half hour of online Scriptures I read through various Internet sources." (Harold)

"Our pastor's excitement and passion for doing God's work is inspiring. He preaches both on topics and on Bible passages. I've been making an effort to read the Bible at least once a day for a good amount of time and sometimes more. Sunday school has helped to hold me accountable for staying up on reading because I have to take part in discussion. We also memorize Scripture in Sunday school. I've also been listening to sermons online from various seminaries which helps me to stay God-conscious throughout the week and not only on the weekends." (John)

"We always pray and read the Bible daily as well as search to make sure what our Pastor has said is true." (Les)

"This older lady started asking me to go to church with her, and I decided to go with her where her son was the pastor of the church. And I went, and the next thing I knew I joined the church. And I enjoy the church, and you know I've been going every Sunday. So my daughter bought me this book

> called *My Time With God*, and I read it every day and a whole lot. And I've really grown a whole lot since I moved my membership over into another church . . . You know, you go to church, and you take your Bible, and sometimes; and I'm one of them, when you come from church, you put it down and you don't pick it up. Well, I mean you should be reading it, but I didn't. I'd just take it over when it was time to go back on Sunday. But since she bought me this little book, I read it every morning. I do that before I do anything. I've learned a lot that I didn't know. I never thought I could read something like that every day." (Annie)

The Importance of the Church

The vast majority of those we interviewed spoke highly of their church involvement. They referenced the importance of fellowship, prayer, preaching, and service. Here are some statements we heard about the church.

> "Well, like I said. It was mostly the church. The people would come up to me and they would talk to me and they would hug you even though they didn't know you . . . It was just the way they welcomed us. They didn't know us and they would walk right up to us and hug us and shake our hand and it made us feel like one of them." (Caty)

> "There are a lot of sermon series that we have been through over the last year. We go through a series about every three months or so. It goes for 40 minutes and it gets real intense.

Plus there is a Bible study that comes right afterwards for those of us who are interested in it of which I did become a part of." (Harold)

"My pastor preaches and teaches (he does a little bit of both) and this did help with my spiritual growth. I am also trying more and more to read and understand the Bible. I have a good friend who has always been involved in church and she influenced me to start going to church and helps me understand things in the Bible." (Crystal)

"I think a lot of it has to do with my recent membership at a church. I've been given a solid church family where I get a lot of encouragement and where I'm held accountable with how I live my life." (John)

"As a backslidden Christian, I rededicated my life to Jesus. Sermons have been very helpful. I always strive to live the fruit of the Spirit and to increase my prayer and reading time. I strive to increase reading and prayer time. Prayers have become more intense and more specific. I read, watch or listen to other resource materials as much as possible." (Dan)

"Well, I would say that the thing that . . . the number one thing that has contributed to my spiritual growth has been finding a church in my area. My husband and I have been searching for a few years and we visited several churches and every time we would go to a church we would find something just wasn't . . . something was lacking. And we found a church close to our house and we started attending. And we are very happy. We felt . . . we really felt the presence of God there. Just going there really inspired me to get closer to God." (Tara)

"You know, so when I first go here we were going to a church, and I just never really was pleased with it, but it was mom's church so we went. And there were a lot of problems in the church. And then we kind of started visiting around, and actually together we've settled on one church. We both love it. It opened its doors. We've been going to it for a year and a half now. And I love the pastor. I mean you know you go in and sometimes you don't think about maybe little things that are bothering you, and it's funny how so many times you go in there and that's what he's preaching on that day. So it really is a church, and the people, we do so much with them. We go to the different services and the different gatherings that we have and stuff. So you know we're really involved." (Susan)

Other Factors

Time and space does not allow me to tell numerous other testimonies of God transforming lives. We listened to stories involving the power of prayer, friendship, and involvement in service. Some told us that sharing the gospel with others caused their growth.

Some mentioned how their spouse was instrumental in encouraging their pursuit of God. Several parents mentioned the powerful motivation of having children and the need to provide them with spiritual instruction in the home and church.

Conclusion

It is abundantly clear that God is at work in the lives of people in every state, city, and town. We can see much evidence of people seeking after God and longing to be part of a church where they can learn, grow, and develop meaningful relationships. We know that God's Word, when faithfully listened to, read, and studied, changes lives. We can see how important the church is in creating opportunities for spiritual formation. By listening to some of our churchgoers share their stories, we know that God uses life events, even the really tough ones, to draw people to Himself.

We can also see the enemy, Satan and his forces, causing uncertainty and confusion. People are shifting in what they believe. Many are dropping out of church. Some are distancing themselves from the very people they need the most.

The battle rages on every day. Many people are hurting, some are seeking, and others are just plain old stuck. We, the body of Christ, have the opportunity to be used by God in reaching out to those who do not know Him and in loving and encouraging one another. In the final chapter I will offer some thoughts about how and why to invest deeply in the lives of others. The future of the church can and must be healthier and stronger. Much is at stake.

Chapter Eleven

So Where Do We Go from Here?

Takeaways and Applications

In Tough Times Leaders Step It Up

I recently stood at the gas pump filling my car and found myself mesmerized by watching the dollar meter rapidly click from one number to the next. It seems like just last year I was paying a little more than a dollar for gas, and now I am paying more than four times that amount. This problem is not limited to gas stations and my thinning wallet; it is indicative of a greater reality. Currently in America, we are experiencing very difficult days. We are in the midst of a global war on terrorism. Our economy is in trouble. The housing market is struggling. Energy prices are skyrocketing. The cost of living is going up every month.

Amidst these difficulties, Americans are crying out for leadership. Many people believe our political leaders are not exercising leadership and doing everything possible for the good of the country. Difficult times require strong, passionate leadership. It is unacceptable for leaders to be focused on self-promotion or petty political party interests. This is not the time for self-interest. This is not a time for mediocrity or trying to solve old problems with the same worn-out solutions.

This is the time for focused, passionate, properly motivated leaders working on solutions. We need a return to the enduring words from the Apollo 13 crisis, "Let's work the problem!"

The title, *The Shape of Faith to Come*, could imply that this book is an attempt to identify future trends. Many books attempt that, and they usually convey the message that we should submissively follow the current trend in order to be successful. This is not my intent. Leaders do not follow trends, they determine them. I am calling out for spiritual leaders to follow God's revealed plan for fostering biblical faith.

Without overstating the human side of the equation, the shape of faith to come will be significantly shaped by how seriously individual Christians and spiritual leaders exert godly influence and get on with the task of making biblical disciples. There is no doubt that cultural trends shape our lives and our churches, but we must not be molded by popular opinion. We cannot determine everything, but we can, by God's grace and according to His will and ways, help create the shape of faith to come.

Some Important Clarifications

Throughout this book I have used the terms *descriptive* and *prescriptive*. Due to the nature of the study that led to this book, much of the content is descriptive in that we have analyzed and described the beliefs, attitudes, and practices of our sample of churchgoers. I have sought to provide some prescriptive or application oriented remarks throughout, and in this final chapter, I am seeking to consolidate various ideas into a strategy for spiritual formation in our churches. I have tried to avoid an overly "preachy" tone and writing as if I have all of the solutions. Nonetheless, these are difficult times and many of us need to be challenged to step up.

Before going further, I want to provide some context and clarification:

- Some of the prescriptive advice is based on what we learned from our study. (Keep in mind that our study was not of church leaders or of churches; it was of individuals.)
- Some of my remarks here are my personal perspective based upon more than twenty years of church pastoral/staff experience, plus several years of teaching and consulting other leaders and churches.
- I tried to avoid loading this book with a lot of "how-to" methods, programs, or resources. As the old saying goes, "Methods are many, principles are few. Methods always

change, principles never do." I could describe in detail what I have done in the past, or what some church is doing currently, only to find that some of this advice would quickly become outdated.

Lastly, we are expending much effort in the development of the SFI (Spiritual Formation Inventory) so that you and other leaders can access a biblically based and relevant diagnostic tool that will provide individual Christians and leaders with a means of assessing spiritual formation for themselves, or for an entire church. The report that will be generated from the use of the SFI will contain very specific advice and will direct you to a number of resources and guidelines that can help you or your church implement specific discipleship strategies. As stated in the Introduction of this book, you can go to www.lifeway.com/sfi to obtain more information about using the diagnostic tool.

Now, let us move toward some conclusions, challenges, and passionate pleas.

Soil Test

Two years ago my wife and I moved into our new home. We loved the backyard and the open commons area that provided a lot of green space and trees. The only negative is the grass in our backyard which looks like it was planted by a church committee. It is a combination of Zoysia, Bermuda, fescue, and several other grasses and weeds. It drives me crazy. The worst part is a six-foot circle where absolutely nothing grows, not even weeds. Now I am not an agronomist, but I know there is something wrong with the soil. It will not fix itself. I am going to have to intervene. It does little good to say, "Well, nothing wants to grow." I have to help provide a proper environment for growth.

I do not intend to place all of the responsibility on the pastor or other spiritual leaders. Sadly, some of those who attend church will not grow spiritually no matter what leaders do. Some churches would survive the rapture predominately intact.

Nonetheless, I believe most of the time the overall spiritual climate of a church is largely determined by the pastor and other key leaders.

Authenticity and Credibility

We cannot take people where we have not been, or where we have not been in a long time. While I have met many authentic leaders who are spiritually vibrant and who lead by example, I have also observed too many who fail the "sniff test." The sniff test has to do with ideas, perspectives, and behavior, or stated differently, KNOWING—BEING—DOING.[1] Leaders must possess a biblical worldview, godly character, and actions that reflect and authenticate both.

KNOWING includes, but goes beyond, theological reflection and beliefs. It is essential that we embrace biblical doctrine, but we must not allow ourselves to divorce doctrine from our daily attitudes and perspectives. The kind of leader who will impact others is the kind that passes the "sniff test" of basic godliness. I am not talking about perfection. I am speaking of the consistent display of Christlike character. I am talking about BEING. This is the bedrock of authenticity and integrity. Much can be gained from a renewed focus on clear biblical expectations regarding the character, heart, and motives of those called by God to shepherd the flock. The Bible has more than a little to say in its description of who is qualified to teach, serve, and lead.

Demonstrating the fruit of the Holy Spirit in how we act and treat others is the DOING part of the equation. If the knowing and being are solid and God honoring, the doing will follow.

Who Gets the Credit?

For fear of placing too much importance on the human side of leadership, I must emphasize that only God causes spiritual formation. Leaders can influence the environment, but only God can change hearts, minds, and character.

> I planted, Apollos watered, but God gave the growth. So then neither the one who plants nor the one who waters is anything, but only God who gives the growth. (1 Cor. 3:6–7)

With this understanding, I want to highlight several factors essential for moving our churches toward spiritual productivity.

Raise the Bar

I was on an airplane recently and one of the persons next to me on the flight was reading the book *Do Hard Things: A Teenage Rebellion Against Low Expectations.* I was intrigued by the title and as soon as I got back to my office I ordered the book. The book is written by teenage twin brothers who claim that many of today's young adults are rebelling against low expectations.

> "Society doesn't expect much of anything from young people during their teen years—except trouble. And it certainly doesn't expect competence, maturity, or productivity. The saddest part is that, as the culture around them has come to expect less and less, young people have dropped to meet those lower expectations. Since most of us have grown up surrounded by these low expectations, meeting them is like breathing to us—we never give it a thought. And we never realize what we've lost."[2]

The Harris twins go into detail about the tragedy of low expectations and the power of high ones. In many ways the same diagnosis could be offered regarding the church. Many of our churches swim in the pool of low expectations. The good news is most believers will rise to the level of expectation.

Leaders are the key. Leaders set the tone for the church. Leaders help create the soil conditions for spiritual productivity. Credibility comes from authenticity. Credible leaders stand upon the foundation of God's authoritative Word and call others to join the journey of spiritual formation and biblical discipleship. This is how it works. This is how it has always worked.

Sometimes It Is the Obvious

I recently walked into a large bookstore and saw a huge section of books under the heading "Diet and Weight Loss." There were hundreds of titles related to losing weight. However, casual observation shows that the availability of literature is not leading to success. After billions of dollars spent in America on weight loss, it comes down to a very simple and basic truth: eating less and exercising more. We search for new ways to make this look easy or attractive, but the reality remains that you have to burn more calories than you take in. Some things may not be easy, but they are not complicated.

Similarly, when it comes to spiritual formation, what we discovered is not complicated. Statistically, ***the number one issue*** correlated to higher maturity scores was the discipline of ***daily Bible reading***. Being consistent in this discipline can be challenging, but it is doable.

After obtaining the results from our statistician related to the influence of Bible reading, I reflected back on my years of attending and serving churches. I tried to recall how much emphasis others or I placed upon getting church members to read their Bibles. My conclusion is that this was an emphasis, but not emphasized enough.

How can we as leaders make Bible reading a stronger emphasis?

- Set the example. How much time do you spend in God's Word (other than for sermon preparation)? Do you recall how, early in your Christian experience, God's Word was alive and powerful? Most of us need to deepen and strengthen this discipline. Your people can tell if you are in God's Word. It is like one of the Gatorade commercials where athletes sweat Gatorade after consuming it in large quantities. It will be evident if you are a man or woman of the Word. It will come out of your pores.
- Make Bible reading (as well as all of the spiritual disciplines) a major part of both new believer training and new member orientation. Never assume anyone new to your church has been adequately trained in the spiritual disciplines. Make sure you have someone, either on staff or a lay volunteer, who is responsible for this training. Provide your people with Bible reading tools and materials. It is no less important than our military being equipped with the proper weapons and resources. Make it essential!
- Emphasize Bible reading from the pulpit. I know that you cannot turn the pulpit into a promotional platform for everything. Nevertheless, remember, reading the Bible was the top factor correlated to spiritual maturity. Talk about it during worship. Occasionally preach and teach on this discipline. Draw attention, through illustrations and testimonies, to those who drink deeply from God's Word. Talk about the fruit of Bible reading in your own life.

- Consider launching a church-wide Bible reading emphasis like a "Read through the Bible in a Year" program.
- Provide access to tools like journals, Bibles with a 365-day reading format, Bible reading plans, devotionals, and books that teach believers how to properly read and interpret the Bible.
- Make sure all of the ministries in your church emphasize Bible reading: children's ministry, student ministry, women's ministry, men's ministry, etc.
- Help parents emphasize this in the home.

The Plumb Line

We noted earlier that it is easy for people to think they are more spiritual than reality would support. This "perception gap" reveals the need for preaching, teaching, meaningful fellowship, and accountability. We are all subject to self-deception. It is easy to play the game of comparing my strengths to your weaknesses. We are also subject to judging ourselves by our intentions, but others by their actions. God's Word, when properly understood and taught, cuts through false subjectivity and self-deception. One friend of mine used the metaphor of a plumb line. A plumb line is a string with a weight on one end. When hanging down, the plumb line will be perfectly aligned vertically and you can use it to expose anything that is not "true."

God's Word exposes things that are not true or perfectly aligned. It is our fallen human nature to think we are better, more mature or healthier spiritually than we really are. We must expose our thoughts, attitudes, and actions to God's Word. This is for our own good. We are never served by believing something false. A good friend of mine often uses the phrase "facts are our friends." The more accurately we see ourselves, the more we are able to align with God and His standards. It is the responsibility of spiritual leaders to faithfully, yet humbly, communicate God's standards and call others to strive to live accordingly.

It Starts at Home

Recently I was speaking with a twenty-two-year-old who seemed to be very solid spiritually and theologically. I asked him what one issue most affected his spiritual growth. He immediately said that growing up in a Christian home was the factor that most influenced his spiritual development.

Our Spiritual Formation Study did not investigate the influence of the home.[3] However, LifeWay Research has conducted quantitative research that highlights the significance of the home environment. In the Teenage Dropout Study, we analyzed the factors that contributed to teens dropping out of church as well as the factors that influenced their remaining active in church. Regarding the latter, here were some important observations.[4]

- One of the most predictive elements correlated to a teenager not dropping out of church was that at age seventeen both parents were still married to each other and both attended church.

- 39 percent of those who returned to church after a period of absence indicated that the influence of parents and family was a major cause for returning.
- 43 percent of those who never left church indicated that the example set by parents and family was a major cause for never dropping out of church.

Over the past few years, a debate has arisen related to the role of parents in the spiritual formation of their children. What is not debated is that parents should embrace the main responsibility for the spiritual nurture of their children. Additionally, there are few who will debate that many parents are not stepping up to this important task.

What is debated is the way many churches approach the discipleship of children and teenagers. A few leaders have been very outspoken against the age-graded strategies of many churches. While I differ with many of their radical and unhelpful "solutions," I agree with their conviction that parents are to be the primary source of spiritual formation in the home.

Church leaders need to develop clear strategies for equipping parents to teach and disciple their children.

It Moves to the Body: Corporate Worship

The corporate worship experience of a church sets the spiritual tone for the community of faith. Gathering for fellowship, prayer, preaching, and worship is indispensable for the development of faith. The next two verses are not a clear reference to a worship service per se, but they contain a description of the Christian faith that most certainly pertains to what the body of Christ does when gathered.

> Speaking to one another in psalms, hymns, and spiritual songs, singing and making music to the Lord in your heart, giving thanks always for everything to God the Father in the name of our Lord Jesus Christ, submitting to one another in the fear of Christ. (Eph. 5:19–21)

> Let the message about the Messiah dwell richly among you, teaching and admonishing one another in all wisdom, and singing psalms, hymns, and spiritual songs, with gratitude in your hearts to God. And whatever you do, in word or in deed, do everything in the name of the Lord Jesus, giving thanks to God the Father through Him. (Col. 3:16–17)

Warm fellowship, joyous praise, corporate prayer, and reverence for the Word are all essential for spiritual formation. It is tragic when we allow our worship services to become routine, dry, predictable, and passionless. It is also sad when they become personality driven in such a way that Christ is not the focus. It is not about the preacher hitting a home run with his sermon or those singing doing so with perfection. It is about Jesus being the focus and our people being edified. Too many of our worship services have become spectator sports rather than true corporate worship.

In many ways preaching sets the tone for a church. The preaching ministry of the church must be substantive. God's Word transforms hearts, minds, and character. We must avoid the temptation merely to draw a crowd with entertaining talks. Pastors are called to teach and preach the precepts of God. I believe that expositional preaching allows the preacher to be true to God's Word. I do believe preachers must carefully explain what God's Word means and how it is to be lived out. Application is essential. Preaching is not about a pastor proving how much he knows and feeling good about his sermon. Rather it is about life transformation. It is about people understanding and applying God's Word.

A Discipleship Strategy

Every church needs some type of disciple making strategy, other than just falling into the routines represented on the weekly church calendar. It is not too difficult to come up with a strategy that sounds good and looks good on paper. But it takes a tremendous amount of energy and focus to break away from the inertia of the normal church practices.

Going beyond strategy, church leaders need intentionality, accountability, and sustained focus.

Strategy ▶ Intentionality ▶ Accountability ▶ Focus

Strategy

I taught leadership classes at a seminary for seven years. One of the major assignments I required of my students was the development of a *strategic plan*. Students normally dreaded this assignment. Why? Because some students loved reflecting more on theology than actually placing concerted energy toward applying their theology to the practice of ministry.

Each semester a few students expressed concern that the development of a strategic plan reflected an attitude of "pragmatism" and was an exercise filled with human ingenuity rather than trusting in the power of God (a fear that can be justified if not approached in a biblical fashion and with proper motives). Some held to the attractive call, "Just preach the Word." They were fine with applying a strategy of exegesis when developing a sermon, but were not all that excited about developing a comprehensive strategy for evangelism and discipleship.

The good news is that not a semester would go by without some former student in the field of ministry making contact with me to express appreciation for the strategic planning assignment. They were actually implementing the plan, or at least some version of it, and seeing the results.

It is beyond the scope of this book to offer a "one size fits all" strategy. I must also state that there is no silver bullet that makes the practice of disciple-making easy. What I do want to offer are some principles of effective strategy.

- First and foremost, any strategy for the church must be grounded in solid theology. The Bible has a lot to say about the nature and purpose of the church. If you decide to complete the Spiritual Formation Inventory, you will be directed to some excellent sources related to ecclesiology (the Doctrine of the Church) and other helpful materials related to thinking about the church from a distinctly biblical point of view.

- A strategy must be simple and yet comprehensive. There is not just one way to foster spiritual formation. Many approaches can be used to motivate and equip believers in spiritual development. However, there must be a clear and intentional process of maturation. Thom Rainer and Eric Geiger have provided church leaders with significant insight in the book *Simple Church* by creating a vision for a disciple-making process built on four keys concepts:

Clarity ▶ Movement ▶ Alignment ▶ Focus[5]

I will not attempt to summarize this book, but if you have not read it, I urge you to do so. This book goes way beyond the concept of simplicity. It calls leaders to make sure the churches they serve and lead have an intentional and clear process that moves the entire body of Christ incrementally toward spiritual maturity. It is too easy for churches to continue week after week through the same routines, regardless of the existence, or lack, of fruitfulness.

Intentionality

I have served three different churches for more than twenty years combined. I have led or participated in a number of staff planning retreats. It is relatively easy for church leaders to identify and form strategic plans. But how easy it is to go back to the daily demands of church ministry and lose intentionality.

Intentionality involves specificity. It means that ministry plans are stated in measurable terms. It is easy to be vague. For instance, it is easy for me to say I want to be a better husband. But this intent is not very measurable. It is a lot different if I say, "I am going to set aside time every day during dinner to tell my wife about my day" (something she has expressed that is important to her).

For the purpose of this book, intentionality means that various people will have very specific responsibility for different aspects of the disciple-making strategy. Ultimately it is the pastor's responsibility to make sure that *intentions* get executed.

Accountability

This is a term that most of us do not like. However, in my experience I have grown to believe that we all need some type of accountability. When we conducted our Standout Church Study, one of the things that really stood out to me was how the pastors of the nineteen churches we visited held the staff members and lay leaders accountable with reference to evangelism. As the old saying goes, "People do what we inspect, not what we expect."

I have personally seen the harm that can come to a church when the leaders pretty much do what they want without any form of accountability. Wise leaders initiate some type of accountability.

Focus

A great example of focus is the golfer Tiger Woods. He possesses an amazing ability to focus. When many golfers approach a putt on the eighteenth green at the end of the tournament, they feel the pressure mounting and become distracted. Tiger has the ability to remove all distractions from his mind and focus completely on the task at hand. The result of this focus is obvious to those who watch golf. Tiger regularly makes incredible putts on the eighteenth green to win tournaments.

Effectiveness in the church is far more important than winning golf tournaments. *Focus is strategy held by intentionality and accountability.* Focus implies that those who lead will refuse to allow anything to keep them from implementing the most essential and important aspects of church ministry.

So, with strategy, intentionality, accountability, and focus in place there is good reason to believe that spiritual formation will take on new and stronger forms in the life of the church. Be patient. It takes time to change the culture of a church or organization. In my experience it takes three to five years for the culture of the church to begin to clearly reflect the passions and priorities of the key leaders. Only on rare occasions have I failed to see this pattern emerge. What leaders embrace will eventually be embraced by the people.

Some Essentials

As I have expressed more than once, I am not attempting to offer a programmatic approach to spiritual formation and disciple making. Some churches have made effective use of structured programs like *Master Life*. Others have used Navigator programs and materials. Some rely on home groups or Sunday school classes. I know some leaders who have relied almost exclusively upon one-on-one disciple-making strategies.

There is not one way to do this. I believe a comprehensive approach that includes preaching, discipleship classes, small groups, men's ministry, women's ministry, parenting classes, etc., can all contribute to conforming believers into the image of Christ.

When it comes to strategy, what follows are a few things that deserve special attention.

Serve as a Role Model

As I have repeatedly stated, spiritual leaders must lead by example. The phrase "Speed of the Leader: Speed of the Team" is a timeless truth. A classic book that can refresh your desire to lead by example is the book *Spiritual Leadership* by Oswald Sanders.

Practice Personal Disciple Making

The concept is simple but powerful. A spiritual leader makes it a priority to invest deeply in the lives of a few people. There is no one way to do this. I personally have enjoyed praying and asking for God to provide two or three faithful, available, and teachable men who want to grow spiritually. If possible, I try to meet with these men as a group once per week and then supplement the group time with some one-on-one interaction.

It goes beyond the scope of this book to provide a lot of detail regarding how to do this. It is basically a life-on-life experience. A couple of classic resources for this disciple-making ministry are Robert Coleman's book *The Master Plan of Evangelism* and Bill Hull's book *The Disciple Making Pastor.*

At some point in the disciple-making process, you need to encourage those in whom you have invested to do the same for others. Over the years I have seen this process unfold repeatedly, and there are untold numbers of godly men and women all over the world who were nurtured in this manner.

I have often been disappointed when pastors, staff members, and other leaders in the church get so busy administrating, counseling, or conducting the public ministry of the church that they lose their focus on investing deeply in the lives of others. To be honest, I have also fallen prey to urgency and busyness and failed to invest deeply in the lives of others.

When leaders invest in people in this manner, it has a way, over time, of creating a disciple-making culture in the church. It also keeps pastors grounded and exposed to the real issues people encounter and face every day.

Be prepared to be accused of partiality if you become seriously involved in discipling others. Do what you can to diffuse this perception, but do not let this push back decrease your intent to invest your life more deeply into a few who will in turn do so for others. In the long run, focusing on a few is not exclusive; rather it is inclusive in that many lives will be impacted by this practice of multiplication discipleship.

Disciple from the Pulpit

There is no doubt about it, God calls His leaders to regularly and passionately preach and teach His revealed Word. Throughout this book, I have expressed my concern that too many pastors fail to provide biblically substantive sermons. I realize there are diverse opinions about topical sermons versus preaching verse by verse through one book of the Bible at a time. Homiletics (the technical term for preaching) is not my professional expertise, but it is difficult to deny that our churches are suffering from lack of biblical depth. It is impossible to think that this is not in part due to superficial preaching and teaching.

Let me address a related problem. I deeply sympathize with the desire many pastors have to reach the lost. I applaud this desire. In fact, I support it with zeal. The first major study that Dr. Thom Rainer and I initiated when we started LifeWay Research dealt with churches that possess a ten-year track record of reaching people for Christ. You can access the findings of this study at the LifeWay Research Web site and look for the Standout Church Study. You will be greatly encouraged to learn about these churches and their hearts and strategies for reaching the lost.

However, the weekly gathering of God's people is for the purpose of worship, praise, fellowship, prayer, and edification of God's people through the faithful teaching of His Word. In other words, it is God-centered and designed for the spiritual formation of God's people. Those yet to come to faith in Christ should be invited, welcomed enthusiastically, treated warmly, and guided toward an understanding of the gospel. Yet, the weekly worship time is not to be designed for the lost. Every service should, and can, have an evangelistic appeal, but not at the exclusion of the edification of God's people.

Substantive preaching should never be boring, and it most definitely should never be done without significant application to daily life. No preacher should be content with a sermon that is well prepared theologically but poorly delivered. Preaching is for life change and it should be interesting and aimed at application.

One other word about preaching is needed. Some pastors mistakenly think that all you have to do to make disciples is prepare and deliver substantive sermons. It most certainly is a major component of making disciples but should never be the only strategy. Moreover, it is arrogant for any leader to think that he can single-handedly disciple the entire church. It takes the entire body of Christ to nurture and disciple one another.

Commit to a Small Group Strategy

God has designed us to live and grow in community. As important as private devotions and individual Bible study are, no Christian will experience maximal spiritual formation in isolation from the body of Christ. Every discipleship strategy should include some type of small group experience where people can experience ongoing support, encouragement, prayer, fellowship, and accountability.

For many years I developed and directed two types of small groups. The first type was an on-campus, open-group Sunday school ministry. Anyone could show up on any Sunday and find a life-stage or age appropriate class. I also organized weekly off-campus affinity based groups in homes, restaurants, work places, etc. There are pros and cons to both strategies. I again refer you to the Spiritual Formation Web site (www.lifeway.com/sfi) to obtain information, including the pros and cons of various small group strategies.

A church serious about spiritual formation will create a high quality, theologically sound, well-led small group ministry where people can experience spiritual growth in community. It must be part of your strategy.

Develop a Strategy for Involvement and Service

Many churches have made the mistake of thinking that great worship services and solid educational approaches are adequate for spiritual formation. However, real growth cannot occur without service. People need to be giving of themselves.

In LifeWay's 2006 research project aimed at learning more about young adults, two of the major findings were that young adults are looking for community and they are looking for involvement. The study suggests that if a church does not help young adults find a place for service within six months of their joining, they will likely start looking for another church more committed to mobilizing Christians for service.

My favorite passages dealing with service are found in the book of Titus.

> He gave Himself for us to redeem us from all lawlessness and to cleanse for Himself a special people, eager to do good works. (Titus 2:14)

> And our people must also learn to devote themselves to good works for cases of urgent need, so that they will not be unfruitful. All those who are with me greet you. Greet those who love us in the faith. Grace be with all of you. (Titus 3:14–15)

The good news is that in recent years churches have become much more effective in teaching about service, offering classes on spiritual gifts, and developing strategies that guide believers through a process of discovering who they are, how they are gifted, and how and where they can find a place of service. Our Web site will provide a good overview of this process and how you can more effectively move in that direction.

Equip the Laity to Feed Themselves

I have stated several times that the number one behavior most correlating to spiritual maturity is reading the Bible. I have already addressed this, but I want to emphasize it one more time. Make sure people are constantly being taught to read and study the Bible. Refuse to fall prey to the temptation to think that sermons and Bible studies, as important as they are, replace private devotion.

Push against Arrogance

We must go to great extent to avoid fostering an environment where people get so focused upon their own personal development that they end up becoming either self-absorbed or proud of how much they know, or how "spiritual" they are. Some of the most difficult Christians I know to be around are those who are very theologically informed, and very proud of it! True growth in knowledge and movement toward biblically based maturity will be manifested in part by humility.

Guard against the Juxtaposition of Evangelism and Discipleship

During my college years I was exposed to various campus ministries. One group was known for outreach and evangelism.

Another group was known for in-depth discipleship. A third group was known for intellectual dialogue and debating issues.

Perhaps it is impossible to find and maintain a perfect balance, but it should be sought nonetheless. Spiritual formation and discipleship should lead to more vibrant evangelism and vice versa. Few things have increased my desire to grow as a Christian more than engaging in sharing the gospel with others. Maturity should lead to more evangelism, not less.

Conclusion

There is an old fable about a man who was riding a horse through the desert. During this dry and wearisome journey, a stranger appeared and said, "As you continue on your way, you will come to a dry riverbed. You will see old, dry rocks. Pick some up and the next morning you will be both glad and sad." Then the stranger disappeared. The dusty traveler indeed came to the dry riverbed. He almost passed without following the stranger's advice. At the last minute he threw a few rocks into his travel bag. The traveler camped later that night. The next morning as he was gathering his things he dropped his bag and out spilled some precious jewels. The rocks had turned into possessions of great worth. Indeed, as the stranger had prophesied, the traveler was both glad and sad. He was glad for the stones he picked up, but was sad for all he left back in the dry riverbed.

I have thought of this fable often when reflecting on the importance of investing in things of great worth. It reminds me of the words of a godly man I met during my college years who told me there are three things that last for all of eternity: God, His people and His Word. What a joy and privilege it is to be given the opportunity to invest in eternity! We get to be part of seeing ordinary people become citizens of God's kingdom.

God's kingdom is within His full control. He is on His throne and will build up, guide and protect His bride, the church, until the day Christ returns. He is at work in the lives of people all around us. He is at work in your church and in your neighborhood.

Our responsibility is to live in a manner that pleases Him, to make Him known to others, and to "mature the saints." I pray this book has served both as a "wake-up call" to you and has provided increased insight into and vision for the task at hand.

> We proclaim Him, warning and teaching everyone with all wisdom, so that we may present everyone mature in Christ. I labor for this, striving with His strength that works powerfully in me. (Col. 1:28–29)

---

1. See the diagram on page 75 in chapter 3 that illustrates KNOWING, BEING, and DOING.

2. Alex and Brett Harris, *Do Hard Things: A Teenage Rebellion Against Low Expectations* (Colorado Spring, CO: Multnomah Books, 2008), 36.

3. One of the issues we had to deal with in terms of the scope of the survey, including the number of questions we asked, is the fact that response rates begin to decline when a survey takes more than ten minutes to complete. There are a lot of significant issues, like the

influence of the home, that we would have liked to investigate, but we were unable to due to concerns about the length of the survey.

4. Teenage Dropout Study. LifeWay Research, Nashville, TN, 2007, www.lifewayresearch.com.

5. Thom S. Rainer and Eric Geiger, *Simple Church* (Nashville, TN: B&H Publishing Group, 2006), 57.